d School Language Literacy Development in Migrant Children

SECOND LANGUAGE ACQUISITION

Series Editors**: Professor David Singleton**, *University of Pannonia, Hungary* and *Fellow Emeritus, Trinity College, Dublin, Ireland* and **Dr Simone E. Pfenninger**, *University of Salzburg, Austria*

This series brings together titles dealing with a variety of aspects of language acquisition and processing in situations where a language or languages other than the native language is involved. Second language is thus interpreted in its broadest possible sense. The volumes included in the series all offer in their different ways, on the one hand, exposition and discussion of empirical findings and, on the other, some degree of theoretical reflection. In this latter connection, no particular theoretical stance is privileged in the series; nor is any relevant perspective – sociolinguistic, psycholinguistic, neurolinguistic, etc. – deemed out of place. The intended readership of the series includes final-year undergraduates working on second language acquisition projects, postgraduate students involved in second language acquisition research, and researchers, teachers and policy-makers in general whose interests include a second language acquisition component.

Full details of all the books in this series and of all our other publications can be found on http://www.multilingual-matters.com, or by writing to Multilingual Matters, St Nicholas House, 31-34 High Street, Bristol BS1 2AW, UK.

SECOND LANGUAGE ACQUISITION: 119

Heritage and School Language Literacy Development in Migrant Children

Interdependence or Independence?

Edited by

Raphael Berthele and Amelia Lambelet

MULTILINGUAL MATTERS
Bristol • Blue Ridge Summit

DOI 10.21832/BERTHE9047
Library of Congress Cataloging in Publication Data
A catalog record for this book is available from the Library of Congress.
Names: Berthele, Raphael, editor. | Lambelet, Amelia, editor.
Title: Heritage and School Language Literacy Development in Migrant Children: Interdependence or Independence?/Edited by Raphael Berthele and Amelia Lambelet.
Description: Bristol, UK; Blue Ridge Summit, PA: Multilingual Matters, [2018] | Series: Second Language Acquisition: 119 | Includes bibliographical references and index.
Identifiers: LCCN 2017028959| ISBN 9781783099047 (hardcover : acid-free paper) | ISBN 9781783099030 (softcover : acid-free paper) | ISBN 9781783099054 (pdf) | ISBN 9781783099061 (epub) | ISBN 9781783099078 (Kindle)
Subjects: LCSH: Multilingualism in children. | Interlanguage (Language learning) | Code switching (Linguistics) | Education, Bilingual. | Sociolinguistics.
Classification: LCC P115.2 .H47 2017 | DDC 372.6–dc23 LC record available at https://lccn.loc.gov/2017028959

British Library Cataloguing in Publication Data
A catalogue entry for this book is available from the British Library.

ISBN-13: 978-1-78309-904-7 (hbk)
ISBN-13: 978-1-78309-903-0 (pbk)

Multilingual Matters
UK: St Nicholas House, 31-34 High Street, Bristol BS1 2AW, UK.
USA: NBN, Blue Ridge Summit, PA, USA.

Website: www.multilingual-matters.com
Twitter: Multi_Ling_Mat
Facebook: https://www.facebook.com/multilingualmatters
Blog: www.channelviewpublications.wordpress.com

The policy of Multilingual Matters/Channel View Publications is to use papers that are natural, renewable and recyclable products, made from wood grown in sustainable forests. In the manufacturing process of our books, and to further support our policy, preference is given to printers that have FSC and PEFC Chain of Custody certification. The FSC and/or PEFC logos will appear on those books where full certification has been granted to the printer concerned.

Typeset by Deanta Global Publishing Services Limited.
Printed and bound in the UK by CPI Group (UK) Ltd, Croydon, CR0 4YY
Printed and bound in the US by Edwards Brothers Malloy, Inc.

Contents

Contributors

Nicole Bayer, a former primary school teacher, is a senior researcher at the Institute for Educational Evaluation (Associated Institute of the University of Zurich). She wrote her doctoral thesis on an intervention programme for immigrant students in kindergarten, especially on the development of linguistic competencies in the heritage and school language. Some of her further research interests include educational measurement with a focus on test design and test development, school effectiveness research as well as diagnostic, formative and summative student assessment.

Raphael Berthele is Professor in multilingualism at the University of Fribourg. He directs the MA programmes in multilingualism studies and in foreign language didactics and he co-founded the Fribourg Institute of Multilingualism in 2008. His research interests cover different areas from cognitive to social aspects of multilingualism. During the last years, he has been focusing on the empirical investigation of receptive multilingualism and on convergence phenomena in the semantic and syntactic patterns in linguistic reference to space in multilinguals.

Magalie Desgrippes studied German language, literature and history as well as French as a foreign language in Caen and Rouen in France, and holds a master in multilingualism studies from the University of Fribourg, Switzerland. She is currently writing her PhD on the influence of family, input and social factors on the development of literacy by bilingual children in the Swiss context. She is also working on a new project at the crossroads of subject and heritage language teaching in the School for Teacher Education in the University of Applied Sciences Northwestern Switzerland.

Edina Krompàk is a lecturer in the School of Teacher Education at the University of Applied Sciences and Arts Northwestern Switzerland. Her PhD, which was conducted at the University of Zurich and funded by the Swiss National Science Foundation, examined first and second language development in the context of heritage language courses. Her main research field is multilingual language use and identity in educational contexts and her current central research interests are ethnic and local identities in linguistic landscapes and the exploration of individual translanguaging profiles of future teachers.

Amelia Lambelet works at the Institute of Multilingualism (University of Fribourg and University of Teachers Education, Fribourg, Switzerland) as a senior researcher. Her current research concerns foreign/second language learning at school and within extra-curricula activities with a particular focus on transfers, the impact of individual differences on language learning, aptitude and the age factor in relation to L2 learning.

Urs Moser is the director of the Institute for Educational Evaluation (Associated Institute of the University of Zurich) and adjunct professor of educational research at the University of Zurich. His research focuses on large-scale educational assessments for monitoring and accountability, school-effectiveness research and educational measurement. He is currently developing a system for a computer-based adaptive assessment based on item response theory. The very general research question is how to arrive at an empirical alignment between an assessment system, new national educational goals (performance standards) and a new curriculum.

Lea Nieminen PhD is working as a research coordinator in the Centre for Applied Language Studies, University of Jyväskylä. Her major research interests are first language development and literacy learning in a first, second or foreign language. Currently, she is involved in research on how children can be supported with digital tools in practicing the basic skills of reading (GraphoLearn). Nieminen has authored several scientific articles in national and international journals and other publications, and co-authored the book *The Diagnosis of Reading in a Second or Foreign Language*. She is also an editor of the Finnish linguistic journal *Puhe ja kieli* (*Speech and Language*).

Carlos Pestana teaches French didactics at the Higher School of Education in Bern, Switzerland. He was a research assistant for the HELASCOT project at the Institute of Multilingualism in Fribourg. He wrote an MA thesis on colonial linguistics at the University of Fribourg. For more than 10 years, he has been a foreign languages teacher at secondary level in Switzerland.

Martin Tomasik has studied psychology at the Free University of Berlin, received his doctoral degree in developmental psychology at the University of Jena and his *venia legendi* in psychology at the University of Zurich. Currently, he works as an assistant professor at the Institute for Educational Evaluation (Associated Institute of the University of Zurich). He does research on the role of social contexts (families, schools, neighborhoods) in the development of children, adolescents, and young adults and is particularly interested in the determinants and consequences of educational transitions as well as methodological aspects of developmental and educational measurement.

Riikka Ullakonoja PhD is currently a post-doctoral researcher in applied linguistics at the Department of Language and Communication Studies at the University of Jyväskylä, Finland. Her main research focus is second/foreign language learning, more specifically oral skills, phonetics, reading, writing, motivation and vocabulary. In addition, she has also studied immigrant learners. Ullakonoja is also a teacher of Russian, French and English and has authored many international and national scientific articles and co-authored the book *The Diagnosis of Reading in a Second or Foreign Language.*

Jan Vanhove is a senior assistant at the Department of Multilingualism in Fribourg, Switzerland. He has done research on receptive multilingualism, crosslinguistic influence between closely related languages and lexical richness. He blogs semi-regularly about research design and statistics in applied linguistics and multilingualism research at http://janhove.github.io.

1 Investigating Interdependence and Literacy Development in Heritage Language Speakers: Theoretical and Methodological Considerations

Raphael Berthele and Amelia Lambelet

Multilingualism, Transfer and Literacy Development

Bilingualism and multilingualism in migrant children has been a research topic in applied linguistics for many years (see Polinsky & Kagan [2007] for an overview). The sociolinguistic situation of children who are confronted with a minority language at home (their heritage language) and a majority language in their everyday life has also been widely documented and compared to other types of bilingual and multilingual development (Montrul, 2012). Historically, linguists' engagement with the topic has gradually developed from deficit views to a resource-oriented view. Deficit-oriented views put the emphasis on the *difficulties* encountered by these multilingual children, as the term 'incomplete acquisition' (Montrul, 2008) suggests. Some authors even argued that in certain contexts, individuals fail to develop functional skills in either of their two languages, as in the semilingualism view advocated by Hansegård (1975; see discussion of this notion below). The resource-oriented views, on the other hand, put the emphasis on the *possibilities* that bi- and multilingualism enable (e.g. Gawlitzek-Maiwald & Tracy, 2005). This positive view of multilingualism puts the emphasis on the potential of transfer on different levels: on the linguistic level and on the level of strategies of language learning and use. Today, it is quite common in scholarly debate to stress this positive transfer potential together with the idea of an added value of being bi- or multilingual (e.g. in the domain of cognitive control cf. Bialystok *et al.* [2004]; but see also Paap & Greenberg [2013] for a critical discussion of the evidence on the bilingual advantage).

The purpose of this book is to describe migrant children's language development, and in particular the potential residing in shared or transferred resources between their heritage languages and the languages spoken in the region where their family has immigrated. More precisely, the focus of the book lies on the development of their literacy skills in both languages. In this book, we refer to literacy as the skills necessary for reading and writing, although we are well aware of the fact that it is 'impossible to give a clear and bounded definition of [it]' (Brockmeyer & Olson, 2009: 4). Our take on literacy is deliberately focusing literacy as a skill (Baker, 2006: 321), although we are aware that other, more critical and more wide-ranging approaches to literacy (e.g. New London Group, 1996; Street, 2006) have been proposed. We chose our focus to match the literacy objectives of the educational systems in which our studies are situated. Skills required in such 'traditional' reading and writing tasks are considered central in educational selection, which justifies the focus in the research reported in this book.

Thus, this book contributes to the scholarly investigation of the potential beneficial effects in academic proficiency across languages in migrant children. After addressing the most central terminological and theoretical issues (Chapter 1), we discuss evidence from four empirical studies on heritage language speakers in different educational and linguistic contexts (Chapters 2–9). The common research goal of all studies was to understand the factors, both linguistic and non-linguistic in nature, that contribute to the development of language skills in the heritage and the school languages. To use a term that is well established in the literature in this field, the research presented in this book attempts to assess the level of 'interdependence' of different languages in the individual multilingual speakers' repertoires.

The theories and terminology used in this book mainly stem from bilingualism and heritage language speakers research. However, since in most situations discussed, more than two languages are part of the speakers' repertoires, we also draw on multilingualism research. Therefore, the participants in the studies are referred to both as 'multilinguals' and as 'bilinguals'. All participants in the studies presented in this book are multilinguals with at least three languages or varieties in their linguistic repertoires: their heritage language(s), their language of instruction, often a local dialect in informal communication (e.g. Alemannic Swiss German) and additional foreign languages taught at school. The children in the non-heritage language comparison groups use a repertoire composed of at least the latter two languages and varieties. The authors of this book also use the terms 'bilingualism' and 'bilinguals' since in all research projects the focus lies on two particularly important languages in this repertoire, the language of instruction and the heritage language.

The deficit-oriented view of bi- and multilingualism, the semilingualism concept, has been questioned by bilingualism scholars (MacSwan, 2000; Martin-Jones & Romaine, 1986). Most contemporary scholars working on bi- and multilingual development tend to emphasise the futility of comparisons of bi- or multilingual repertoires to idealised monolingual norms, since bilingualism and multilingualism unavoidably lead to a different type of language competence (Bley-Vroman, 1983; Cook, 2002; Grosjean, 1985, 1989; Herdina & Jessner, 2002). This is often done by explicitly referring to the idea of crosslinguistic influence and transfer across languages (Jarvis & Pavlenko, 2007) and/or to resources shared by all languages in the repertoire (Cummins, 1980, 2005). As discussed in the section 'Metaphor of Transfer', it is often difficult to clearly distinguish the idea of transfer and the idea of interdependence of languages in the repertoire in the scholarly literature.

As the literature in this field often construes the notion of transfer very broadly, including the effects of a common underlying proficiency for academic language use that are the typical instantiations of linguistic interdependence (see Cummins, [1980] 2001: 131), it is important to start by clarifying the theoretical foundations and the terminological conventions adopted for our book.

The metaphor of transfer

The literature on transfer and interdependence involves a confusing degree of conceptual and terminological heterogeneity due to various reformulations and revisions of some of the central ideas. Our intention in this chapter is not to give a comprehensive account of the various versions of the hypotheses of the dynamics within the bilinguals' or multilinguals' languages. The main goal is instead to discuss the most central assumptions underlying transfer and interdependence research and to come up with a suitable set of terms for the discussion of the empirical research presented in this book.

The notion of transfer in second language acquisition (SLA), third language acquisition (TLA), multilingualism research and bilingualism research is always metaphorical. Literal transfer would mean that a linguistic phenomenon is taken from a donor language and carried into another (receiving) language, and is thus no longer present in the source language. Instead, most definitions of transfer capture processes such as copying (Johanson, 2002) or the replication (Matras, 2009) of matter or patterns of the model or source language in the replica or target language. The term 'pattern replication' refers to the replication of a (semantic or syntactic) feature of the model language using matter of the recipient language. The term 'matter replication' refers to the replication of morphemes, words or even longer chunks from a model language in a receiving language – an example of matter replication is the emergence of loanwords in language contact situations. An example of 'pattern replication' is discussed in Berthele (2015): multilingual speakers of Romansh, when speaking Swiss German, tend to replicate the semantic category represented by a general verb 'metter' ('to put') in their dominant language Romansh. They do this by overgeneralising a German-caused posture verb 'legen' ('to lay' [transitive]), even when referring to events where monolingual speakers of German use other caused posture verbs such as 'setzen' ('to sit' [transitive]) or 'stellen' ('to stand' [transitive]). Depending on the normative point of view, such differences in the use of German can be considered 'deviations from the monolingual norm' or, within a multicompetence view of bi- and multilingualism, as 'convergence'. As research on bilinguals consistently shows, bilingualism both entails the borrowing of linguistic matter from one language into the other, as well as the convergence of linguistic patterns, e.g. on the level of syntax (Jarvis & Pavlenko, 2008) or semantics (Berthele, 2012; Lambelet, 2012, 2016).

However, many influential definitions of transfer, e.g. the one by Odlin quoted below, include a wide variety of phenomena beyond matter and pattern replication:

> Transfer is the influence resulting from similarities and differences between the target language and any other language that has been previously (and perhaps imperfectly) acquired. (Odlin, 1989: 27)

Odlin's definition regards transfer in a much wider sense by including target language use patterns that can be explained very generally as the *influence of the coexistence* of two languages in the bi- or multilingual repertoire. Avoidance of constructions that are different (and perceived difficult) in the target language is an example of transfer in the wider sense: a multilingual might deliberately avoid the French 'il faut que...' (It is necessary/obligatory that...) that requires a subjunctive form of the subordinate clause if she or he is uncertain about the correct subjunctive morphology of that particular verb (see Laufer and Eliasson [1993] for a study of lexical avoidance). Other examples are stylistic and pragmatic choices. For instance, in the argumentative letters collected in the Heritage Language and School Language: Are Literacy Skills Transferable? (HELASCOT) research project (see the section 'Outline of the Book' and Chapters 2 and 5 of this book), some participants used emotional and affective ways of addressing the addressee for their letters to have more impact. As this socio-pragmatic *plus* often appears in both of the participant's languages, it could be argued that this particular pragmatic competence is transferred from one language to the other, or at least that

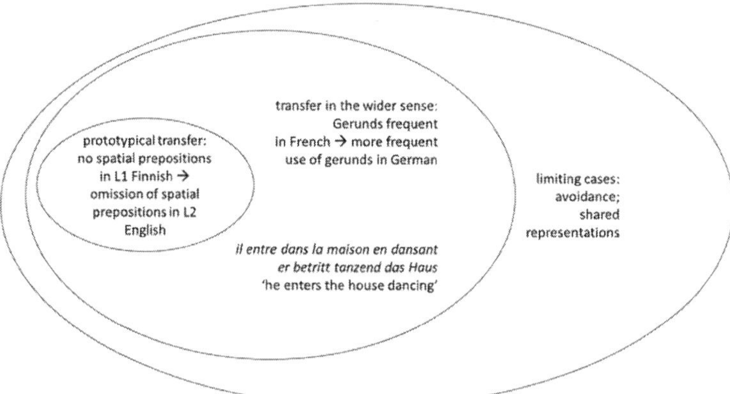

Figure 1.1 The radial category 'transfer'. The prototypical example is inspired by Jarvis and Odlin (2000) and the example 'transfer in the wider sense' is by Berthele and Stocker (2016)

it forms part of some kind of trans-linguistic pragmatic competence. This example illustrates the difficulty of distinguishing transfer in the wider sense from the idea of common underlying resources for two or more languages.

As a preliminary conclusion, we argue that the notion of transfer in bi- and multilingual repertoires can be considered a radial category with relatively good examples (prototypical transfer, transfer in the narrow sense) at its centre, and less typical examples (transfer in the wider sense) and fuzzy boundaries where transfer and shared resources overlap (see Figure 1.1).

Odlin's definition quoted above covers both *positive* and *negative* transfer (Odlin, 1989: 36). As can be observed in production data from many different types of multilinguals and second language (L2) users, there is ample evidence for negative *and* positive transfer (for a review, see Pavlenko & Jarvis, 2002). Positive transfer potentially occurs when there is a match between the structures of a language x (Lx) and a language y (Ly), and negative transfer is likely to occur when there is a mismatch between both structures. The learners' mental processes underlying both kinds of transfer are the same. Positive transfer is particularly well-documented in the domain of receptive skills: research on the comprehension of cognate words (Berthele & Lambelet, 2009; Vanhove & Berthele, 2015), on L2 and third language (L3) reading (Kaiser *et al.*, 2012; Lambelet & Mauron, 2015; Ringbom, 1992), as well as L3 listening comprehension (Haenni Hoti *et al.*, 2010) suggests that transfer from previously learnt languages can help learners to break into a new foreign language.

Assumptions in transfer and interdependence research

As we have seen, the notion of transfer can refer to rather diverse processes (matter or pattern replication) leading to very different outcomes (avoidance, underproduction, rapid comprehension of the target language, but also errors, etc.). To come to grips with the notion of transfer and with the idea of shared proficiency in the literacy domain, we discuss three assumptions that inspire, as far as our knowledge of the literature is concerned, many studies on language transfer:

(a) Some instances of transfer are easily observable (surface elements) while others are more covert (underlying elements).
(b) There is an underlying proficiency that is not separate, but shared between an individual's languages: thus, what appears as transfer from one language into the other can also be explained by postulating a basis of shared, transversal abilities that are not tied to a particular language.
(c) Unfolding the potential of this shared underlying proficiency (b) may only be possible once a certain level of (first language [L1] and/or L2) proficiency is attained.

Overt and covert transfer

A first observation is that there are two kinds of transfer: some instances of transfer are easily observable while others are covert and therefore harder to investigate. Matter and pattern replication relate to what Shuy (1978) considers the 'visible' aspects of language proficiency (vocabulary, grammar and pronunciation). Shuy's iceberg metaphor, distinguishing between the visible and the invisible aspects of language proficiency, has been made widely known by Jim Cummins to scholars in bilingualism research. Cummins uses the iceberg metaphor to illustrate his dichotomy of basic interpersonal communication skills (BICS) and cognitive/academic language proficiency (CALP) (Cummins, 2008). CALP is 'students' ability to understand and express, in both oral and written modes, concepts and ideas that are relevant to success in school' (Cummins, 2008: 71). CALP is the locus of the covert forms of transfer. For instance, in reading comprehension, we can hypothetically assume that bilinguals, provided they have developed reading skills in their L1, can fruitfully make use of them in their other language. More specifically, knowing how to scan a newspaper article for specific information is similar in most languages, so knowledge of the text genre in question and how to exploit this knowledge in reading is useful for this task, regardless of the language the text is written in.

In Figure 1.2, we try to give an overarching taxonomy that integrates both the transfer of overt (e.g. linguistic matter and patterns) and covert elements (e.g. literacy-related elements such as knowledge about text genres). The figure is an attempt to give an overview of the various

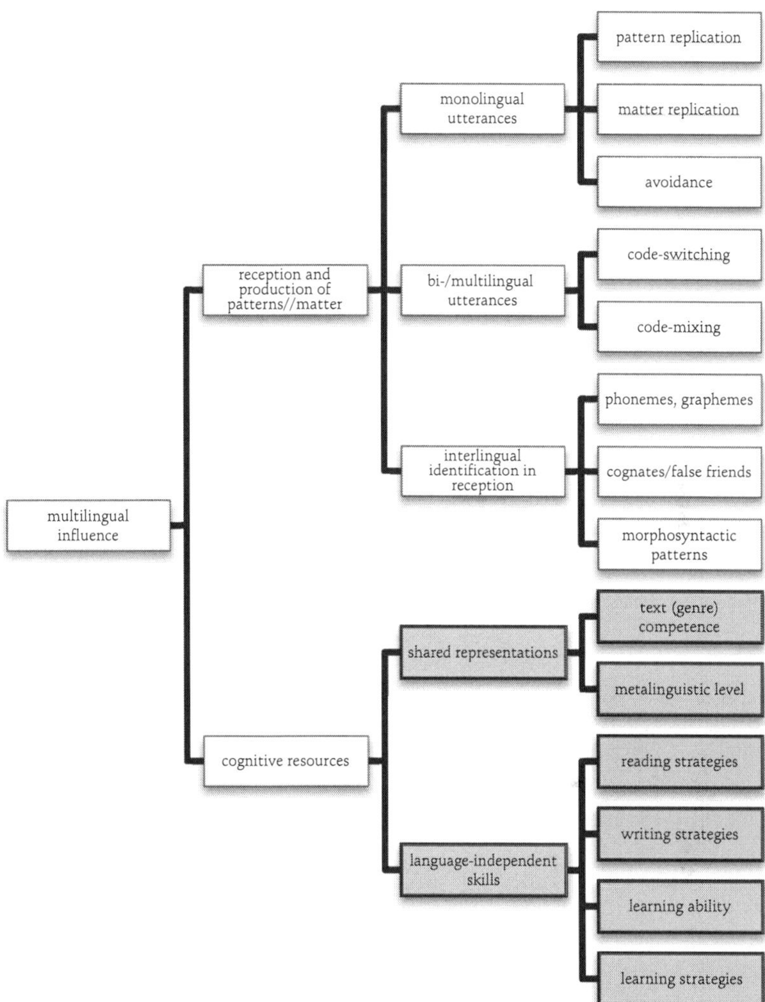

Figure 1.2 Overarching taxonomy of influence across languages

dynamics caused by the acquisition and use of the bi- or multilingual's languages. These processes are often referred to as *crosslinguistic influence* (see Kellerman & Smith, 1986; Jarvis & Pavlenko, 2008: 3).

As suggested in Figure 1.2, we start from the notion of multilingual influence as the most general term referring to any effects that the presence of different languages in the individual repertoire may have on cognition and on linguistic outcomes in production and reception. Thus, this term is even more general than Odlin's definition of transfer, since it also covers phenomena that are unrelated to the influence of similarity or difference (e.g. reading strategies that are shared across languages in the repertoire). Such interaction is generally diagnosed based on a comparison of the linguistic behaviour of multilinguals to observed or idealised patterns of monolinguals (whatever a monolingual or 'native speaker' of a language in reality may be [see Davies, 2003]).

In Figure 1.2, we distinguish between influences across languages that manifest themselves in the production and reception of linguistic patterns and linguistic matter ('overt transfers') and those that pertain to the strategic–cognitive level ('covert'). On the linguistic level, all kinds of bilingual and language contact phenomena are part of this taxonomy, ranging from matter and pattern replication to avoidance (Dagut & Laufer, 1985; Schachter, 1974) and bi- and multilingual speech (e.g. code-switching as discussed in Bullock and Toribio [2009]). Some of the phenomena on the linguistic level lead to increased similarity in the systems of the multilingual speaker. Such tendencies are often referred to with the term *convergence* (Toribio, 2004). The bottom of Figure 1.2 shows types of multilingual influence at the strategic–cognitive level. These include metalinguistic ability, learning strategies, as well as text competences at the receptive (e.g. our text scanning example) or at the productive level (e.g. the text structure example).

As stated above, the focus of our book is not on the transfer that is detectable directly in linguistic matter and patterns[1] (syntax, morphology, lexicon and semantics) but on the transfer of these literacy skills (reading, writing) subsumed at the bottom of Figure 1.2 under 'cognitive resources'. This level corresponds to Shuy's (1978) hidden part of the iceberg, and it involves important components of Cummins' CALP dimension of language proficiency. Hulstijn's (2015) distinction between basic and higher language cognition (BLC-HLC) is orthogonal to the main distinction made in Figure 1.2, for both HLC and BLC rely on the learning and use of linguistic items in the narrow sense (words, constructions and pragmatic elements), but his notion of HLC involves higher-level cognitive operations (e.g. 'reflective, meta-linguistic awareness'; Hulstijn, 2015: 61). Transfer on this level has already been investigated in terms of (reading or writing) strategies, metacognitive knowledge (about reading or writing) or more general reading/writing ability (see, for instance, Egli Cuenat, 2008; García *et al.*, 1998; Idiazabal & Larringan, 1997; Muñiz-Swicegood, 1994; Schoonen *et al.*, 1998; van Gelderen *et al.*, 2007).

Shared underlying resources

A closer examination of the literature shows that there is no clear line between resources that are transferred and cognitive resources that are considered to be shared among the languages of the individuals (e.g. Cummins' notion of common underlying proficiency): influential authors such as Cummins ([1980] 2001: 119) and Genesee (1979: 74) use the term *transfer* to refer to the use of shared underlying skills of proficiencies in bilinguals. Moreover, bilingualism and SLA researchers tend to use the term transfer, as already exemplified in Odlin's quote above, in a rather wide sense that is synonymous with crosslinguistic influence (e.g. Jarvis & Pavlenko, 2007: xi; see also Hulstijn, 2015: 130).

If text competences are acquired by a language user in L1, and then applied to a text in an L2, this can be argued to be an example of transfer from one language into the other, even though text competence, e.g. knowledge about how a narrative text is structured, does not obligatorily 'belong' to a particular language but can be considered at least partly language-neutral. If, however, text competence is not acquired in one language but in two or more languages simultaneously, transfer, in the narrow sense of the definition, does not seem to be an appropriate notion: thus, a more apt way of putting it would be that such skills are not language-specific but transversal or shared among the languages used for literacy purposes in the multilingual repertoire. Thus, the finding that literacy skills in two or more languages within the repertoire are associated can be explained to a large extent by 'a range of cognitive abilities' (Hulstijn, 2011: 103) without any need to invoke transfer of skills from one language onto the other. Similarly, even much lower-level skills related to reading fluency such as word-reading are not necessarily due to transfer but can be explained via underlying cognitive abilities such as phonological awareness (see Lesaux & Geva [2006] for a review).

The second assumption in the list presented earlier (b) thus draws on Cummins' ([1980] 2001: 112) extension of Shuy's (1978) bipartite iceberg metaphor and refers to such elements that are somehow represented as a resource shared by all languages. Following this view, a bi-/multilingual repertoire can be conceptualised as being formed of some common elements across languages (a language-independent basis of transversal abilities[2]) and of some elements pertaining to one or the other language (i.e. their surface elements such as vocabulary, phonetic particularities, syntax, etc.). In this sense, a student who is skilled in one language would show equally good skills in another language, provided the skills in question are part of the shared resources. For instance, it can be hypothesised that good learners in L1 will be able to benefit from their language learning and using skills in their L2s, L3s, etc. Conversely, comparatively unskilled users of L1 would experience similar difficulties in their other languages. Arguably, in reading comprehension, the activity of scanning for information can rely on similar mechanisms across the languages of the multilingual individual. Restrictions do apply, obviously, depending on the text's script, orthographic features, etc., where differences can act as a barrier to the transfer of reading skills. As stated in Cummins ([1980] 2001: 119), proficiency in languages is expected to be more highly correlated if the languages are very similar.

Even if CALP is acquired in one language before the other, as is the case in SLA or sequential bilingualism, resources can still be or become shared, e.g. by a process of fusion of the two systems (e.g. at the conceptual level, Kecskes and Papp's [2003] common underlying conceptual base). This fused system is hypothesised to emerge, in the view of Kecskes and Papp, once a certain level of (L1 and/or L2) proficiency is attained (see the section 'Threshold Theories').

To sum up, we are faced with a terminologically rather messy field where central terms are used more or less interchangeably (crosslinguistic influence *is* transfer *is* interdependence), and where the metaphorical entailments of mapping the notion of transfer of an entity from one language into the other are erased as there is a contradiction in the assumption of bi- and multilingual holism: if something is part of a common underlying proficiency, then it is not transferred from one language into the other. Nevertheless, as shown above, some influential authors use the two terms interchangeably. Although we do not think this terminological situation to be very helpful for the conceptual rigor necessary in scholarly research, the use of transfer in this very wide sense seems to be so entrenched in the research community that we do not deem it useful to battle against it. Our goal is to engage with the predictions and assumptions based on interdependence and transfer research in the domain of bilingual literacy acquisition, and we therefore adopt the terminological habits of the field. However, we do think that some of the methodological problems discussed in the section 'Study Designs in Research on Biliteracy Development' are at least partially due to the lack of conceptual rigor regarding the theoretical construal of the skills measured.

Threshold theories

Some scholars assume that transfer and interdependence are constrained by proficiency in the languages of the bi-/multilingual, in the sense that a certain threshold is needed for a child to benefit from the advantages of additive bilingualism. Threshold theories have found a wide appeal in societal debates and have led to linguistic policies that aim to foster one or the other language. Even though relatively similar, the various threshold hypotheses diverge on several points. They differ on the *language* in which the child needs to attain a certain proficiency to benefit from positive transfer (L2 in Alderson's [1984] and Kecskes & Papp's [2003] versions; both L1 and L2 in Cummins' [1979] version), but more fundamentally they also differ on the *type* of linguistic knowledge needed to permit transfer (in particular surface or underlying elements).

A belief still widespread is that it is the L1 that needs to be developed to a certain level in order to guarantee successful cognitive and linguistic development (e.g. Riehl [2013: 78] who makes explicit reference to Cummins' threshold theory). We refer to this belief as the 'first language axiom'. For instance, a common understanding of Cummins' threshold hypothesis states that successful bilingual children's literacy learning cannot occur if the children's L1 is not adequately developed: a low L1 proficiency would impede CALP from developing, and as a consequence would result in low (L1 and L2) literacy skills ('semi-literacy'). The pedagogical implication would therefore be to increase L1 instruction whereas L2 instruction has to come later and is not crucial at the beginning of literacy development. Before we discuss the fallacious nature of this type of threshold theory, we briefly present a different variety of the idea. For some scholars, even if literacy is well developed in L1, this knowledge cannot be accessed in L2 if the L2 linguistic proficiency is too low (see, for instance, Alderson, 1984; Jeong-Won Lee & Schallert, 1997). The problem would then be the *access* to the language-independent basis of transversal abilities. In this view, intensified L2 instruction would be important to exploit the underlying resources. We completely agree with Hulstijn (2011: 105) that the hypothesis that a multilingual can only deploy reading strategies if some knowledge of the target language is acquired (the script, basic vocabulary, etc.) is a rather trivial fact that does not call for further empirical investigation. An open question, however, is whether we are dealing with a linear or a truly non-linear phenomenon: only the latter can be construed as a threshold theory (see discussion below and Chapter 10).

There are several conceptual and empirical problems with threshold theories in general, and specifically with the L1 axiom presented above. First, when focusing on literacy, the L1 axiom postulates that the L1 needs to be developed as a basis involving CALP-style competences before other languages can be added to the repertoire. This idea is both empirically wrong (and has been considered wrong for quite some time, see Karajoli & Nehr, 1994) and sociolinguistically naïve as it presupposes that high language proficiency or dominance automatically entails high levels of literacy. As there are many languages and dialects in the world that are never or hardly ever used in writing, excluding the possibility for literacy to be developed first (and often exclusively) in an L2 or L3 is certainly not very realistic and of little use for educational policies in heterogeneous contexts.

As for the idea of thresholds, the difficulty with the very notion of linguistic thresholds having an impact on skills transfer is to define them theoretically and to provide empirical evidence for their existence (for a discussion, see Hall *et al.*, 2006; Takakuwa, 2003). As Cummins (1979: 230) notes himself, '[t]he threshold cannot be defined in absolute terms; rather it is likely to vary according to the children's stage of cognitive development and the academic demands of different stages of schooling'. This conceptualisation of thresholds as relative (inter-individual) and dynamic (intra-individual) is also problematic when used for policymaking as a reform adapted for one child would not automatically have positive effects for another child (see, for instance, Takakuwa, 2003).

Moreover, these hypotheses may also have implications in terms of teachers' categorisations of their students, and, as a result, on these students' real linguistic development. For instance, a study by Valadez *et al.* (2000) showed that migrant students categorised by their teachers as not having reached a minimal threshold of proficiency in either of their languages (Cummins' [1979] 'semilingualism' concept) were in fact as proficient as students who were categorised by the same teachers as having normal or high linguistic abilities. Even though this paradox could be explained by the kind of tasks assessing proficiency (while the researchers investigated oral competence using a storytelling task, the teachers were mainly focusing on reading and writing abilities) or by the small sample size of the study, this categorisation of students by their teachers as semilinguals can impact on the students' real linguistic development (for a discussion, see MacSwan [2000: 6–7]; Valadez *et al.*, 2000).

To sum up, the literature discussed in this chapter provides hardly any evidence for a discontinuous bilingual development which would then allow the determination of one or several thresholds. Relying on group means and significant differences between groups in order to identify thresholds (for an example, see Lasagabaster, 1998) does not provide any evidence for thresholds, let alone allow us to identify break points in a developmental slope (see Vanhove [2013, 2015] for discussion). Cummins (2000: 175) himself refers to the idea as a 'speculation'. Pending convincing evidence for such theories, we deem it preferable to assume that the null hypothesis holds, i.e. that while there may be interdependence of linguistic and higher-order cognitive competences, this interdependence is not governed by thresholds but is continuous in nature. Evidence to the contrary would have to come from studies that indicate strong non-linearities and discontinuous relationships.

Sociolinguistic variability and heritage language speakers

The migrant children in the research reported on in this book are not linguistically, culturally or socio-economically homogenous. The book covers heritage languages such as Portuguese (Chapters 2–6), Albanian, Bosnian/Croatian/Serbian, Portuguese, Spanish and Tamil (Chapter 7), Turkish and Albanian (Chapter 8) and Russian (Chapter 9). In most studies, the speakers investigated are associated with socio-economically low strata of society. The most notable exception is the situation investigated in Chapter 9, where the heritage language speakers belong to a well-educated and economically thriving stratum of society. From previous sociolinguistic work, we know that the skills we are interested in correlate systematically with social background (Hart & Risley, 1995). Moreover, as Brizić (2007) has shown, migrant children often belong to stigmatised minorities in their countries of origin. Children from such backgrounds often fail to develop literacy or literacy-related competences in their L1, thus there is nowhere to transfer from to the language of instruction. On the contrary, literacy is often developed in the language of instruction for the first time ever. Literacy developed in an L2 or L3 might later be transferred onto the L1. Any stereotypical and idealised representation of L1 as being perfectly entrenched, and in particular the presumption that L1 literacy is a given for those populations, would be completely off target.

Study Designs in Research on Biliteracy Development

Both transfer and interdependence are at the same time conceptually appealing and methodologically tricky to investigate. Whereas we find good methodological advice in the literature on the investigation of transfer of elements on the linguistic level (see Jarvis [2000, 2010] and Jarvis & Crossley [2012] for methodological procedures that allow the detection of this kind of transfer), testing the common underlying proficiency at work is difficult. Thus, the three assumptions discussed above are not equally easily testable: the negative transfer of matter and patterns is easily observable, whereas the positive transfer of surface elements and the interdependence of text competence and/or threshold hypotheses are less obvious to test.

Many researchers rely on correlational studies when making claims about interdependence and transfer: it is certainly the case that scores in a reading task in one language that predict reading scores in another language are consistent with the idea of interdependence. A particularly prolific field is reading research, where many scholars have investigated the factors having an impact on reading in L1 and L2 using correlational methods (cf. Abu-Rabia, 2001; Butler & Hakuta, 2006; Da Fontoura & Siegel, 1995; Eisterhold Carson *et al.*, 1990; Proctor *et al.*, 2010). However, such correlational evidence is not necessarily a reliable indicator for causality (see Geva [2014: 5] for a similar critique of correlational 'proofs' of interdependence). In order to make a case, e.g. for heritage language instruction as a means to develop heritage and school language, longitudinal designs, ideally comparing experimental groups with heritage language instruction to control groups without such instruction, are needed. Thus, the gold standard here would be an experiment with randomly assigned subjects to the two treatment groups. Such research would be very difficult to carry out, both for practical and for ethical reasons (it would involve deciding for a randomly selected participant whether he/she should follow heritage language instruction or not). All projects presented in our volume, however, attempt to go beyond simple correlationist analyses of proficiency in two languages, by modelling longitudinal within- and across-languages effects in combination with other relevant factors.

On testing interdependence

If research on interdependence and transfer often looks for correlations between the (literacy) skills in both languages of the bilingual participants at one point in time (see, for instance, Brisbois, 1995), it is, however, worth questioning what kind of correlational patterns are tests for the presence or absence of the interdependence of literacy skills in multilinguals. In the case of (hypothetically) common underlying skills such as text competence or metacognitive skills (see Figure 1.2), we can imagine potential research results that would disprove their existence. Let us assume that we test multilinguals with high overall language proficiency in all languages under investigation. If, at a given point in time, a skill pertaining to the literacy domain manifests itself in one language exclusively and cannot be observed to be used in another language by the same individual, although this other language is mastered on high levels so that threshold explanations (see the section 'Threshold Theories') can be ruled out, then this is evidence *against* a common resource. As soon as proficiency is low in one of the languages under investigation, the infrequent or non-existent use of skills in that particular language is simply not informative as to its status of being shared or language-specific: as the language specific elements, i.e. what Cummins (2001: 118) refers to as the 'surface features', are a prerequisite for literacy practices, they can always be argued to be insufficiently acquired, which in turn explains the inability to draw on the common underlying proficiency. Unless the linguistic skills in each language and the potentially transferred skills are not measured independently, threshold theories are not helpful, as they do not yield predictions that can be proven wrong.

But it is not only the threshold 'escape route' that makes it difficult to put interdependence and transfer theories to the test. According to contemporary theorising in multilingualism research, the attribution of skills to specific languages in the multilingual system is considered obsolete and reductionist (Cook, 1995; Herdina & Jessner, 2002). The view that an individual's different languages function in isolation from each other should be replaced by a holistic, 'multicompetence' view where a multitude of linguistic and non-linguistic factors interact in complex ways, as the following quote illustrates:

> [E]ach learner will develop a specific factor complex, and some factors may turn out to be predominant and exert a strong influence on the learning situation. Others may become completely unimportant and irrelevant for the individual learning process. (Jessner, 2008: 24)

The problem with such holistic approaches is that, again, most of them are not testable, as no clear predictions are made as to when which factors or skills will exert any influence and when they will not. For the purposes of developing educational policies, it would be useful to have a more specific theory on the mechanisms and directions of transfer and interdependence.

The usefulness, for the development of the field, of the interpretation of a correlation of two measured skills in two languages depends not on the statistics, but on the quality of the theoretical underpinnings of the research. As we will discuss in more detail in Chapters 6 and 10, if all a theory predicts is that skills across languages will correlate unless they don't – which is basically what the complexity and the threshold theories of bi- and multilingual language development do – then there is a lot of room for unfruitful ex-post theorising once the results of a particular study are known.

On research designs

To go beyond a static snapshot at a given point in time, and to be able to search for causality (instead of purely correlational patterns), several studies on biliteracy have investigated transfer using longitudinal designs. Two kinds of longitudinal studies can be distinguished. The first one investigates if the performance of an individual at time T in one language predicts their performance at time T+1 in the other language (cf. Cárdenas-Hagan *et al.*, 2007; Lambelet *et al.*, 2014; Verhoeven, 1994). The second type comprises intervention studies in which a particular competence is taught in one language and is later on tested in the other language to see if the acquired competence is applied in the language in which it has not been taught (see Chapters 7 and 8 in this volume, Idiazabal & Larringan [1997] and Muñiz-Swicegood [1994]).

Compared to cross-sectional studies, longitudinal designs offer the advantage of being able to model the direction of transfer. It is again often unclear if positive cross-lagged correlations (see Figure 1.3) are to be taken as evidence of *transfer* from a skill acquired in one language into another, as evidence of the existence of a language-independent basis of transversal abilities, or even as evidence of the impact of general cognitive (i.e. non-linguistic) development. Thus, in addition to the question of transfer or shared resources (see the section 'Shared Underlying Resources'), it is also difficult to disentangle the effect of bilingualism and the effect of cognitive maturation

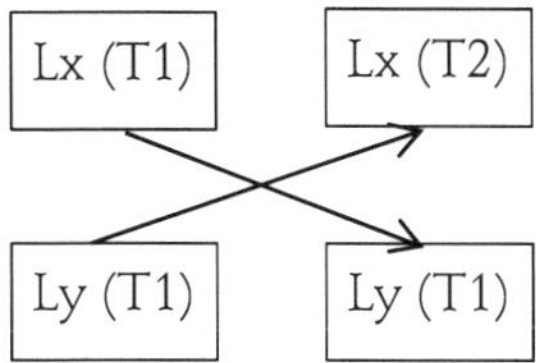

Figure 1.3 Cross-lagged influence

processes on literacy development in each language. For instance, if results indicate that poor readers in one language are also poor readers in their other language (and similarly for good readers), this may well be evidence of the impact of cognitive development in general on language proficiency.

Determining the causes for good or poor literacy development is methodologically difficult but crucial for multilingual language policies: Is the development of skills in the language of education dependent on equivalent skills in the heritage language or rather on more general cognitive predictors? Are the correlational patterns between the heritage and second language due to underlying cognitive skills that are independent from language or due to transfer and interdependence effects? Depending on the answers to such questions, stakeholders are more or less prone to allocate resources to bi- or monolingual curricula. If the focus of curriculum planning lies on the development of skills, it seems important to put widely held beliefs on the transfer potential across languages to the test. As argued in Chapters 7, 8 and 10, the current state of the art on those transfer effects might nevertheless incite scholars to revise their strongly transfer-based rationales in favour of bi- or multilingual education towards other motivations and arguments.

The four projects presented in this book use longitudinal designs with the aim of deepening these questions and assessing heritage and school languages' development from a perspective of interdependence. Cross-lagged (i.e. the influence of an individual's score in one language at T to their score in the other language at T+1, Figure 1.3), cross-sectional (i.e. correlation of the skills in the two languages from each time of data collection, Figure 1.4) and auto-regressive influences (Figure 1.5) are analysed.

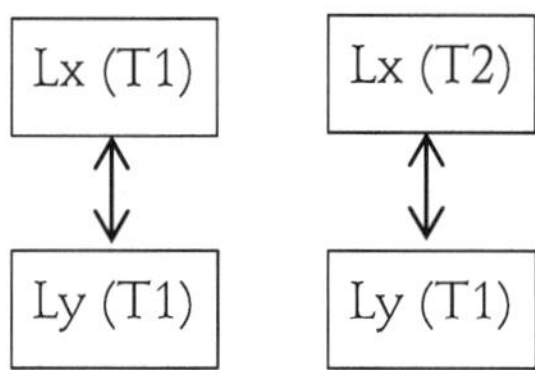

Figure 1.4 Cross-sectional influence

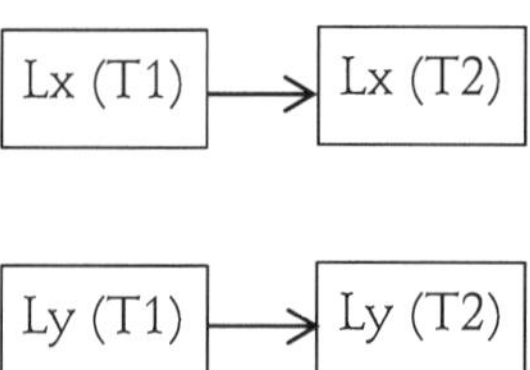

Figure 1.5 Auto-regressive influence

Outline of the Book

Table 1.1. gives an overview of the research questions and methods of the studies presented in this book. Chapters 2 through 6 discuss research results from the HELASCOT project. This is a longitudinal study aiming to investigate biliteracy development and covert transfer processes between the heritage and school languages of migrant Portuguese children in both French- and German-speaking Switzerland. Participants were tested in their heritage and school language (school language only for monolingual French/Portuguese/German comparison groups) at three points in time (beginning of third grade, end of third grade and end of fourth grade).

The background and rationale of the HELASCOT project are described in Chapter 2. The participants' socio-economic characteristics are presented by Magalie Desgrippes and Amelia Lambelet in Chapter 3. Topics of central interest are the children's language environment, their parents' length or stay in the immigration region, their parents' self-assessment of linguistic proficiency in the school language, their home literacy environment and the financial resources of the family.

Chapters 4 and 5 describe the reading and writing tasks that the participants were asked to perform. In Chapter 4, after an explanation of the task design, Carlos Pestana, Amelia Lambelet and Jan Vanhove discuss descriptive analyses of the participants' reading comprehension skills' development. Inter-groups' developmental differences are investigated. As far as results in the school language are concerned, Portuguese children and their French- and German-speaking peers are compared. In the heritage language, migrant children's results are compared to their peers' in Portugal, but also among the two migrant groups in French- and German-speaking Switzerland; differences between the results of participants living in French-speaking Switzerland and the results of participants living in German-speaking Switzerland are displayed and discussed. In Chapter 5 (Amelia Lambelet, Magalie Desgrippes and Jan Vanhove), the same type of descriptive analyses on the participants' performance in two writing tasks (a narration and an argumentation) are discussed.

Chapter 6 by Jan Vanhove and Raphael Berthele presents the inferential analyses of the project data and discusses crosslinguistic longitudinal effects (the extent to which an individual score at T1 in one language influences the individual's score at T+1 in the other language), the effect of literacy training (the extent to which the fact that the literacy training occurs primarily in the school language affects crosslinguistic effects) and the effects of typology (Portuguese being more closely related to French than to German).

In Chapter 7, Urs Moser, Nicole Bayer and Martin J. Tomasik investigate the effect of an intervention aiming to promote the development of heritage language skills of migrant children from different backgrounds in Switzerland, and test the transfer of these skills to the local language (German). The treatment was organised to promote the heritage language

Table 1.1 Summary of the research questions and method of the four studies

Chapters	*Research questions*	*Participants*	*Associations HL-SL*	*Effect of instruction*	*Cognitive variables*	*Sociolinguistic variables*
2–6	(1) Crosslinguistic longitudinal effects: To what extent does an individual's score at time T predict their score in the same skill in the other language at time T+1? (2) Different crosslinguistic longitudinal effects from HL to SL vs. SL to HL: To what extent does the fact that literacy training takes place predominantly in the school language affect crosslinguistic effects? (3) Effects of typology: To which extent does language typology affect crosslinguistic effects?	HL=Portuguese SL=French/German Heritage language speakers (*n*=252) Comparison groups (*n*=256) Age 8 (T1) to 10 (T3)	Cross-sectional Cross-lagged Auto-regressive	Literacy developed in SL (RQ2)	NA	Parental questionnaire (Chapter 2)
7	(1) Does the treatment (in the heritage language) have an impact on proficiency in the heritage language? (2) Does the treatment (in the heritage language) have an impact on proficiency in the school language? (3) Is the development of the linguistic skills in the heritage and school language interrelated across time?	HL: Albanian, Bosnian/ Croatian/Serbian, Portuguese, Spanish, Tamil Treatment group (*n*=63) Control group (*n*=118) Age 4 (T1) to 6 (T4)	Cross-sectional Cross-lagged Auto-regressive	Treatment in HL (HL classes and home literacy activities)	CFT-1 HAWIK	Parents' highest level of education

8	(1) How do heritage language courses impact on first and second language development?	HL: Albanian, Turkish SL=German Age 10 (T1) to 12 (T2)	Cross-lagged Auto-regressive	HL classes	NA	SES, parents' language orientation, motivation
9	(1) How does the writing proficiency in Finnish and Russian develop in two years, assessed by a fine-tuned scale of the Common European Framework of Reference (CEFR)? (2) What kind of relationships can be found between background factors and development in writing proficiency in Finnish and Russian? (3) How do the linguistic and cognitive measures predict the writing performance at Time 1 and Time 2?	HL: Russian SL: Finnish Age 9–15 at T1 (11–17 at T2)	Auto-regressive Cross-sectional Cross-lagged	NA	Phonological awareness; WM; Word recognition; lexical access	'Background variables' (i.e. length of stay, AoA, exposure, etc.)

Note: HL: heritage language; SL: school language (as second/third language); T1, T2, T3: measurement times.

(two lessons/week), coordinate school and heritage language instruction (topics from regular instruction consolidated in the heritage language) and to support the parents in promoting the heritage language in the family. Skills in the heritage and school languages are assessed four times over a period of almost two years. The evidence allows us to assess learning gains in both the heritage and the school languages as well as the impact of heritage language support on these gains.

A second investigation of potential effects of heritage language classes is presented in Chapter 8 by Edina Krompàk. In this research, the impact of Turkish and Albanian heritage language courses on the development of the heritage and school language German is investigated. Both languages are assessed by C-tests, a measure of global proficiency, during two periods of data collection over one year. Again, the learning gains in both the heritage and school languages are measured, and the effects of (non-controlled) voluntary heritage language instruction are assessed.

Chapter 9 by Lea Nieminen and Riikka Ullakonoja investigates migrant children's development of literacy skills in the heritage and school language of Russian migrant children in Finland. As these children's literacy training occurs in Finnish, the development of their Russian literacy skills is of interest for the construct of interdependence and transferability of skills from a broader perspective: the authors discuss this and the effect of cognitive, linguistic and family-related background variables on literacy development in both heritage and school languages.

The concluding chapter (Chapter 10, Raphael Berthele) recapitulates the main insights gathered in the studies reported on in this book, wraps up the discussion and attempts to give a summary of our current evidence-based understanding of interdependence.

Notes

(1) Transfer on the purely linguistic level can help learning a second or third language and can also speed up the acquisition of literacy skills (processes occurring at the strategic–conceptual level of Figure 1.2). However, due to space limitations we do not review the extensive literature on the bidirectional transfer of linguistic matter in L2 and L3 acquisition here.

(2) For instance, Cummins' Common Underlying Proficiency (CUP) hypothesis (also called the Interdependence hypothesis, see Cummins [2005]) or Kecskes' Common Underlying Conceptual Base (CUCB).

References

Abu-Rabia, S. (2001) Testing the interdependence hypothesis among native adult bilingual Russian-English students. *Journal of Psycholinguistic Research* 30 (4), 437–455.

Alderson, J.C. (1984) *Reading in a Foreign Language: A Reading Problem or a Language Problem*.

Baker, C. (2006) Literacy, biliteracy and multiliteracies for bilinguals. In C. Baker (ed.) *Foundations of Bilingual Education and Bilingualism* (4th edn) (pp. 320–345). Clevedon: Multilingual Matters.

Berthele, R. (2012) On the use of PUT verbs by multilingual speakers of Romansh. In A. Kopecka and B. Narasimhan (eds) *Events of 'Putting' and Taking': A Crosslinguistic Perspective* (pp. 145–166). Amsterdam: John Benjamins.

Berthele, R. (2015) Convergence in the domains of static spatial relations and events of putting and taking. Evidence from bilingual speakers of Romansh and German. *International Journal of Bilingual Education and Bilingualism* (ahead-of-print), 1–19.

Berthele, R. and Lambelet, A. (2009) Approche empirique de l'intercompréhension: répertoires, processus et résultats. *Lidil. Revue de linguistique et de didactique des langues* (39), 151–162.

Berthele, R. and Stocker, L. (2016) The effect of language mode on motion event descriptions in German–French bilinguals. *Language and Cognition*, 1–29. See https://doi.org/10.1017/langcog.2016.34.

Bialystok, E., Craik, F.I., Klein, R. and Viswanathan, M. (2004) Bilingualism, aging, and cognitive control: Evidence from the Simon task. *Psychology and Aging* 19 (2), 290–303. See https://doi.org/10.1037/0882-7974.19.2.290.

Bley-Vroman, R. (1983) The comparative fallacy in interlanguage studies: The case of systematicity. *Language Learning* 33/1, 1–17.

Brisbois, J.E. (1995) Connections between first-and second-language reading. *Journal of Literacy Research* 27 (4), 565–584.

Brizić, K. (2007) *Das geheime Leben der Sprachen. Gesprochene und verschwiegene Sprachen und ihr Einfluss auf den Spracherwerb in der Migration*. Münster/New York: Waxman.

Brockmeier, J. and Olson, D. (2009) The literacy episteme. In D.R. Olson and N. Torrance (eds) *Cambridge Handbook of Literacy* (pp. 3–22). Cambridge: Cambridge University Press.

Bullock, B.E. and Toribio, A.J. (2009) *Cambridge Handbook of Linguistic Code-Switching*. Cambridge/New York: Cambridge University Press.

Butler, Y.G. and Hakuta, K. (2006) Cognitive factors in children's L1 and L2 reading. *Academic Exchange* 10 (1), 23–27.

Cárdenas-Hagan, E., Carlson, C.D. and Pollard-Durodola, S.D. (2007) The cross-linguistic transfer of early literacy skills: The role of initial L1 and L2 skills and language of instruction. *Language, Speech, and Hearing Services in Schools* 38 (3), 249–259.

Cook, V. (1995) Multi-competence and the learning of many languages. In M. Bensoussan, I. Kreindler and E. Aogáin (eds) *Multilingualism and Language Learning: 8, 2. Language, Culture and Curriculum* (pp. 93–98). Clevedon: Multilingual Matters.

Cook, V. (2002) *Portraits of the L2 User* (Vol. 1). Clevedon: Multilingual Matters. See http://books.google.ch/books?hl=fr&lr=&id=-_dmdR1ZK_kC&oi=fnd&pg=PR7&dq=individual+differences+multilingualism&ots=_egwTe-ILM&sig=TiVfUKyoxwps7KmSzNQwc2fS77k.

Cummins, J. (1979) Linguistic interdependence and the educational development of bilingual children. *Review of Educational Research* 49 (2), 222–251. See https://doi.org/10.3102/00346543049002222.

Cummins, J. (1980) The construct of language proficiency in bilingual education. In J. Atalis (ed.) *Current Issues in Bilingual Education* (pp. 81–103). Washington, DC: Georgetown University Press.

Cummins, J. (2000) *Language, Power and Pedagogy: Bilingual Children in the Crossfire*. Clevedon: Multilingual Matters.

Cummins, J. (2001) *An Introductory Reader to the Writings of Jim Cummins*. Clevedon: Multilingual Matters.

Cummins, J. (2005) Teaching for Cross-Language Transfer in Dual Language Education: Possibilities and Pitfalls. TESOL Symposium on Dual Language Education: Teaching and Learning Two Languages in the EFL Setting.

Cummins, J. (2008) BICS and CALP: Empirical and theoretical status of the distinction. In N. Hornberger (ed.) *Encyclopedia of Language and Education* (4th edn) (pp. 487–499). New York: Springer.

Da Fontoura, H.A. and Siegel, L.S. (1995) Reading, syntactic, and working memory skills of bilingual Portuguese-English Canadian children. *Reading and Writing* 7 (1), 139–153.

Dagut, M. and Laufer, B. (1985) Avoidance of phrasal verbs: A case for contrastive analysis. *Studies in Second Language Acquisition* 7 (01), 73–79. doi: doi:10.1017/S0272263100005167.

Davies, A. (2003) *The Native Speaker: Myth and Reality*. Clevedon: Multilingual Matters.

Egli Cuenat, M. (2008) *Le langage écrit chez l'enfant bilingue: bilinguisme, bilittératie et production narrative*. University of Basel. See http://edoc.unibas.ch/34092/.

Eisterhold Carson, J., Carrell, P.L., Silberstein, S., Kroll, B. and Kuehn, P.A. (1990) Reading-writing relationships in first and second language. *TESOL Quarterly* 24, 245–266.

García, G.E., Jiménez, R.T., Pearson, P.D. and Hacker, D. (1998) Metacognition, childhood bilingualism, and reading. In G.E. García, R.T. Jiménez, P.D. Pearson and D. Hacker (eds) *Metacognition in Educational Theory and Practice* (pp. 193–219). New York: Routledge.

Gawlitzek-Maiwald, I. and Tracy, R. (2005) The multilingual potential in emerging grammars. *International Journal of Bilingualism* 9/2, 277–297.

Geva, E. (2014) The cross-language transfer journey: A guide to the perplexed. *Written Language & Literacy* 17 (1), 1–15.

Grosjean, F. (1985) The bilingual as a competent but specific speaker-hearer. *Journal of Multilingual & Multicultural Development* 6 (6), 467–477.

Grosjean, F. (1989) Neurolinguists, beware! The bilingual is not two monolinguals in one person. *Brain and Language* 36 (1), 3–15.

Haenni Hoti, A.U., Heinzmann, S., Müller, M., Oliveira, M., Wicki, W. and Werlen, E. (2010) Introducing a second foreign language in Swiss primary schools: The effect of L2 listening and reading skills on L3 acquisition. *International Journal of Multilingualism* 8 (2), 98–116. doi: 10.1080/14790718.2010.527006.

Hall, J.K., Cheng, A. and Carlson, M.T. (2006) Reconceptualizing multicompetence as a theory of language knowledge. *Applied Linguistics* 27 (2), 220–240.

Hansegård, N.E. (1975) *Tvåspråkighet eller halvspråkighet?* Stockholm: Aldus.

Hart, B. and Risley, T.R. (1995) *Meaningful Differences in the Everyday Experience of Young American Children*. Baltimore, MD: Paul H. Brooks.

Herdina, P., and Jessner, U. (2002) *A Dynamic Model of Multilingualism: Perspectives of Change in Psycholinguistics* (Vol. 121). Clevedon: Multilingual Matters. See http://books.google.ch/books?hl=fr&lr=&id=KKM0zlLcagQC&oi=fnd&pg=PR7&dq=individual+differences+multilingualism&ots=46Gu6EOAvc&sig=P2cuB5QgFzouEqnF1OgECwIIxNA.

Hulstijn, J. (2011) Explanations of associations between L1 and L2 literacy skills. In M.S. Schmid and W. Lowie (eds) *Modeling Bilingualism. From Structure to Chaos* (pp. 85–111). Amsterdam/Philadelphia, PA: John Benjamins Publishing Company.

Idiazabal, I. and Larringan, L. (1997) Transfert de maîtrises discursives dans un programme d'enseignement bilingue basque-espagnol. *Acquisition et interaction en langue étrangère* (10), 107–125.

Jarvis, S. (2000) Methodological rigor in the study of transfer: Identifying L1 influence in them interlanguage lexicon. *Language Learning* 50 (2), 245–309.

Jarvis, S. (2010) Comparison-based and detection-based approaches to transfer research. *Eurosla Yearbook* 10 (1), 169–192.

Jarvis, S. and Crossley, S.A. (2012) *Approaching Language Transfer Through Text Classification: Explorations in the Detection-Based Approach* (Vol. 64). Bristol: Multilingual Matters. See http://books.google.ch/books?hl=fr&lr=&id=Pq8BUooF930C&oi=

fnd&pg=PR7&dq=jarvis+approaching+language&ots=xDu-JydWNI&sig=2B2RM0vA5eMwwgl2goRpvySvrn4.

Jarvis, S. and Odlin, T. (2000) Morphological type, spatial reference, and language transfer. *Studies in Second Language Acquisition* 22 (4), 535–556.

Jarvis, S. and Pavlenko, A. (2007) *Crosslinguistic Influence in Language and Cognition*. Mahwah, NJ: Lawrence Erlbaum Associates.

Jarvis, S. and Pavlenko, A. (2008) *Crosslinguistic Influence in Language and Cognition*. New York: Routledge. See http://books.google.ch/books?hl=fr&lr=&id=kniRAgAAQBAJ&oi=fnd&pg=PP1&dq=jarvis+pavlenko+2008&ots=gaPGi2HNLI&sig=6O1HQED6VQSaIHTw4NTgoMzcyrg.

Jeong-Won Lee and Schallert, D.L. (1997) The relative contribution of L2 language proficiency and L1 reading ability to L2 reading performance: A test of the threshold hypothesis in an EFL context. *TESOL Quarterly* 31 (4), 713–739. https://doi.org/10.2307/3587757.

Jessner, U. (2008) Teaching third languages: Findings, trends and challenges. *Language Teaching* 41 (1), 15–56.

Johanson, L. (2002) Contact-induced change in a code-copying framework. *Contributions to the Sociology of Language* 86, 285–314.

Kaiser, I., Peyer, E. and Berthele, R. (2012) Does different mean difficult? Contrastivity and foreign language reading: Some data on reading in German. *International Journal of Bilingualism* 18 (3), 222–243. doi: 10.1177/1367006912440018.

Karajoli, E. and Nehr, M. (1994) Schriftspracherwerb unter Bedingungen der Mehrsprachigkeit. In H. Günther and O. Ludwig (eds) *Schrift und Schriftlichkeit: ein interdiziplinäres Handbuch internationaler Forschung* [*Writing and Its Use: An Interdisciplinary Handbook of International Research*] (pp. 1191–1205). Berlin/New York: de Gruyter.

Kellerman, E. and Smith, M.S. (1986) *Crosslinguistic Influence in Second Language Acquisition*. Oxford: Pergamon Institute of English. See http://books.google.com/books/about/Crosslinguistic_Influence_in_Second_Lang.html?id=FuF4AAAACAAJ.

Lambelet, A. (2012) *L'apprentissage du genre grammatical en langue étrangère: A la croisée des approches linguistiques et cognitives*. Fribourg. See http://doc.rero.ch/record/32546/files/LambeletA.pdf.

Lambelet, A. (2016). Second grammatical gender system and gender linked connotations in adult emergent bilinguals with French as a second language. *International Journal of Bilingualism* 20(1), 62-75

Lambelet, A. and Mauron, P.-Y. (2015) Receptive multilingualism at school: An uneven playing ground? *International Journal of Bilingual Education and Bilingualism*. See http://www.tandfonline.com/doi/full/10.1080/13670050.2015.1114583

Lambelet, A., Desgrippes, M., Decandio, F. and Pestana, C. (2014) Acquis dans une langue, transféré dans l'autre? *Mélanges CRAPEL* 35, 99–114.

Lasagabaster, D. (1998) The threshold hypothesis applied to three languages in contact at school. *International Journal of Bilingual Education and Bilingualism* 1 (2), 119–133.

Laufer, B. and Eliasson, S. (1993) What causes avoidance in L2 learning. *Studies in Second Language Acquisition* 15 (1), 35–48. See https://doi.org/10.1017/S0272263100011657.

MacSwan, J. (2000) The threshold hypothesis, semilingualism, and other contributions to a deficit view of linguistic minorities. *Hispanic Journal of Behavioral Sciences* 22 (1), 3–45.

Martin-Jones, M. and Romaine, S. (1986) Semilingualism: A half-baked theory of communicative competence. *Applied Linguistics* 7 (1), 26–38.

Matras, Y. (2009) *Language Contact*. Cambridge: Cambridge University Press. See http://books.google.ch/books?hl=fr&lr=&id=IOUgAwAAQBAJ&

oi=fnd&pg=PR13&dq=matras+2009&ots=0TPW2BkBkX&sig=Yu2wsX-pGyH1MRew6O3RDbHVCgw.

Montrul, S.A. (2008) *Incomplete Acquisition in Bilingualism: Re-Examining the Age Factor* (Vol. 39). Amsterdam: John Benjamins Publishing. See https://books.google.ch/books?hl=fr&lr=&id=012axJTL-6cC&oi=fnd&pg=PR1&dq=).+Incomplete+Acquisition+in+Bilingualism.+Re-examining+the+Age+Factor&ots=x4uVPeSlLW&sig=Eu9Pog0KMOkjhKKyh8I3uHNqMpc.

Montrul, S.A. (2012) Is the heritage language like a second language? *Eurosla Yearbook* 12 (1), 1–29.

Moser, U., Bayer, N. and Tunger, V. (2008) *Entwicklung der Sprachkompetenzen in der Erst- und Zweitsprache von Migrantenkindern*. See http://www.ibe.uzh.ch/publikationen/Diss13ohneAnhang.pdf.

Muñiz-Swicegood, M. (1994) The effects of metacognitive reading strategy training on the reading performance and student reading analysis strategies of third grade bilingual students. *Bilingual Research Journal* 18 (1–2), 83–97.

New London Group (1996) A pedagogy of multiliteracies: Designing social futures. *Harvard Educational Review* 66 (1), 60–92.

Odlin, T. (1989) *Language Transfer: Cross-Linguistic Influence in Language Learning*. Cambridge: Cambridge University Press.

Paap, K.R. and Greenberg, Z.I. (2013) There is no coherent evidence for a bilingual advantage in executive processing. *Cognitive Psychology* 66 (2), 232–258. See https://doi.org/10.1016/j.cogpsych.2012.12.002.

Pavlenko, A. and Jarvis, S. (2002) Bidirectional transfer. *Applied Linguistics* 23, 190–214.

Proctor, C.P., August, D., Snow, C. and Barr, C.D. (2010) The interdependence continuum: A perspective on the nature of Spanish–English bilingual reading comprehension. *Bilingual Research Journal* 33 (1), 5–20. See https://doi.org/10.1080/15235881003733209.

Riehl, C.M. (2013) *Sprachkontaktforschung: eine Einführung* (3 Auflage ed.). Tübingen: Narr.

Ringbom, H. (1992) On L1 transfer in L2 comprehension and L2 production. *Language Learning* 42, 85–112.

Schachter, J. (1974) An error in error analysis. Language learning. *Language Learning* 24, 205–214.

Schoonen, R., Hulstijn, J. and Bossers, B. (1998) Metacognitive and language-specific knowledge in native and foreign language reading comprehension: An empirical study among Dutch students in grades 6, 8 and 10. *Language Learning* 48 (1), 71–106.

Shuy, R. (1978) Problems in assessing language ability in bilingual education programs. In H. Lafontaine, H. Persky and L. Golubchick (eds) *Bilingual Education* (pp. 376–381). Wayne, NJ: Avery.

Street, B.V. (2006) Autonomous and ideological models of literacy: Approaches from new literacy studies. *Media Anthropology Network Working Papers* 1–15.

Takakuwa, M. (2003) Lessons from a paradoxical hypothesis: A methodological critique of the threshold hypothesis. In *El Előadás: 4th International Symposium on Bilingualism. Arizona State University, April* (Vol. 30).

Toribio, A.J. (2004) Convergence as an optimization strategy in bilingual speech: Evidence from code-switching. *Bilingualism: Language and Cognition* 7 (2), 165–173.

Valadez, C.M., MacSwan, J. and Martínez, C. (2000) Toward a new view of low-achieving bilinguals: A study of linguistic competence in designated "semilinguals". *Bilingual Review/La Revista Bilingüe* 238–248.

van Gelderen, A., Schoonen, R., Stoel, R.D., de Glopper, K. and Hulstijn, J. (2007) Development of adolescent reading comprehension in language 1 and language 2: A longitudinal analysis of constituent components. *Journal of Educational Psychology* 99 (3), 477.

Vanhove, J. (2013) The critical period hypothesis in second language acquisition: A statistical critique and a reanalysis. *Plos One* 8 (7), e69172. See https://doi.org/10.1371/journal.pone.0069172.

Vanhove, J. (2015, October 16) The problem with cutting up continuous variables and what to do when things aren't linear. See http://janhove.github.io/analysis/2015/10/16/nonlinear-relationships.

Vanhove, J. and Berthele, R. (2015) The lifespan development of cognate guessing skills in an unknown related language. *IRAL* 1–38.

Verhoeven, L.T. (1994) Transfer in bilingual development: The linguistic interdependence hypothesis revisited. *Language Learning* 44 (3), 381–415. See https://doi.org/10.1111/j.1467-1770.1994.tb01112.x.

2 Testing Interdependence in Portuguese Heritage Speakers in Switzerland: The HELASCOT Project

Amelia Lambelet, Raphael Berthele, Magalie Desgrippes, Carlos Pestana and Jan Vanhove

Background

Heritage Language and Culture (HLC) courses in Switzerland are organised by the countries of emigration, with support (to a greater or lesser extent) from the cantonal Ministries of Education.[1] This support can take several forms: (1) classrooms are made available for the lessons, but the lessons take place outside school hours and no information is given by the school to the parents; (2) HLC classes take place outside school hours but migrant parents are encouraged to register their children; (3) HLC marks are integrated in the official grading documents and therefore enjoy official recognition from the school; and even, in some cases, (4) HLC lessons are integrated in the curriculum and take place during school hours. Switzerland is a federal state in which educational policies are predominantly shaped by cantonal and not federal authorities. This also applies to the level of support provided to HLC courses. The accessibility of HLC courses therefore depends on the canton and often also on the local school context where the migrant children and their parents live.

It is nevertheless worth mentioning that, in Switzerland, HLC courses have received a generally increasing degree of support in the last two decades. For instance, migrant children's linguistic repertoires are mentioned in the most recent federal laws and ordinances on languages, which state that cantons can receive federal funds to help promote their heritage languages (Art. 16: Law on Languages, 2007; Art. 11: Languages Ordinance, 2010). This legal mention and support of heritage languages follows the recommendations made by a report commissioned by the Swiss Conference of Cantonal Ministers of Education (EDK) in 1998 that stakes off educational linguistic policies of the Swiss Confederation and its cantons. In this report, the authors recommend fostering heritage languages as they 'play a fundamental role for the construction of [these children's] identity' (EDK, 1998, our translation) and are 'an important financial resource for Switzerland' (EDK, 1998, our translation). The report also states that their development is 'essential to successfully acquire the local national language and other languages' (EDK, 1998, our translation). This last argument, which concerns the influence of HLC classes on the *local* language, is widely reused in official documents, like the Directive P-DGEP-02A-02 from the Department of Education of the canton of Geneva, which begins as follows:

> The non-French-speaking child can only learn French if their mother tongue is well structured. Therefore it is important to encourage students to take heritage language courses. (Directive P-DGEP-02A-02, page 1, our translation[2])

Though the 1998 EDK report gave a variety of (more or less empirically verified) pragmatic reasons for supporting HLC classes and fostering the heritage language of migrant children, it is interesting to see that it is particularly their usefulness in learning the local language that is frequently cited in favour of HLC classes. This argument marks a shift of perspective on HLC courses, which were initially developed to facilitate the children's reintegration in the school system of their home country should they return. This shift of perspective on the role of HLC courses is a consequence of a more fundamental shift in the Swiss immigration profile as immigration has evolved from being essentially work related and short lasting in the 1960s to the 1980s to being more permanent in the newer waves of immigration.

More importantly, in our view, this widely used argument is implicitly based on a hypothesis from the field of applied linguistics that postulates interdependence between the various languages of a bi-/multilingual individual (see Chapter 1 of this book for a discussion). Nevertheless, besides one sentence on page 14 of the 2014 EDK report on HLC courses, empirical evidence validating the hypothesis is never mentioned in support of this argument. As the interdependence hypothesis is one of the key rationales for promoting heritage languages in the Swiss educational policy discourse, the need for its empirical verification is critical for both stakeholders and researchers.

The HELASCOT Project: Genesis and Aims

In this context, the Heritage Language and School Language: Are Literacy Skills Transferable? (HELASCOT) project has been conceived as part of the 2011–2015 research programme of the Research Center on

Multilingualism (Institute of Multilingualism, Fribourg). The Research Center on Multilingualism was set up by a mandate from the Swiss Confederation to intensify and coordinate research on multilingualism in Switzerland, based on the 2007 Swiss law on languages which aims to foster multilingualism in Switzerland. The HELASCOT project has therefore received full institutional support from the Swiss government. The Camões Institute, which is responsible for Portuguese HLC courses, also supported the project by giving the researchers access to HLC classes in Switzerland (see the section 'Participants'). Finally, for the sake of comparison, classes in Portugal and Switzerland were made accessible by the Portuguese Ministry of Education and the respective Swiss cantonal departments of education.

The first goal of the HELASCOT project was to put a fundamental tenet of interdependence theory to the test: is there empirical evidence for the crosslinguistic influence of one language of heritage language speakers on the development of the other language(s) in their repertoire. As discussed in Chapter 1, the transfer of competence in children with an immigration background has been researched using both cross-sectional methods (assessment of those children's linguistic skills in both languages at a specific time in their development) and longitudinal methods (with or without intervention). For the HELASCOT project, we chose a longitudinal design with three periods of data collection (see the section 'Methodology').

More precisely, the HELASCOT project aimed to describe the development of literacy in Portuguese heritage speakers in Switzerland from the beginning of Grade 3 (roughly 8 years of age) to the end of Grade 4 (10 years of age) in both of their languages, and to document instances of the crosslinguistic transfer of literacy skills.

The Portuguese population was chosen for several reasons. The Portuguese make up the third largest immigrant community in Switzerland and constitute 13% of the foreign population (267,500 people according to the 2015 census). Most of the Portuguese living in Switzerland (or their parents) arrived in the country in the 1980s and 1990s as labour immigrants. They therefore form a well-established immigrant community in Switzerland, benefiting from a large network of cultural and sports associations as well as high participation in HLC classes. Following Fibbi *et al.* (2010: 87), 70% of the Portuguese children take HLC classes.

Nevertheless, Portuguese adults in Switzerland have lower educational levels than other populations: 58% stopped their schooling at the end of compulsory education. By way of comparison, only 16% of the Swiss citizens and 26% of migrants from other origin countries don't have a higher degree. Only 11% of the Portuguese adults hold a tertiary education degree, compared to 34% of the Swiss citizens and 39% of migrants from other origins. This pattern seems to reproduce in the next generation: Portuguese children are under-represented in the most demanding school curricula and over-represented in the lowest levels (Statistics on Pupils and

Students 2014–2015, Federal Office of Statistics). Consequently, it seemed important to us (and to the stakeholders on the Swiss federal and cantonal levels) to investigate Portuguese children's literacy development.

From a transfer research perspective, the decision to investigate Portuguese heritage speakers' literacy development was also a strategic one that allowed us to explore the influence of linguistic typology on transfer processes. Participants of the study were children living in either the French- or German-speaking part of Switzerland. Their linguistic repertoires consequently consisted of either two closely related languages (Portuguese and French) or two more distantly related languages (Portuguese and German).

Methodology

Participants performed two tasks during three periods of data collection in both of their languages: reading comprehension (see Chapter 4 for details) and written production (see Chapter 5). The data collection took place at the beginning of Grade 3 (when the pupils were roughly 8 years of age), end of Grade 3 and end of Grade 4 (when the pupils were roughly 10 years of age). The participants' parents also completed a questionnaire on the children's exposure to languages, the family literacy practice, their own level of proficiency in the school language and their socio-economic status (see Chapter 3 for more details) (Figure 2.1).

Participants

The design of this study called for a considerable number of participants. As a result, our efforts to recruit participants took place throughout the whole German- and French-speaking part of Switzerland, as well as Portugal for comparison. A total of 508 pupils participated in the study.

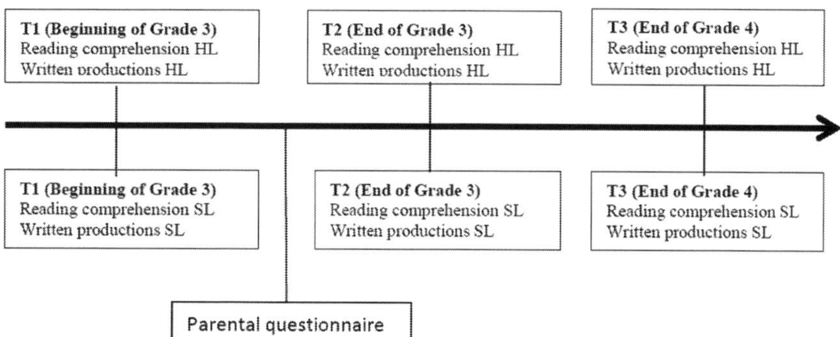

Figure 2.1 Research design of the HELASCOT project. HL=heritage language (i.e. Portuguese), SL=school language (i.e. French or German)

Their parents gave written consent. More precisely, the sample consists of five groups:

- Portuguese heritage speakers living in French-speaking Switzerland (*n*=124); 73% of them were taking HLC courses at the time of the study.
- Portuguese heritage speakers living in German-speaking Switzerland (*n*=128); 97% of them were taking HLC courses at the time of the study.
- Comparison group in French-speaking Switzerland (*n*=82) and comparison group in German-speaking Switzerland (*n*=81): the two Swiss comparison groups were composed of children following the regular Swiss curriculum.
- Comparison group in Portugal (*n*=93): data were collected in two schools in Portugal.

Among Portuguese heritage speakers in French- and German-speaking Switzerland, the over-representation of children taking HLC courses is due to recruiting difficulties. The HELASCOT project benefited from the support of the coordinator of Portuguese HLC courses in Switzerland and its leading institution, the Camões Institute. Thanks to this support, 13 Portuguese HLC course teachers accepted our invitation to participate in the study, and gave us access to their classes. They helped us convince students and parents of the importance of the study and collected the consent forms signed by the parents.

Recruiting Portuguese children not taking HLC courses, on the other hand, turned out to be difficult, even if we rewarded them with a small present and a modest sum of money. Ninety-nine Portuguese associations as well as the Ministries of Education of all French- and German-speaking Swiss cantons were contacted by either phone or mail. Some of them forwarded the information to primary school principals, others allowed us to contact schools with a high percentage of foreign children and others gave us permission to get in touch directly with parents of Portuguese-speaking children registered to start Grade 3. Portuguese-speaking assistants contacted 324 parents, mainly by phone. Furthermore, over 1500 information flyers were distributed, 400 of which had a prepaid return envelope. Yet, in total, only 38 Portuguese children not taking HLC classes could be recruited for the project. This very low rate of success can be explained by several factors. The first one, as mentioned above, is linked to the particularities of the Portuguese diaspora in Switzerland and its high loyalty to the HLC; 70% of the school-age Portuguese children in Switzerland take HLC classes. The second explanation is the additional time to be devoted to participate in the study. Participants from the four other groups answered the tasks during their (regular school or HLC) class hours, while Portuguese children who did not take HLC courses were expected to do it during their free time, due to a lack of any organisational alternatives. This perspective was often mentioned by parents as a decisive reason to turn down our invitation.

Dropout rate

Longitudinal studies often must deal with the attrition of its sample as time goes by (see, for instance, Cotter, 2005; Epstein & Botvin, 2000; Foss *et al.*, 2013). In our case, the aim was to retain as many participants as possible for a rather charged research design: bilingual participants had to participate in six data collections and participants from the comparison groups in three data collections in two calendar years. In the following, we discuss the dropout rate for each group of participants.

The above-mentioned numbers per group represent participants who completed at least one test (at T1, T2 or T3). Among the bilinguals, there are some who, at a certain time of data collection, participated in only one session (in their school language but not in their heritage language, or vice versa). Besides the number of participants who completed at least one test, two other measures are used to define the dropout rate: the number of participants who completed all tests at T1, and the number of participants who completed all tests at T1, T2 and T3. These three measures allow the calculation of two dropout rates (see Table 2.1): the low dropout rate compares the number of participants who completed all tests (T1, T2, T3) with the number of participants who completed all tests at T1. The high dropout rate compares the number of participants who wrote all tests (T1, T2, T3) with the overall number of individuals who took part in at least one period of data collection.

As Table 2.1 shows, most of the bilingual participants could be recruited in the German-speaking part of Switzerland. At the same time, the biggest dropout rate among HLC participants also occurred in this part of Switzerland. This high dropout rate can be explained by a misunderstanding at one time of data collection which resulted in a group failing to complete a test. Besides this singular event, the highest sample attrition concerned the non-HLC group in the French part of Switzerland. A closer look at the 18 participants who did all 6 tests shows that 8 did the tests during their normal school time (most of the times, this was also the case for the four non-HLC German bilinguals). From the remaining 10 participants, the majority (8) completed the tests at home or in their own city. By comparison, among the 16 who did not participate in all 6 tests, 13 were supposed to do the tests outside normal school time. Out of these 13, 6 had to travel to the place where the data collection took place.

Even though our dropout figures are similar to those mentioned in the literature (see, for instance, Foss *et al.*, 2013; Moser, 2008), we might have been more successful in both recruiting and retaining participants if we had more insistently called for the support of the participants' teachers and schools. This would have increased the possibility of taking the tests during regular school time (and therefore not forcing participants to give up

Table 2.1 Number of participants per group who completed at least one test, completed all tests at T1 and completed all tests at T1, T2 and T3

	No. of participants who completed at least one test	*No. of participants who completed all tests at T1*	*No. of participants who completed all tests at T1, T2, T3*	*Dropout high (%)*	*Dropout low (%)*
HLC bilinguals (German)	124	107	67	46	37
Non-HLC bilinguals (German)	4	4	4	0	0
HLC bilinguals (French)	90	79	68	24	14
Non-HLC bilinguals (French)	34	25	18	47	28
Control (French)	82	78	65	21	17
Control (German)	81	80	74	9	8
Control (Portuguese)	93	89	76	18	15
Total bilinguals	252	215	157	38	27
Total	508	462	372	27	20

Note: The high dropout rate compares the number of participants who wrote all tests with the number of participants who completed at least one test. The low dropout rate compares the number of participants who completed all tests with the number of participants who completed all tests at T1.

their free time or to travel to take the tests). Furthermore, the support of an institution that has strong links with children and parents might have increased their understanding of the pertinence of the project.

The HELASCOT Project: Development of Skills and Interdependence between Heritage and School Languages

The low number of non-HLC participants made it impossible to compare Portuguese children that did and did not take HLC classes. The specific question of the impact of HLC classes on both heritage and school language is therefore not part of our investigation.[3] The data collected in the HELASCOT project, however, allow us to describe the development of writing and reading comprehension skills in the heritage and school languages and to put the interdependence hypothesis regarding the transfer or shared nature of literacy skills to the test. In particular, in this book we compare the development of literacy in heritage speakers to its development in monolingual comparison participants (reading comprehension, Chapter 4; writing skills, Chapter 5), and test the interdependence hypothesis and the influence of linguistic typology in transfer processes (Chapter 6).

Acknowledgement

We thank all students and research assistants who participated in the project – Fabricio Decândio, Monique Schoch, Mirjam Andexlinger, Eglantine Dousse, Carole Brülhart, Rebecca Schaer, Susanne Christen, Sandra Bucheli, Barbara Wucherer, Anne-Laure Aubry, Audrey Bonvin, Ladina Stocker, Catia Parente da Silva and Lavinia Lainsbury – for their work throughout the project. We also thank our participants: pupils, parents, compulsory education teachers in Switzerland and Portugal and teachers of Portuguese heritage language courses in Switzerland. This research could not have taken place without the support of António Proença from the Portuguese Ministry of Education and the different coordinators of Portuguese heritage courses in Switzerland: Mariana Gois Neves, Anabela Albino and Maria Lurdes Gonçalves, thank you!

Notes

(1) In Switzerland, each of the 26 cantons has the primary responsability for compulsory education.

(2) *L'élève allophone ne peut véritablement apprendre le français que si sa langue d'origine est bien structurée. Dans cette optique, il est important d'encourager les élèves à participer aux cours de langue et culture d'origine.* (Directive P-DGEP-02A-02, page 1, our translation)

(3) See Chapters 7 and 8 of this book for two longitudinal intervention studies from Switzerland that allow an investigation of this question, although drawing on different samples and different heritage languages.

References

EDK (Swiss Conference of Cantonal Ministers of Education) (1998) *Quelles langues apprendre en Suisse pendant la scolarité obligatoire?* Bern: CDIP.

Cotter, R.B., Burke, J.D., Stouthamer-Loeber, M. and Loeber, R. (2005) Contacting participants for follow-up: How much effort is required to retain participants in longitudinal studies? *Evaluation and Program Planning* 28 (1), 15–21.

Epstein, J. and Botvin, G.J. (2000) Methods to decrease attrition in longitudinal studies with adolescents. *Psychological Reports* 87 (1), 139–140.

Foss, E., Druin, A. and Guha, M.L. (2013) Recruiting and retaining young participants: Strategies from five years of field research. In *Proceedings of the 12th International Conference on Interaction Design and Children* (pp. 313–316). New York: ACM.

3 On the Sociolinguistic Embedding of Portuguese Heritage Language Speakers in Switzerland: Socio-Economic Status and Home Literacy Environment (HELASCOT Project)

Magalie Desgrippes and Amelia Lambelet

Introduction

The study of language and literacy development and of possible transfers of competencies by bilinguals is at the crossroads of several fields of study: psycholinguistics, sociolinguistics and applied linguistics, but also developmental psychology and educational science. Especially in the latter fields, language development is seen in a holistic or ecological view (Bronfenbrenner, 1979), with many factors at play. These may be individual factors, for instance, health, motivation, attitude or cognitive abilities; proximal factors, for example, the qualitative and quantitative input provided by the parents; or more distal factors like socio-economic status (SES), the overall language environment, linguistic properties of the languages and their possible interplay in contact situations, as well as language policies in the family and in the society. As proximal factors and distal factors were found to be related (e.g. Hoff, 2012), we should strive for a unified model considering all forces at play in the investigation of heritage language speakers' language development. Unfortunately, this is often not empirically possible given the available samples' sizes. Therefore, choices must be made following theoretical and methodological considerations. In this chapter, we shed some light on our manner of investigating proximal and distal factors that are deemed to have an impact on migrant Portuguese children's literacy development.

This study is part of the 'Heritage Language and School Language: Are Literacy Skills Transferable?' (HELASCOT) project. It is based on a questionnaire answered by a majority of the participants' parents, and therefore gives a valuable insight into the participants' linguistic and social backgrounds. The results also allow a discussion of the particularities of Portuguese speakers in Switzerland, in particular in contrast to other groups in Switzerland and Portugal.

We answer the following research questions:

- What are the specificities of Portuguese heritage speaker participants in terms of language environment, SES and home literacy environment in comparison to children from the comparison groups (monolingual and migrant with other origins)?
- Are there differences between Portuguese heritage speakers living in French- and German-speaking Switzerland in terms of language environment, SES and home literacy environment?

After a discussion of the terms 'heritage language' and 'heritage language speakers', we review different proximal and distal factors known to have an impact on heritage speakers' language and literacy development. In the remainder of the chapter, we provide a description of our study, questionnaire and results.

On the terms 'heritage language' and 'heritage language speakers'

We frame our analyses using the terms 'heritage language' and 'heritage language speaker'. Alternative terms with somewhat different entailments can be found in the literature on interdependence and the transfer of literacy skills in multilingual migrant children. In what follows, we briefly discuss our conceptual frame.

In the HELASCOT project, the participants are children whose parents are mostly Portuguese immigrants in Switzerland. If they live in the French-speaking region, these children have the possibility to access courses called *'cours en langue et culture d'origine'*, while their peers in the German-speaking region can go to *'Heimatliche Sprache und Kultur'* courses. Both terms convey different semantic features: the French term refers to a past migration and its geographical starting point with its language and culture, even if the speaker is from the third generation living in the country. The German word 'Heimat' (homeland) relates to a current situation of belonging and identity, thus constructing the speaker as not belonging to the society they are living in.

Also found in German academic literature and politics, the term 'Kinder mit Migrationshintergrund' (children with a migration background) has been coined and mostly relates to the study of the children's deficits in the school system or of the politics set to counter this situation. Using the English term 'heritage language' thus seems to be more neutral. Indeed, *heritage* can be understood as 'a trait or an asset gained through birth' (King & Ennser-Kananen, 2013; Melo-Pfeiffer, 2015). Moreover, heritage is characterised by variation in the inherited resources' quantity and quality, in the bond between the heir and the person they inherit from, in the heir's agency (i.e. their acceptance or denial of the heritage) and in the environmental factors that influence how the inherited resources are going to be managed and nurtured (even in the case of DNA, whose expression, as epigenetics show, also depends on environmental influence). Furthermore, 'heritage' isn't linked to past traditions and more 'primitive times' in the European multilingual context (see the fears expressed by Baker & Jones, 1998; Van Deusen-Scholl, 2003).

Most research on heritage language speakers relies on the definition used in foreign language teaching and set out by Valdés (2005) for the US context: 'a student of language who is raised in a home where a non-English language is spoken' and who 'speaks or merely understands the heritage language and who is to some degree bilingual in English and the heritage language'. Adapting this definition to a context where English is not the official language inevitably brings us to use the concepts of minority and majority languages; the minority languages being spoken mostly at home and in the community, while the majority language(s) are also the one(s) of the school system.

Attention towards heritage languages grew in the United States at the end of the last century with the First National Conference on Heritage Language in America focusing on the challenges of heritage language education. From an American point of view, heritage languages subsume immigrant, indigenous and colonial languages other than English (Fishman, 2001). In other contexts, the terms used are immigrant, indigenous and 'world' languages, and some scholars have pointed out that even English can be a heritage language (Benmamoun *et al.*, 2013b, citing Viswanath, 2013).[1]

In Switzerland, a country with four official languages/linguistic regions (in decreasing order: German, French, Italian and Rumantsch), two official languages (Italian and French) are taught as heritage languages outside of their linguistic regions; the other two (German and Rumantsch) are not taught as such in any canton.[2] The existence of heritage language courses for Italian and French has nevertheless nothing to do with their status as official languages. Both have been organised by migrant communities, Italian even being the first language taught in that context in the 1930s (Giudici & Bühlmann, 2014), and French heritage courses being apparently a new trend, existing in parallel with some French schools connected to the school system of France.

For German and French in particular, but also for other languages taught at school, like Italian or Spanish, the situation described by Valdés (2005) for the United States can be found in Swiss classes: these languages are taught at school as foreign languages;[3] French and German are even taught in primary school. Thus, students may attend foreign language classes of (one of) their native language(s) if they live in another linguistic region. This is not the case for Portuguese speaking students, or very sporadically in some cantons where Portuguese is taught as a foreign language at the secondary school level. The need for differentiating between heritage and foreign language learning is therefore less acute in that particular pedagogical context.

One might ask with Meisel (2013) if the distinction between bilinguals and heritage language speakers really needs to be made, and what the added value of this distinction is. Meisel (2013) as well as Rothman (2009) see the heritage language differentiation as essentially sociolinguistic, which, following Meisel, is a reason to discard its importance in the study of bilingualism. On the contrary, we argue that the sociolinguistic features conveyed by the concept of heritage language are essential in the study of heritage language speakers' language development: heritage language speakers may be speakers of varieties that evolved differently in the community than in the 'home country' because of different patterns of language use and different contact situations (with the majority language(s) in the 'host' country or with other languages and dialects in the country 'of origin'). Therefore, from a normative and prescriptive point of view, they might not be acknowledged as legitimate (bilingual) speakers of any of the two languages (see Muysken, 2013; Valdés, 2005).

As far as the heritage language speakers' needs are concerned, Valdés (2005) thus considers that heritage language students' literacy development should be seen as second language literacy development in the majority language, and maybe second dialect literacy development in the heritage language (comparable to literacy development in standard German which dialect speakers have to go through in Switzerland). Valdés (2005) also points to the differences in registers that heritage language speakers may be fluent in, and takes as an example the goal that they can have to extend their 'repertoires to include styles and registers of the heritage language appropriate for communicating in academic or professional settings'.

This last point leads us to the importance of heritage language speakers' SES. SES is at the centre of many researches on heritage language speakers. This line of research shows that heritage language speakers often suffer from disadvantages in the society they are living in. These disadvantages can be of a socio-economic nature, but even at the higher end of the socio-economic scale, heritage language speakers might have to fight with interpretations of their bilingualism as an impairment in educational contexts (Kirsch, 2012).

We thus consider that using the term 'heritage language speakers' is appropriate as they are minorities living with inherited resources that they might want to develop or retain. This is particularly evident in the case of the Portuguese in Switzerland, as we will argue in the remainder of this chapter.

Portuguese in Switzerland

The Portuguese community is the third biggest foreign community in Switzerland. It represented 13% of the foreign population in 2015. Because of this, this population has been the subject of particular attention from the Federal Office of Migration, who ordered a study on the Portuguese diaspora in Switzerland. Relevant features of the Portuguese diaspora are that it is mostly a form of labour migration, with a high probability of remigration to the home country in the third age (Fibbi *et al.*, 2010). This goes hand in hand with a small proportion of naturalisation and a weaker tendency to learn the majority language, at least as far as the first generation is concerned.

Marked by the long-lasting authoritarian regime of Salazar, Portugal established an obligatory school system of four years until the late 1960s and of six years until the 1980s. However, the implementation of this system remained patchy. Therefore, the first wave of migrants, who arrived before 1980 were mostly from rural regions of Portugal, was less educated than other immigrant populations in Switzerland (Fibbi *et al.*, 2010). Today, Portugal has caught up with European standards in education; therefore, the new waves of migrants (since the last economic crisis) have a different educational background than former immigrants. Nevertheless, when comparing Portuguese speakers with other groups in terms of educational level, differences are still striking: in 2016, 58% of the adult Portuguese living in Switzerland had completed only compulsory school (compared to 16% of the Swiss and 26% of foreigners from other countries), 30% have a secondary II degree (50% of the Swiss and 34% of foreigners from other EU countries) and only 11% have a tertiary degree (34% of the Swiss and 39% of foreigners from other EU countries). We will discuss these characteristics of Portuguese heritage language speakers in Switzerland based on our data in the 'Results' section.

The pressure to learn the majority language of the linguistic region is high in both the French- and the German-speaking part of Switzerland. Based on detailed analyses of the 2000 census data, it seems to be somewhat higher in the French-speaking area than in the German-speaking area (cf. Lüdi & Werlen, 2005: 31). However, there are also policies favouring the maintenance and development of the heritage language. Both the law on languages (*'Sprachengesetz'*) from 2007 and the directive on languages ('Sprachenverordnung') from 2010 pursue a 30-year federal tradition of encouraging the cantons responsible for the educational institutions to respect the right of heritage language speakers to speak and learn their languages. Cantons are encouraged to help the organisation of heritage language courses (provide classrooms and materials, and allow the courses to take place during normal school time) and to valorise the resources and work of the heritage language learners in their curriculum (indicate the results on the grade sheet, organise contacts between heritage language and school teachers, and take the children's heritage language background into account when decisions concerning their future orientation are made) (Calderón *et al.*, 2013; EDK, 1991). Some cantons have newly developed special guidelines or general curricula for heritage language courses that must be followed if school premises and materials are used (for instance, Zürich's 'Bildungsdirektion des Kantons Zürich', 2011). Nevertheless, the heritage language courses are organised and paid for by the heritage country. In the case of Portuguese, the heritage language courses are under the responsibility of the Camões Institute, which also hires the teachers and sets the curriculum. In cantons where an accreditation system exists, the Portuguese courses are accredited and thus take place in school buildings. Most of the time, though, courses take place outside normal school time, in general on Wednesdays (afternoon or evening) and Saturdays.

Background Factors Influencing Literacy Development

The Portuguese heritage speakers' sociolinguistic embedding requires researchers to consider a great number of factors known to potentially influence their language competence. A first set of factors pertains to the children's *language environment*, i.e. the quantitative and qualitative input they receive in each of their languages (De Houwer, 2007; Meisel, 2013; Place & Hoff, 2011; Scheffner Hammer *et al.*, 2014). Also, the *socio-economic status* of the family, the *home literacy environment* (Farver *et al.*, 2013; Reese *et al.*, 2000), the *parents' length of stay and language competence in both languages* (Place & Hoff, 2011) and the *community's sociolinguistic background and activities* (Brizić, 2007; Melo-Pfeifer, 2015) are all potentially relevant for shaping the children's literacy acquisition process.

We briefly discuss these different factors in the next subsections, before giving an insight into the characteristics of the HELASCOT project's participants.

Sociolinguistic background

Several features of the society and of the community are known to have an influence on heritage language competence. Among them are family representations of linguistic power and prestige (Tse, 2001), family's length of stay in the host country and its well-being (Carreira & Kagan, 2011), social linguistic attitudes and representations regarding migrant communities' languages and culture, social pressure regarding the mastery of the host language (Oriyama, 2011), political support in the form of linguistic policies (Shohamy, 2006), sociocultural context (Oriyama, 2011) and community initiatives to improve the learning of heritage and host languages (García *et al.*, 2013).

Language environment

In a critical review of the language and literacy development of young dual language learners, Hammer *et al.* (2014) report the influence of two main factors: the amount of language exposure and the learner's usage of their two languages. The more a child is exposed to a language, the more they will develop this language (Hammer *et al.*, 2014; Oller & Eilers, 2002; Parra *et al.*, 2011; Quiroz *et al.*, 2010). Several components of language exposure having an impact on language development have been identified. For instance, the number of words that parents pronounce in an hour has been found to be related to the child's vocabulary size (De Houwer, 2009). In bilingual language development, the relative amount of exposure in each language is related to the vocabulary size in the respective languages (Place & Hoff, 2011). The syntactic complexity of the input is also meant to play a role (Huttenlocher *et al.*, 2002), as well as the way that parents communicate with their child (Sohr-Preston *et al.*, 2013) and the use of code-mixing in the family (Byers-Heinlein, 2013; but see Bail *et al.*, 2015). This influence of the input has a long-term impact, as the results of Gathercole and Thomas (2009) on Welsh–English bilinguals in Wales suggest.

Socio-economic status

SES refers to the 'relative position in a social hierarchy based on access to, or control over, wealth, prestige and power' (Hoff *et al.*, 2012). It is a construct building on different sorts of resources, or 'capitals' (Coleman, 1988; Hoff *et al.*, 2012). Even if most research in psychology relies on the mother's educational level as a marker of SES, thus emphasising human capital and the importance of mothers in education, SES is also meant to be composed of both parent's educational levels and financial and social capital (Coleman, 1988), as well as occupational status and financial income (Bornstein *et al.*, 2003; Hoff, 2006). One of the most cited studies on the relationship between SES and input and its influence on vocabulary development is Hart and Risley (1995), who state that higher SES children not only hear more but also more different words from their parents than children from working-class parents, and even more than low-SES children. These often-cited results have also been highly criticised methodologically, in particular in terms of data collection (lower-SES populations might talk less in an intimidating laboratory condition) and treatment (as the features coded and used for the measure of quality are known features of middle-class talk, their correlation with the social class constitutes a circular argument; see, for instance, Michaels [2013]). Language development has also been found to be related to SES without the mediation of language input. For example, Fernald *et al.* (2013) found disparities in vocabulary and language processing between 18-month-old children from low- and high-SES families, which extend to a 6-month gap by the age of 24 months.

Home literacy environment

Given the HELASCOT's focus on literacy competencies and their transferability across languages, we cannot ignore the whole body of research dedicated to the influence of the home literacy environment on language and on literacy development, a construct that had already been found to play a role in monolingualism (Davis-Kean, 2005; Payne *et al.*, 1994).In a state of the art review highly relevant to the context of heritage language speakers, Dixon and Wu (2014) include studies that document home literacy practices in immigrant families. They shed light on factors having an impact on the occurrence of home literacy practices, the impact of these practices on children's literacy development and the mediators and moderators involved. A whole range of home literacy practices were reported to be part of the families' routine of immigrants: the most studied are book reading (e.g. Farver *et al.*, 2013; Scheele *et al.*, 2010), schoolwork, reading for fun or religious purposes, literacy teaching following the respective pedagogical cultures and oral literacy practices (e.g. Sneddon, 2000). Literacy practices at home were found to be positively related to child language and literacy outcomes, without cross-language effects in one study (Farver *et al.*, 2013), and with a longitudinal cross-lagged effect of home literacy environment on seventh-grade school language English, mediated by Spanish literacy skills and oral English proficiency in Kindergarten, in another study (Reese *et al.*, 2000). Book reading to the child is one of the practices found to have a positive impact on both heritage and school languages (e.g. Farver *et al.*, 2013; Quiroz *et al.*, 2010), whereas library use has been found to have an impact only in the case of families having fewer books at home (Dixon & Wu, 2014).

In the HELASCOT project, we tried to take into account all the aforementioned factors in our description of Portuguese heritage speakers' biliteracy development. We describe the principal results of this investigation in the next section.

Method

As our participants were eight years old at the beginning of the project, we decided to assess their language environment, home literacy and SES background by means of a questionnaire sent to all parents (Portuguese living in Switzerland and comparison groups). Two versions of the questionnaire were developed: one for monolingual families (comparison groups in Switzerland and Portugal) and one for multilingual families (Portuguese families in Switzerland, but also families from the comparison groups). As about one quarter of the population living in Switzerland are foreigners,[4] many children of the comparison groups speak more than one language. These questionnaires, as well as the data collection design, are presented in the next subsection.

Data collection

In the HELASCOT project, three measurement times were used to collect the longitudinal literacy data (see Chapter 2 of this book for details on the sample, tasks and longitudinal design). Between T2 and T3, parents completed the questionnaire. Portuguese parents of children following heritage language courses answered the questionnaire during parental meetings. One or two researchers attended the meetings and helped some of the parents to fill out their questionnaires. Parents from the comparison groups received the questionnaire from the class teachers and filled it out at home. The questionnaires were handed back to the teachers who sent them back to the researchers. In cases of incomplete questionnaires, researchers called the parents directly by phone to obtain accurate answers. Overall, the response rate was about 80%. Some differences between groups were observed (see Table 3.1).

Table 3.1 Number of questionnaires by group

	Amount of languages				*Total answered questionnaires*	*n*	*Response rate*
	1	*2*	*3*	*4*			
German-speaking comparison group	50	24	3	0	77	80	0.96
French-speaking comparison group	25	23	2	0	50	80	0.62
Portuguese-speaking comparison group	68	7	0	0	75	85	0.88
German-Portuguese group	0	84	6	0	90	116	0.78
French-Portuguese group	0	90	6	1	96	120	0.80

Note: The distribution of children per number of languages spoken is given for each group, as well as the response rate per group.

Questionnaire

The questionnaire was designed and translated for monolingual and multilingual families into Portuguese, French and German. The Portuguese version was piloted in Portuguese with the parents of 21 Portuguese children in the presence of a bilingual student who intervened when questions were too difficult, sensitive or lacking a response possibility that would be relevant.

Questions and variables correspondence

Language environment

The language environment questions distinguish four age periods: from birth to age 3, from age 3 to the start of preschool, during preschool and from starting school. Parents were asked to estimate in percentage (total obligatory=100) which languages the child had been in contact with during each of those periods. The same question design (percentage of use) was used to ask for the current language environment in the family. These data are complemented with the parents' length of stay in the language region, as well as their auto-estimated level of proficiency in each language (school language, Portuguese and other languages on Likert scales from 0 [not at all] to 6 [perfectly]). As the parents were asked to indicate the number of years of residence and their age, we are also able to distinguish between first- and second-generation immigrants.

Socioeconomic status

The questionnaire features two widely used indicators of SES status: (1) the parents' educational level and (2) their financial resources. The educational level is operationalised via a 5-point Likert scale (0=no primary school, 1=primary school level, 2=compulsory [9 years] education, 3=achieved secondary school [12 years], 4=apprenticeship or professional school, 5=tertiary educational level, university or similar). Financial resources were elicited in two ways: first of all, five items of the 'Family Resources scale' (Dittmeier & Dunst, 2001) were chosen: standard bills, salary, healthcare and health insurance, savings and travel/holidays. For each of these items, parents were asked if their resources were sufficient or not (Likert scales from 1 to 5, from 'not at all enough' to 'always enough'). The second, more direct question on financial resources asked about the family's income in five categories: less than 5000 CHF (a bit above the poverty line for a family with two children in Switzerland[5]); between 5000 and 10,000 CHF; between 10,000 CHF and 15,000 CHF; between 15,000 CHF and 20,000 CHF; and more than 20,000 CHF. This scale was adapted to the economic context in Portugal: below €700 (also a bit above the poverty line defined for a family with two children in Portugal); between €700 and €1400; between €1400 and €2800; and above €2800.

Home literacy environment

The home literacy environment can either be reduced to the reading habits of the child and the number of books they own (Davis-Kean, 2005), or it can be elicited with a longer questionnaire. We opted for the second solution and adapted the Stony Brook Family Survey (Whitehurst, 2001) to our context. Two questions were asked without mentioning the language of the activity: the frequency of reading activities initiated by the child and the frequency of visits to the library. Other questions were asked separately for each language: frequency of parents' story reading (before literacy development); number of children books owned (5-point Likert scale: 0–2; 3–10; 11–20; 21–40; more than 40); time spent watching television, videos or films in a day (5-point Likert scales: never; less than half an hour; 30–60 minutes; 1–3 hours; more than 3 hours); and frequency with which the child sees each parent read a newspaper or a book. All the frequency questions were to be answered on a 4-point Likert scale (almost never; once or twice a month; once or twice a week; almost every day).

Results

Due to length restrictions, we only provide a partial overview of the evidence gathered in this questionnaire-based survey. Our goal is to describe the sample and show similarities and differences between Portuguese migrant children's and comparison groups' sociolinguistic background. We therefore display boxplots and data points representing the answers in each group to give a good overview of the distribution of the data and make differences visible instead of running inferential statistics systematically. The only exception is for the SES markers, which are intended to be aggregated, and therefore are explored by means of correlations. The answers on home literacy environment are shown in a table (means and standard deviations by group).

Differences between Portuguese children living in French- and German-speaking Switzerland are discussed. The 'Results' section is organised into three subsections. First, the particularities of our participants' language environment are presented. Then, the discussion focuses on their SES background and on their home literacy environment.

Language environment

As detailed above, the children's language environment was described by questions on the percentage of contact with each language, as well as parents' length of stay and self-assessment of their proficiency in the school language.

The first item we describe is the percentage of time the children are exposed to the school language. This information was collected on about

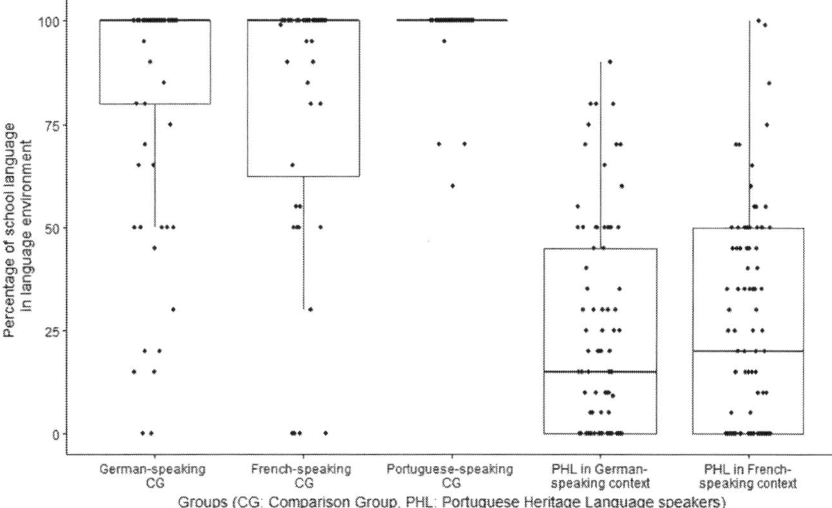

Figure 3.1 Proportion of the school language in the multilingual (Portuguese and other origins) children's language environment before preschool. The middle line of the plot gives the median answer to the question (which means that 50% of the group answered above the value), upper and lower ends of the boxes give the upper and lower quartiles of the data (25% of the group has answers less or greater than this value, respectively) and the vertical lines connect the minimum and the maximum values excluding outliers

all the multilingual children (i.e. Swiss German speakers and those with a Portuguese or other non-local language background). The answers are therefore also interesting from a comparative perspective, as the Portuguese diaspora is considered to be more communitarian than other diasporas in Switzerland (see above, and Fibbi *et al.*, 2010). The answer to these questions being almost identical for the first two age periods (from birth to 3, and between 3 and preschool), and for the next two (during preschool and since starting school) these four variables were merged into two (before preschool and after entering school). As Figure 3.1 shows, before starting preschool, the Portuguese-speaking children living in Switzerland have much less contact with the school language than the other multilinguals from the comparison classes. Most of them are in contact with their future school language less than 50% of the time, and 50% of them less than 25% of the time. The ceiling effect in the Portuguese comparison group shows the very little contact with other languages in this group, as only outliers seem to hear less than 100% Portuguese before preschool.

After starting preschool, we observe an increase in contact with the school language for Portuguese children, while it remains quite stable

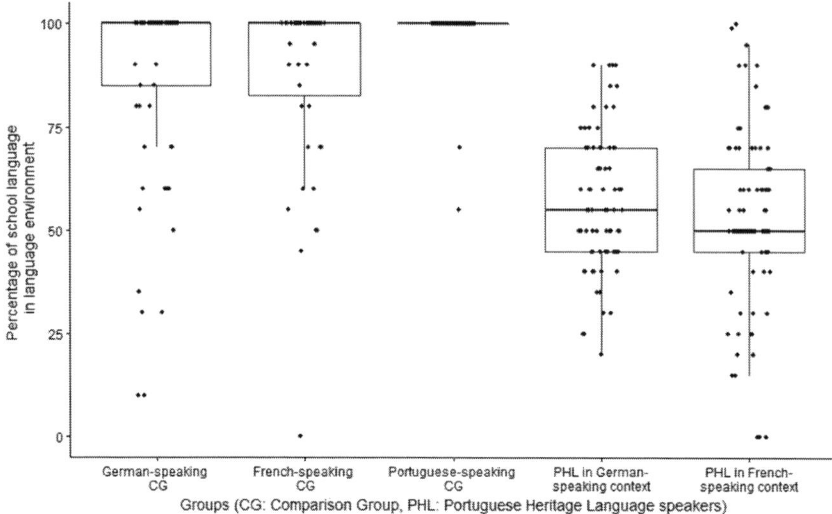

Figure 3.2 Proportion of the school language in (Portuguese and other origins) children's language environment after entering the school system

for the other multilinguals from the comparison group (Figure 3.2). This probably reflects a division between family life in one language and school in the other language for the Portuguese children living in Switzerland (with contact with the school language for 50% of the time or more). Nevertheless, for all the groups, the distribution of the data is narrower after entering the school system (Figure 3.2) than before (Figure 3.1).

The predominance of Portuguese in the children's environment before starting preschool could in theory be explained by the recent immigration of a substantial proportion of members of this group. Nevertheless, as can be inferred from Figure 3.3, almost all children were born in Switzerland. It seems that all the Portuguese parents arrived in Switzerland during an approximately 10-year migration wave, whereas the parents of the multilingual children in the comparison groups arrived over a more extended period.

This difference in length of stay might have an impact on the learning of the school language, which is an important feature of the family's language environment when it comes to the support parents give to their children for homework. This is indeed what Figure 3.4 shows regarding parents' self-assessed competence level in the school language. As all parents were asked this question (i.e. also the monolingual children's parents), the comparison groups' data converge towards the monolinguals' patterns. Nevertheless, Portuguese parents living in German-speaking Switzerland display strikingly low self-assessment scores of their proficiency in the school language (compared to parents of all other groups).

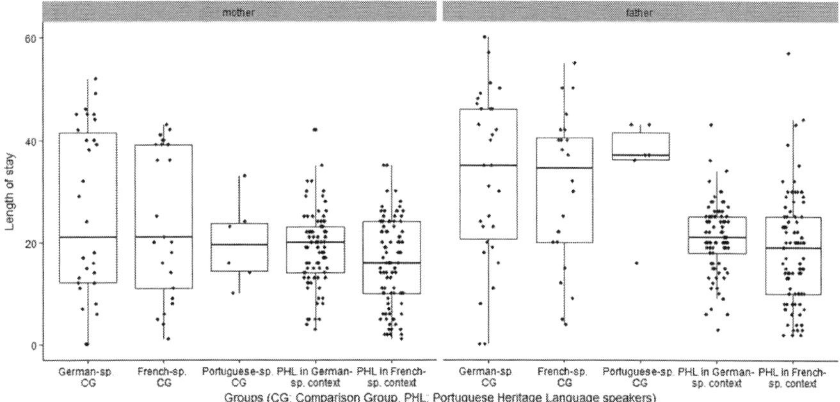

Figure 3.3 Length of stay of migrant (Portuguese and other origins) fathers and mothers in a region where the school language is the official language

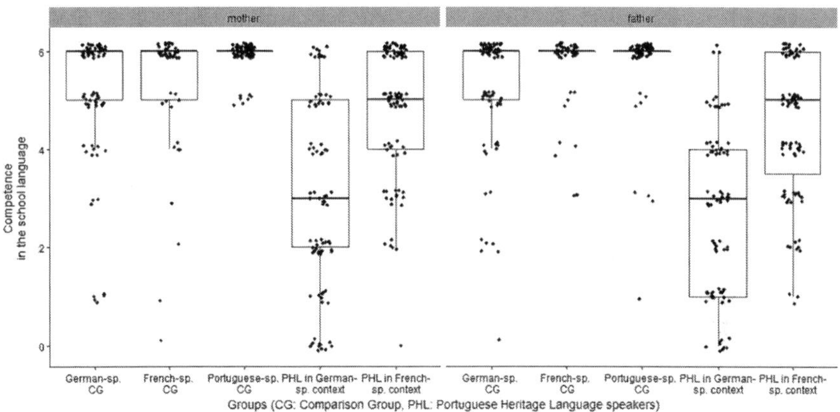

Figure 3.4 Self-assessed competence of the parents in the school language (standard for German). The comparison groups include monolingual children's parents

This difference in proficiency in the school language can be explained in several ways. One of them is the typological proximity of Portuguese and French (two Romance languages), which could account for a faster learning of French than of German. Another explanation could lie in the diglossic situation of the German-speaking part of Switzerland. Migrants in this region are often confronted in their everyday life with at least two languages: the Swiss-German dialect spoken in the region they're living in, and standard German, which is the language that their children develop literacy in. Parents might therefore acquire language skills (in dialect) not useful for helping their children in school-related learning in standard German (homework, for instance).

Finally, the last explanation of the difference between Portuguese living in French- and German-speaking Switzerland might also be linked to the foreign languages education system in Portugal: asked how they learnt the language of the country, 34 fathers and 30 mothers answered that they had learnt French at school in Portugal, whereas only three mothers had learnt German in Portugal.

Socio-economic status

SES in our data was measured in two dimensions and four types of questions: level of education (from the mother and the father) and financial resources (objective and subjective). As can be seen in Figure 3.5, Portuguese parents have a lower educational level than parents from the comparison groups (even if the Portuguese comparison group shows a wider distribution than the two Swiss comparison groups). Most of the Portuguese fathers living in Switzerland did not get any professional education: they have at best finished secondary school (or only compulsory school as far as fathers living in the German-speaking part of Switzerland are concerned).

The situation is somewhat different for Portuguese mothers living in both Swiss linguistic regions: 50% have finished obligatory school. Nevertheless, like the fathers, Portuguese mothers living in the German-speaking part of Switzerland have lower educational levels than their peers living in the French-speaking part.

Despite these differences in the level of education between the Portuguese living in German- and French-speaking parts of Switzerland, the other indicators of SES don't show financial dissimilarities between those two groups. In terms of objective income, the biggest difference is

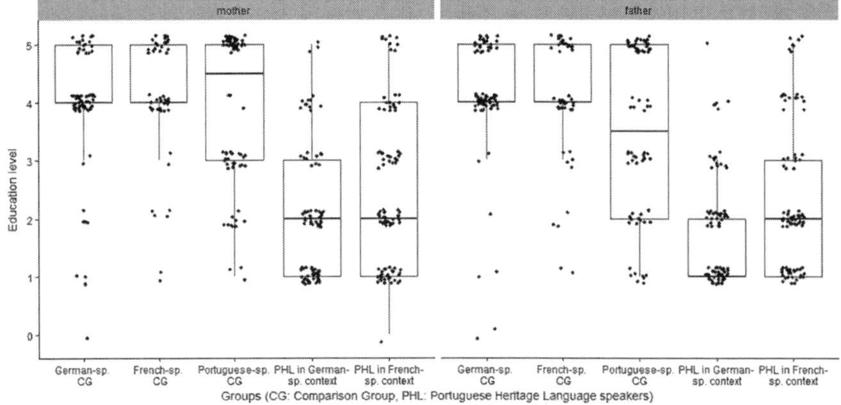

Figure 3.5 Educational level of the parents (from 1=primary school to 5=university or comparable). The comparison groups include monolingual children's parents

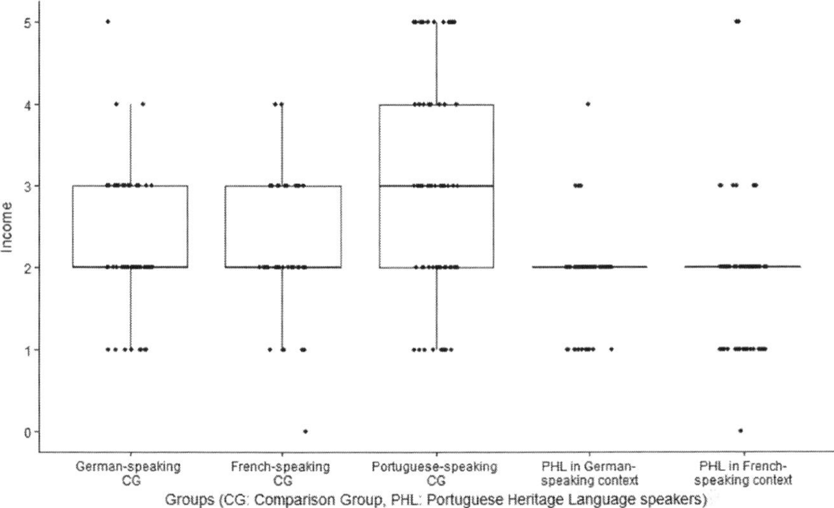

Figure 3.6 Income categories (the scale used in Portugal was adapted to Portuguese context).[6] The comparison groups include monolingual children's parents

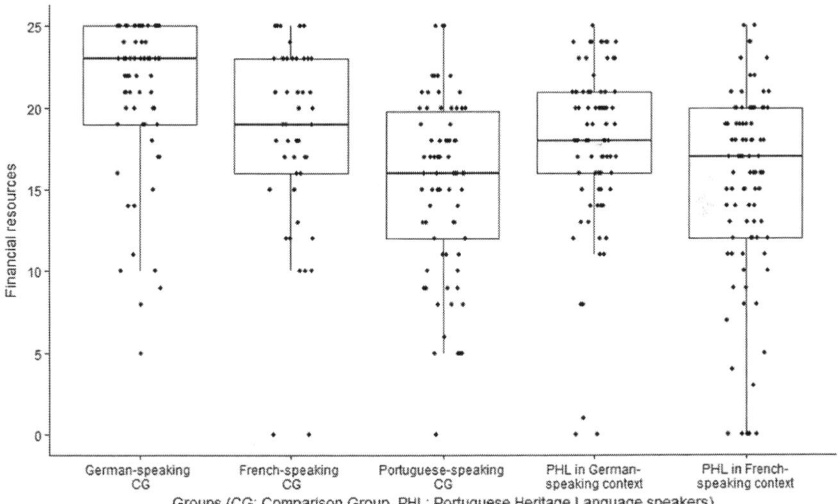

Figure 3.7 Index of financial resources covering the basic needs of the family. The comparison groups include monolingual children's parents

not between the Portuguese living in French- or in German-speaking parts of Switzerland, but between them and the comparison groups. As can be seen in Figure 3.6, almost all the Portuguese families living in Switzerland have an income between 5,000 CHF and 10,000 CHF,[6] while 50% of the families from the comparison groups have an income above 10,000 CHF. As the categories are different for Portugal (see above), the data are not really comparable. It is nevertheless worth noting that 50% of the Portuguese parents living in Portugal earn more than twice the amount fixed for the poverty line, and 25% earn even three times this amount. Therefore, participants from the monolingual Portuguese group seem to belong to quite privileged social groups in Portugal.

The second indicator of financial resources was more subjectivity oriented as it asked the participants if they had enough income for several basic needs (see above). Figure 3.7 shows a substantial overlap between the groups whereby the German-speaking comparison group seems to have a higher satisfaction level than the other groups, while the Portuguese comparison group and the French-Portuguese heritage speakers show the lowest level of satisfaction with the resources available.

Link between level of education, income and basic needs covering

As our participants' SES was measured in four dimensions, we ran correlation tests to see if they measure a unified construct, and to shed light on the relationships between level of education, income and the subjective evaluation of basic needs covering.

Over the whole sample, all the Spearman correlation coefficients calculated between the four variables are significant ($p<0.001$). Nevertheless, only the correlation between mothers and fathers' educational levels is strong ($r=0.74$, $n=370$), whereas the correlation between basic needs and income is moderate ($r=0.45$, $n=342$), as well as the correlation between income and fathers' ($r=0.42$, $n=334$) or mothers' educational levels ($r=0.48$, $n=339$). Furthermore, the correlation between basic needs covering and educational level is rather weak (fathers: $r=0.32$, $n=364$; mothers: $r=0.27$, $n=369$).

The picture is quite different if we take only the Swiss Portuguese sample: the index of basic needs covering and the income category correlate ($r=0.43$, $p<0.001$, $n=162$), as well as the educational levels of the mother and father ($r=0.54$, $p<0.001$, $n=176$), but the basic needs covering is not related to the educational level of the parents. This lack of relation is probably due to the overall low educational level of the Portuguese living in Switzerland. The Portuguese, on average, thus work in jobs at the lower end of the income scale (as seen in Figure 3.6). At first sight, the index of basic needs covering shows a surprisingly large overlap between the Portuguese comparison group and the Swiss Portuguese (Figure 3.7). This index represents a self-evaluation of the adequation of resources and needs. Thus, it is not impossible that the Portuguese living in Switzerland are similarly satisfied with their living conditions as the Portuguese with higher educational levels in Portugal.

Home literacy environment

Home literacy environment was measured by the means of several questions (see above). Except for two, all were collected for both languages of the children (Portuguese or other heritage language and school language). The means and standard deviations of the answers per group appear in Table 3.2.

The answers show several trends of inter-group differences and similarities. Portuguese parents living in Switzerland report reading more stories in Portuguese (between 'once or twice a week' and 'almost every day') than in the school language to their children (between 'once or twice a month' and 'once or twice a week'). In terms of differences between groups, French- and Portuguese-speaking comparison groups seem to read more to their children than the German-speaking comparison group, and more than the Portuguese living in Switzerland if we take languages separately. Nevertheless, if reading in heritage and school languages is added, Portuguese migrant parents read to their children just as much as, or even more, than their respective comparison groups.

Table 3.2 Mean and standard deviation for the home literacy environment questions

Mean (SD)	*Comparison groups*		*Swiss Portuguese*		
	German	*French*	*Portuguese*	*German*	*French*
Parental reading SL	2.04 (1.11)	2.48 (0.90)		1.07 (1.19)	1.48 (1.25)
Parental reading P			2.42 (0.76)	2.27 (0.87)	2.05 (0.97)
Books SL	3.19 (1.00)	3.51 (0.96)		2.24 (1.18)	2.49 (1.23)
Books P			3.28 (0.93)	1.93 (1.10)	1.82 (1.02)
Media time SL	1.81 (0.87)	1.94 (0.80)		2.12 (0.85)	2.10 (0.96)
Media time P			2.43 (0.86)	2.02 (0.99)	1.66 (1.16)
Father's reading SL	2.23 (1.06)	2.27 (1.09)		1.37 (1.30)	1.54 (1.18)
Father's reading P			1.61 (1.04)	1.39 (1.11)	1.22 (1.16)
Mother's reading SL	2.45 (0.88)	2.37 (1.01)		1.28 (1.14)	1.88 (1.07)
Mother's reading P			1.77 (1.01)	1.72 (1.12)	1.37 (1.10)
Library visits	1.26 (0.55)	0.98 (0.69)	1.29 (0.80)	1.37 (0.66))	1.01 (0.86)
Child's reading motivation	2.08 (1.04)	2.33 (0.85)	1.96 (0.89)	1.96 (0.83)	2.25 (0.90)

Note: All the frequency questions are answered on 4-point Likert scales: almost never (0), once or twice a month (1), once or twice a week (2), almost every day (3). The number of books is built on a 5-point Likert scale: 0–2 (0), 3–10 (1), 11–20 (2), 21–40 (3), more than 40 (4), as watching television: never (0), less than half an hour (1), 30– 60 minutes (2), 1–3 hours (3), more than 3 hours (4).

The data on parents' literacy habits show mainly differences between Swiss and Portuguese comparison groups. One of the questions tapping into this construct was 'How often does your child see you read in Lx?'. Fathers and mothers from the two Swiss comparison groups answer between 'once or twice a week' and 'almost every day', while parents from the Portuguese comparison groups tend to answer either 'once or twice a month' or 'once or twice a week'. But, for story reading, when adding the two languages, they seem to read more than the comparison parents.

The number of books the families have at their disposal also seems higher in the comparison groups when comparing only the school language; but, again, adding the responses for the two languages, i.e. adding the number of books in the heritage language and in the school language, shows that the Portuguese families own as many books as their counterparts. They do, however, possess more books in the heritage language than in the school language.

The contrary appears to be true for time spent watching television, videos or films in a day: Portuguese children living in Switzerland spend more time watching media in the school language than in their heritage language. On average, when adding their two languages, they spend more time watching TV, videos or films than their peers from the monolingual groups.

Finally, visits to the library and interest in reading show some inter-group differences. In particular, children schooled in French (comparison and heritage speaker groups) seem to initiate more reading activities (child's reading motivation in Table 3.2) than the other groups (especially the monolingual Portuguese and Portuguese living in the German-speaking part of Switzerland). This pattern is nevertheless contradicted by the answer to the number of library visits, which shows that children from the German-speaking comparison groups and Portuguese–German bilinguals borrow books more often than the children from the other groups (which might be explained by a tradition to visit libraries during school time in Swiss-German schools).

Summary

Several relevant features of the Portuguese-speaking community in Switzerland appear in our data. We discuss them in relation to another study on the Portuguese in Switzerland (Fibbi *et al.*, 2010), and to the transfer and literacy development investigated in the HELASCOT project.

One first point worth mentioning concerns the socio-economic background of our participants. Fibbi *et al.* (2010) showed that the Portuguese community in Switzerland is characterised by overall rather low levels of education. In our data, this is also the case, especially as far as the fathers are concerned. Overall, the Portuguese in Switzerland tend to have low income, and very little variation, in contrast to our other comparison groups. It thus seems that the Portuguese community's financial resources have not evolved greatly between 2010 and 2017. This lack of educational and financial improvement had already been discussed by Fibbi *et al.* (2010) in their historiographical description.

Besides differences between Portuguese and other participants, intra-group differences are also important, most notably so between the Portuguese living in French- and German-speaking parts of Switzerland. The Portuguese living in German-speaking Switzerland assess their proficiency in German at a strikingly low level. This fact can have an impact on their children's (Swiss-)German language development, as they are also more in contact with Portuguese than (Swiss-)German speakers (as shown in Figures 3.1 and 3.2).

Nevertheless, when considering the home literacy environment, differences between Portuguese heritage speakers and comparison groups on the one hand, and Portuguese living in French- and German-speaking Switzerland on the other, are less salient. Portuguese families living in French-speaking Switzerland own on average more books and report more story reading in the school language than Portuguese living in German-speaking Switzerland, but Portuguese living in German-speaking Switzerland visit libraries more often. This trend seems to be shared by the German-speaking comparison group in contrast to the French-speaking comparison group: in general, participants living in French-speaking Switzerland (Portuguese and others) own more books but visit libraries less often.

In conclusion, taken all together, the sociolinguistic variables collected in the HELASCOT project show differences between Portuguese heritage speakers and their peers from the comparison groups (in Switzerland and Portugal). They also show differences between Portuguese heritage speakers living in French- and German-speaking Switzerland. These differences are discussed in Chapters 4 and 5 of this book, as inter-group differences also appear in the answers to the two literacy tasks the participants were asked to do (reading comprehension, see Chapter 4; and essay writing, see Chapter 5). The inferential analyses of these factors' influence on the children's biliteracy development are part of the PhD thesis of the first author of this chapter.

Acknowledgement

The authors acknowledge the help and advice of Raphael Berthele in the graphic presentation of the data.

Notes

(1) Another way to include all these groups is to use the broad definition as opposed to the narrow one by Polinsky and Kagan (2007).

(2) See http://www.edudoc.ch/static/web/arbeiten/migrationssprachen/1_kursangebote_f.pdf.

(3) Depending on the linguistic region of Switzerland; that is French for the German speaking part and German for the Swiss speaking part of the country.

(4) See http://www.bfs.admin.ch/bfs/portal/de/index/themen/01/07/blank/key/01/01.html.

(5) See http://www.bfs.admin.ch/bfs/portal/fr/index/themen/20/03/blank/key/07/01.html.

(6) This category is therefore too large to show potential variation.

(7) The categories are described in the section 'Questions and Variables Correspondence': (1) <5000 CHF or <€700; (2) 5000–10,000 CHF or €700–€1400; (3) 10,000 CHF–15,000 CHF or €1400–€2800; (4) 15,000 CHF–20,000 CHF or >€2800; (5) >20,000 CHF.

References

Bail, A., Morini, G. and Newman, R.S. (2015) Look at the gato! Code-switching in speech to toddlers. *Journal of Child Language* 42 (5), 1073–1101.

Baker, C. and Prys Jones, S. (eds) (1998) *Encyclopedia of Bilingualism and Bilingual Education*. Clevedon: Multilingual Matters.

Benmamoun, E., Montrul, S. and Polinsky, M. (2013a) Keynote article. Heritage languages and their speakers: Opportunities and challenges for linguistics. *Theoretical Linguistics* 39 (3–4), 129–181.

Benmamoun, E., Montrul, S. and Polinsky, M. (2013b) Defining and 'ideal' heritage speaker: Theoretical and methodological challenges. Reply to peer commentaries. *Theoretical Linguistics* 39 (3–4), 259–294.

Bildungsdirektion des Kantons Zürich (2011) Rahmenlehrplan für Heimatliche Sprache und Kultur (HSK). Erlassen vom Bildungsrat am 28. Februar 2011. Mit Erläuterungen zu den Rahmenbedingungen des Unterrichts. Vollständig überarbeitete Zweitauflage | September 2011. Lehrmittelverlag Zürich.

Bornstein, M.H. and Bradley, R.H. (eds) (2003) *Socioeconomic Status, Parenting, and Child Development*. Mahwah, NJ: Lawrence Erlbaum Associates.

Brizić, K. (2007) *Das geheime Leben der Sprachen. Gesprochene und verschwiegene Sprachen und ihr Einfluss auf den Spracherwerb in der Migration*. Münster/München [u.a.]: Waxmann.

Bronfenbrenner, U. (1979) *Ecology of Human Development*. Cambridge MA: Harvard University Press.

Byersheinlein, K. (2013) Parental language mixing: Its measurement and the relation of mixed input to young bilingual children's vocabulary size. *Bilingualism: Language and Cognition* 16, 32–48. doi:10.1017/S1366728912000120.

Calderón, R., Fibbi, R. and Truong, J. (2013) Situation professionnelle et besoins en matière de formation continue des enseignant-e-s des cours de langue et culture d'origine (LCO). Une enquête dans 6 cantons : BE, GE, JU, LU, SO, VD. Rc Consulta/SFM Bern. See http://www.erz.be.ch/erz/fr/index/kindergarten_volksschule/kindergarten_volksschule/interkulturelle_bildung/hsk-unterricht/materialien.assetref/content/dam/documents/ERZ/AKVB/fr/04_Migration_Integration/interkultur_hsk_Erhebung_Arbeitssituation_HSK_f.pdf (accessed 22 November 2016).

Carreira, M. and Kagan, O. (2011) The results of the National Heritage Language Survey: Implications for teaching, curriculum design, and professional development. *Foreign Language Annals* 44 (1), 40–64. doi: 10.1111/j.1944-9720.2010.01118.x.

Coleman, J.S. (1988) Social capital in the creation of human capital. *American Journal of Sociology* 94, S95–S120. doi 10.2307/2780243.

Davis-Kean, P.E. (2005) The influence of parent education and family income on child achievement: The indirect role of parental expectations and the home environment. *Journal of Family Psychology* 19 (2), 294–304. doi: 10.1037/0893-3200.19.2.294.

De Houwer, A. (2007) Parental language input patterns and children's bilingual use. *Applied Psycholinguistics* 28 (3), 411–424. doi: 10.1017/S0142716407070221.

De Houwer, A. (2009) *Bilingual First Language Acquisition*. Bristol: Multilingual Matters.

Dittmeier, H.L. and Dunst, C.J. (2001) Family Resource Scale (FRS). In: J. Touliatos, coord: *Handbook of Family Measurement Techniques, 3e tome*. (pp. 387–388). Thousand Oaks, Calif: SAGE.

Dixon, L.Q. and Wu, S. (2014) Home language and literacy practices among immigrant second-language learners. *Language Teaching* 47 (4), 414–449. doi: 10.1017/S0261444814000160.

EDK (1991) EDK-RECHT-2007-155: Recommandations concernant la scolarisation des enfants de langue étrangère du 24 octobre 1991; 1991-10-24. See http://edudoc.ch/record/25485/files/EDK-Empfehlungen_f.pdf (accessed 22 November 2016).

Farver, J.A.M., Xu, Y., Lonigan, C.J. and Eppe, S. (2013) The home literacy environment and Latino Head Start children's emergent literacy skills. *Developmental Psychology* 49 (4), 775–791.

Fernald, A., Marchman, V.A. and Weisleder, A. (2013) SES differences in language processing skill and vocabulary are evident at 18 months. *Developmental Science* 16 (2), 234–248. doi: 10.1111/desc.12019.

Fibbi, R., Bolzman, C., Fernandez, A., Gomensoro, A., Kaya, B., Christelle, M., Mercay, C., Pecoraro, M. and Wanner, P. (2010) *Les Portugais en Suisse*. Bern: Office des Migrations.

Fishman, J.A. (2001) 300-plus years of heritage language education in the United States. In J.K. Peyton, D.A. Ranard and S. McGinnis (eds) *Heritage Languages in America: Preserving a National Resource* (pp. 81–98). Washington, DC/McHenry, IL: Center for Applied Linguistics & Delta Systems.

García, O., Zakharia, A. and Otcu, B. (eds) (2013) *Bilingual Community Education and Multilingualism*. Bristol: Multilingual Matters.

Gathercole, V.C.M. and Thomas, E.M. (2009) Bilingual first-language development: Dominant language takeover, threatened minority language take-up. *Bilingualism: Language and Cognition*, 12 (2), 213. doi: 10.1017/S1366728909004015.

Giudici, A. and Bühlmann, R. (2014). Les cours de langue et de culture d'origine (LCO). Un choix de bonnes pratiques en Suisse. Etudes+Rapports 6B. CDIP, Berne.

Hammer, C.S., Hoff, E., Uchikoshi, Y., Gillanders, C., Castro, D.C. and Sandilos, L.E. (2014) The language and literacy development of young dual language learners: A critical review. *Early Childhood Research Quarterly* 29 (4), 715–733. doi: 10.1016/j.ecresq.2014.05.008.

Hart, B., Risley, T.R. (1995) *Meaningful Differences in the Everyday Experience of Young American Children*. Baltimore, MD/London: P.H. Brookes.

Hoff, E. (2006) How social contexts support and shape language development. *Developmental Review* 26 (1), 55–88. doi: 10.1016/j.dr.2005.11.002.

Hoff, E., Laursen, B. and Bridges, K. (2012) Measurement and model building in the studying the influence of socioeconomic status on child development. In M. Lewis and L. Mayes (eds) *A Developmental Environment Measurement Handbook* (pp. 590–606). Cambridge: Cambridge University Press.

Hoff, E. Core, C. Place, S. Rumiche, R. Señor, M. Parra, M. (2012) Dual language exposure and early bilingual development. *Journal of Child Language*, 39 (1), p. 1–27. DOI: 10.1017/S0305000910000759.

King, K.A. and Ennser-Kananen, J. (2013) Heritage languages and language policy. In C.A. Chapelle (ed.) *The Encyclopedia of Applied Linguistics*. Oxford: Blackwell Publishing Ltd. doi: 10.1002/9781405198431.wbeal0500.

Kirsch, C. (2012) Ideologies, struggles and contradictions: An account of mothers raising their children bilingually in Luxembourgish and English in Great Britain. *International Journal of Bilingual Education and Bilingualism* 15 (1), 95–112. doi: 10.1080/13670050.2011.607229.

Lüdi, G. and Werlen, I. (2005) *Le paysage linguistique en Suisse*. Neuchâtel: Office Fédéral de la Statistique.

Meisel, J.M. (2013) Heritage language learners: Unprecedented opportunities for the study of grammars and their development? *Theoretical Linguistics* 39 (3–4), 225–236.

Melo-Pfeifer, S. (2015) The role of the family in heritage language use and learning: Impact on heritage language policies. *International Journal of Bilingual Education and Bilingualism* 18 (1), 26–44. doi: 10.1080/13670050.2013.868400.

Michaels, S. (2013) Commentary. Déjà vu all over again: What's wrong with Hart & Risley and a 'Linguistic Deficit' framework in early childhood education? *LEARNing Landscapes* 7 (1), 23.

Muysken, P. (2013) Challenges of comparability. *Theoretical Linguistics* 39 (3–4), 237–239.

Oller, D.K. and Eilers, R.E. (eds) (2002) *Language and Literacy in Bilingual Children* (Child Language and Child Development, 2). Clevedon: Multilingual Matters.

Oriyama, K. (2011) The effects of the sociocultural context on heritage language literacy: Japanese–English bilingual children in Sydney. *International Journal of Bilingual Education and Bilingualism* 14 (6): 653–681. doi:10.1080/13670050.2011.570739.

Parra, M., Hoff, E. and Core, C. (2011) Relations among language exposure, phonological memory, and language development in Spanish–English bilingually developing 2-year-olds. *Journal of Experimental Child Psychology* 108 (1), 113–125. doi: 10.1016/j.jecp.2010.07.011.

Payne, A.C., Whitehurst, G.J. and Angell, A.L. (1994) The role of home literacy environment in the development of language ability in preschool children from low-income families. *Early Childhood Research Quarterly* 9 (3–4), 427–440. doi: 10.1016/0885-2006(94)90018-3.

Place, S. and Hoff, EE (2011) Properties of dual language exposure that influence 2-year-olds' bilingual proficiency. *Child Development* 82 (6), 1834–1849. doi: 10.1111/j.1467-8624.2011.01660.x.

Polinsky, M. Kagan, O. (2007) Heritage Languages: In the 'Wild' and in the Classroom. *Language and Linguistics Compass* 1 (5), 368–395. doi: 10.1111/j.1749-818X.2007.00022.x.

Quiroz, B.G., Snow, C.E. and Jing Z. (2010) Vocabulary skills of Spanish–English bilinguals: Impact of mother–child language interactions and home language and literacy support. *International Journal of Bilingualism* 14 (4), 379–399. doi: 10.1177/1367006910370919.

Reese, L., Garnier, H., Gallimore, R. and Goldenberg, C. (2000) Longitudinal analysis of the antecedents of emergent Spanish literacy and middle-school English reading achievement of Spanish-speaking students. *American Educational Research Journal* 37 (3), 633–662. See http://www.jstor.org/stable/1163484.

Rothman, J. (2009) Understanding the nature and outcomes of early bilingualism: Romance languages as heritage languages. *International Journal of Bilingualism* 13, 155–163.

Scheele, A.F., Leseman, P.M. and Mayo, A.Y. (2010) The home language environment of monolingual and bilingual children and their language proficiency. *Applied Psycholinguistics* 31 (1), 117. doi: 10.1017/S0142716409990191.

Shohamy, E. (2006) *Language Policy: Hidden Agendas and New Approaches*. London: Routledge.

Sneddon, R. (2000) Language and literacy: Children's experiences in multilingual environments. *International Journal of Bilingual Education and Bilingualism* 3 (4), 265–282. doi: 10.1080/13670050008667711.

Sohr-Preston, S.L., Scaramella, L.V., Martin, M.J., Neppl, T.K., Ontai, L. and Conger, R. (2013) Parental socioeconomic status, communication, and children's vocabulary development: A third-generation test of the family investment model. *Child Development* 84 (3), 1046–1062. doi: 10.1111/cdev.12023.

Tse, L. (2001) *'Why Don't They Learn English?' Separating Fact from Fallacy in the U.S.* Language debate. New York: Teachers College Press.

Valdés, G. (2005), Bilingualism, heritage language learners, and SLA research: Opportunities lost or seized? *The Modern Language Journal* 89, 410–426. doi:10.1111/j.1540-4781.2005.00314.x.

Van Deusen-Scholl, N. (2003) Toward a definition of heritage language: Sociopolitical and pedagogical considerations. *Journal of Language, Identity & Education* 2 (3), 211–230. doi: 0.1207/S15327701JLIE0203_4.

Viswanath, A. (2013) Heritage English in Israeli children. Honors thesis, Harvard University.

Whitehurst, G. J. (2001) Stony Brook Family Reading Survey (SBFRS). In: J. Touliatos, coord.: *Handbook of Family Measurement Techniques, 3e tome.* (pp. 337–343) Thousand Oaks, CA: SAGE.

4 Reading Comprehension Development in Portuguese Heritage Speakers in Switzerland (HELASCOT Project)

Carlos Pestana, Amelia Lambelet and Jan Vanhove

Introduction

A good understanding of written texts is a key competence for almost all school subjects. Written text is involved in linguistic disciplines (school language and foreign languages), but also in non-linguistic subjects like history or geography. In the Heritage Language and School Language: Are Literacy Skills Transferable?' (HELASCOT) project, we investigated the development of reading comprehension (and writing skills, see Chapter 5) in children aged 8–10 in their heritage language (Portuguese) and in their school language (either French or German).

In this chapter, we focus on the HELASCOT reading comprehension task. After a brief theoretical discussion of the processes involved in (first language [L1] and second language [L2]) reading comprehension, we describe the task and main developmental results. In a nutshell, participants read an extract of *Alice in Wonderland* and answered 15 questions designed to measure 4 subskills adapted from the Swiss Intercantonal Agreement on Compulsory Education standards for Grades 2 and 6. The goals of the analyses presented in this chapter are to discuss whether the subskills represent separate dimensions in the present data, to describe our participants' progression, and to compare this development across the different groups in our sample, i.e. to compare the scores of the bilingual children to their peers of the comparison groups in each language. In particular, we answer the following research questions:

- To what extent do reading comprehension skills improve between Grade 3 and Grade 4 in Portuguese heritage speakers living in Switzerland and in their (monolingual) peers in the comparison groups?
- Are there between-group differences in the rate of reading comprehension skills development?

Processes involved in (L1 and L2) reading comprehension

Literature on the development of children's reading skills often focuses on the processes of learning the principles of the writing system of their language of instruction (i.e. its orthographical encoding) and their ability to decode words in context and without context (for research in this paradigm, see, for instance, Aarnoutse *et al.*, 2001; Gough & Tunmer, 1986). In this chapter, we focus on a second dimension of the reading construct, which is *reading comprehension* or, in other words, the process of drawing meaning from the text and interpreting the information conveyed by it appropriately. We structure our discussion from the more general to the specific, beginning with reading models, followed by a description of the processes at stake in comprehension, and ending with the abilities necessary for good text comprehension.

Several models of reading have been proposed in the last few decades, construing reading comprehension as a product of bottom-up (word decoding to semantic comprehension), top-down (influence of semantic comprehension on word decoding) or mixed processes (for a comprehensive overview, see Grabe & Stoller [2013]). Furthermore, some models conceive of reading comprehension as the simple product of word decoding and general linguistic comprehension (see, for instance, the 'Simple view of reading', Hoover & Tunmer, 1993), while others integrate several levels of factors including individual and social dimensions (for instance, the dynamic multilevel non-hierarchical model of reading, Rosebrock & Nix [2008]).

On the process level, comprehending a written text consists of several steps. To begin with, decoding words and analysing the syntactic structure of the sentences allows the reader to build a first representation of the intended message. This representation is then processed and the new information is mapped onto the developed mental structure (in particular, regarding time, reference and cause, see Mckee [2012]), and if the new information doesn't match with already-acquired (i.e. background) knowledge, a new substructure is built (Walter, 2007). Grabe and Stoller (2013) categorise these processes in terms of lower-level and higher-level processes. The lower level includes word recognition, syntactic parsing (disambiguating the meaning of the words based on their context and their place in a sentence) and semantic proposition formation, while the higher-level processes consist of building a comprehension model for the entire text, interpreting its meaning, and making inferences about the intended message by integrating the new information and background knowledge. Lower-level processes generally take place 'automatically' as they occur effortlessly and unconsciously, while the higher-level processes need an 'attentional monitor', allowing the speaker to 'use strategies as needed, reassess and re-establish goals, and repair comprehension problems' (Grabe & Stoller, 2013: 22; see also Rosebrock & Nix, 2008). However, while fluent adult readers use several reading abilities to achieve reading comprehension either quickly and globally (scanning the text, skimming for important information, etc.), or at a slower pace for a more precise understanding of the text, children developing their literacy skills are still in a process of automating the several components of reading comprehension, including the lower-level processes of recognising the words, analysing the structure of the sentences and of the text, and building a mental representation of its general meaning.

Concerning the abilities having an impact on reading comprehension success, as posited by the Simple View of Reading and confirmed by several studies, listening comprehension is a key factor in L1 reading comprehension (among others, see Catts & Weismer, 2006; Dreyert & Katzt, 1992). Another decisive factor is the size of the vocabulary: percentages of known lexemes in a text necessary to allow comprehension have been suggested by various authors (see Mckee [2012] for a review). Therefore, if L1 reading is conceptualised as influenced by decoding abilities, listening comprehension and vocabulary size, children whose L1 is not the school language (i.e. the language in which they acquire literacy) may have more difficulties in reading comprehension than their monolingual peers, in particular if their listening comprehension skills are less developed. Following other research results, good readers tend to rely on semantic cues whereas bad readers rely more on syntax (Clarke, 1980). According to Clarke, this implies that bad readers need to focus more on syntax during reading than good readers do. In L2, however, the good and bad readers show the same types of errors, both groups needing to concentrate on syntax in order to understand the text.

Reading comprehension in a subsequent language

In the following sections of this chapter, we will use the term *subsequent language* to refer to reading in a language in which literacy has not been primarily learnt (i.e. the term can refer either to an L2 or to a heritage/home language, depending on the individual's language biography). In this perspective, we assume that for many children, literacy is developed in one language and one context (i.e. generally in school and in the L1/school language). Several scholars have postulated that reading skills are transferred from the language in which literacy is developed to other, subsequent languages – either at the decoding level (see, for instance,

Koda, 2008) or at the comprehension level. Geva and Wiener (2015) propose a framework for understanding reading comprehension in L2 learners based on the theory of the Simple View of Reading, where cross-language transfer is one of the factors influencing L2 language and literacy development, besides socio-emotional, contextual, sociocultural, home and family factors. Nevertheless, for reading, the transfer hypothesis is often linked to threshold hypotheses to a greater extent than other literacy skills (see Chapter 1 of this book for a comprehensive discussion of threshold, interdependence and transfer hypotheses).

As Lutjeharms (2006) points out, good L1 readers often become bad readers in L2, particularly if their general L2 proficiency is low. Following this author, readers are more susceptible to using top-down strategies in the non-dominant language than in their literacy language to compensate for their lack of linguistic skills. In the same vein, Clarke (1980: 206) proposed already in 1980 the notion of *short circuit* in L2 reading (or more generally in readers confronted with a difficult text): 'limited control over the language "short circuits" the good reader's system, causing him/her to revert to poor reader strategies when confronted with a difficult or confusing task in the second language'. This 'limited control over the language' includes lexical knowledge as well as syntax as both skills contribute decisively to enhance reading ability (Shiotsu & Weir, 2007). Some authors have even hypothesised the existence of three threshold levels: a fundamental level, before which L2 language ability is very low and has no influence on L2 reading ability; a second level, on which L2 ability makes a contribution to L2 reading, but doesn't allow the transfer of L1 reading skills; and finally, a third level, in which L2 comprehension is mostly explained by L1 reading skills, with L2 proficiency losing its explanatory power (see Yamashita, 2001).

The difficulties experienced even by good L1 readers in their non-dominant language(s) have been extensively discussed by Alderson in his 1984 paper called 'Reading in a Foreign Language: A Reading Problem or a Language Problem?', and in various empirical studies following it. The main question of this paradigm is to understand the relative weight of general reading abilities as developed in the literacy language and proficiency (in particular in terms of vocabulary size and syntax) in the target language for reading comprehension in a non-dominant language. In a meta-analysis by Jeon and Yamashita (2014), L2 proficiency is mentioned as the main indicator for L2 reading comprehension. However, the authors also report significant correlations between L2 reading comprehension and L1 reading. In a review of the literature taking into account a large number of studies on this question, Bernhardt (2000) modelled L2 reading comprehension as the result of general literacy ability (20%), L2 syntax and lexical knowledge (30%) and unexplained variance (50%). These percentages of variance explained depend on the task's difficulty: the more difficult the task, the more variance is explained by L2 proficiency (see Walter, 2007). In this sense, difficulties in L2 reading are at the same time a language problem and a reading problem: successful L2 reading comprehension is mainly dependent on L2 language proficiency at the lower levels of L2 proficiency (i.e. it is a *language problem* in Alderson's terminology) and on general linguistic proficiency (i.e. *reading problem)* at the higher levels of L2 proficiency.

The linguistic distance between the two languages has also been shown to have an impact on the relationship between literacy skills in both languages, in particular if the writing system is different in the two languages (Bérubé & Marinova-Todd, 2012). In other studies, however, linguistic distance is not a significant predictor (for instance, in a study on L2 English reading learning in Eritrea by Asfaha *et al.* [2009]).

Design of HELASCOT's Reading Comprehension Task

The divergent models of reading comprehension have led to the development of different types of instruments to measure the construct (for research in our field, see, for instance, Da Fontoura & Siegel, 1995; Proctor *et al.*, 2010; Verhoeven, 1994). For this study, we aimed to construct a test similar to the tasks that the children are confronted with daily at school. This test was designed not only to provide information about general reading performances, but also to analyse whether specific subskills were transferred. For an appropriate construction of the task, we consulted the relevant curricula. As most of our Portuguese participants attend Swiss compulsory education as well as Portuguese heritage language classes, we considered both curricula and the educational goals set for these two learning environments.

Portuguese heritage courses are regulated by the QuaREPE curriculum (Grosso *et al.*, 2011), which uses the Common European Framework of Reference for Languages (CEFR) proficiency levels. The QuaREPE uses the same descriptors as the CEFR for the different proficiency scales (as, for instance, 'The student is capable of understanding information in texts, or parts of texts, of a reasonable size, selecting it in order to accomplish a specific task'[1] (Grosso *et al.*, 2011: 25–26)). These descriptors were not precise enough to serve as a basis for constructing our tests; therefore, we also used the standards developed by the HarmoS concordat (Lindauer *et al.*, 2010) for Swiss compulsory education. In Switzerland, each of the 26 cantons has the primary responsibility for compulsory education, and is represented in the coordinating Swiss Conference of Cantonal Ministers of Education (EDK). In 2004, the EDK agreed on an intercantonal agreement on education, called the 'HarmoS concordat', aiming to set overall objectives for compulsory education and to develop national educational standards monitored at the end of Grades 2, 7 and 9. In order to design the reading comprehension task, we used the descriptors for Grade 2 (Lindauer *et al.*, 2010: 55–56) and Grade 6 (Lindauer *et al.*, 2010: 57–58), and particularly the following subskills: the retrieval of implicit information; the retrieval of explicit information; the establishment of a global coherence; and the ability to have an empathic understanding of the mental states of characters during the reading process.

The reading task consists of reading a text of about 500 words (see below for more details on each language version) and answering 13 multiple-choice questions and two open questions requiring a short response. The use of multiple-choice questions was motivated by the fact that it is a widely used method both in the research field and in the school context, and is easily quantifiable as the score is assessed by counting the number of correct or incorrect answers. Multiple-choice questions are also time efficient and allow us to address both details and the general content of a text. However, this format also poses challenges. For instance, it is not always clear why a specific answer was chosen. Furthermore, the use of distractors can induce the respondents to wrongly assume answers they may not have thought of (Alderson, 2000: 211).

Texts used

The texts used for the reading comprehension task were two passages extracted from *Alice in Wonderland* by Lewis Carroll. *Alice in Wonderland* is a popular character among children of our participants' age; however, its popularity is mainly based on movies and book editions for children. We therefore assumed that the original text was not well-known to the vast majority of our participants, and that it was unlikely that a group of participants could take advantage of knowing the exact content of the story. Furthermore, its comprehension is not highly dependent on the participants' knowledge of the world.

The French (Carroll, 1979) and the German (Carroll, 1998) versions are translations of the same extract, in which shrunken Alice, who is taken for a housemaid by the rabbit, is sent into his house in order to get gloves and a fan, where she also finds a bottle which she wants to drink hoping to grow large again. In the Portuguese version of our reading task (text based on Carroll [2000]), Alice has just fallen down the rabbit hole and starts pursuing the rabbit, ending in a hall from which she can't escape as the door leading out is too small (see Appendix A for the Portuguese version, and Appendices B and C for the French and German versions). The choice of these passages corresponds to the following HarmoS requirements (Lindauer *et al.*, 2010: 139ff):[2]

- The story is narrated linearly and the episodes have a beginning, an evolution and an ending.
- The language is familiar to the children.
- The story is focused on the world of the children.

- The text makes it possible for participants to look for implicit and explicit information.
- The sentences are simple.
- The difficult words have no influence on the understanding of the text.

The French version contains 531 words, the German version 479 words and the Portuguese version 438 words. Some modifications on content and vocabulary were made to adjust the texts to a similar level of difficulty. All tests have the same number of questions and the type and quality of the information required is similar. The order of the questions corresponds to the order in which the content appears in the text. The whole reading part takes 25 minutes to complete (5 minutes to read the text, 15 minutes to answer the questions and 5 minutes for revision). At all collection times, the same tests were used, making it possible to evaluate the same skills at every moment and thereby allowing us to evaluate the development of reading skills.

Reading comprehension subskills

Following the HarmoS standards' descriptors, questions were designed in order to measure four subskills: the retrieval of explicit information, the retrieval of implicit information, the establishment of a global coherence and the building of empathy during the reading process.

The *explicit information* questions (four question items) contained elements having the exact same form in text and questions. An example of this type of question is Question 9 of the German-language text:

> Question 9: Was glaubt Alice, wer Marie ist? (*Who does Alice think Marie is?*)
>
> ☐ Das Dienstmädchen des Kaninchens. (*The rabbit's maid* – the correct answer)
>
> ☐ Die Tante des Kaninchens. (*The rabbit's aunt*)
>
> ☐ Die Mutter des Kaninchens. (*The rabbit's mother*)
>
> ☐ Die Tochter des Kaninchens. (*The rabbit's daughter*)

The correct answer to the question appears with the exact same wording in the text ('Er hat mich für sein Dienstmädchen gehalten', *'He thought I was his maid'*, Appendix C, line 13).

By contrast, the *implicit information* questions (four question items) couldn't be solved without reformulating/inferring the information. For instance, to find the appropriate answer to Question 14, participants had to be aware that no information was given in the text on how the bottle got on the table:[3]

Question 14: Alice findet eine kleine Flasche auf dem Tisch. Wer hat diese Flasche dort drauf gestellt? (*Alice finds a small bottle on the table. Who put it there?*)

- ☐ Das Kaninchen (*The rabbit*)
- ☐ Die Königin (*The queen*)
- ☐ Die Mutter von Alice (*Alice's mother*)
- ☐ Man weiss es nicht (*We don't know* – the correct answer)

The third type of question focuses on *global coherence*, or the 'establishment of a structured perception of the text content as a whole' (Rosebrock & Nix, 2008: 19). An example of a question verifying the establishment of global coherence is the following:

Question 1: Die Geschichte findet statt (*The story takes place*)

- ☐ In der Wirklichkeit (*In reality*)
- ☐ In einer Phantasiewelt (*In a fantasy world* – the correct answer)
- ☐ Unter Wasser (*Under water*)

Finally, the fourth type of question (three question items) aimed to test the participants' *empathic reading*, i.e. their capacity to perceive and feel the emotions of a figure (Olsen, 2011). For instance, the participants need to perceive Alice's surprise in the sentence 'Wie sonderbar das doch ist', sagte Alice zu sich, 'für ein Kaninchen etwas zu erledigen!' (*'How peculiar it is to do a job for the rabbit!', said Alice to herself.* Appendix C, line 20) to answer Question 11.

Question 11: Etwas für ein Kaninchen zu erledigen ist für Alice... (*For Alice, to do a job for the rabbit is...*)

- ☐ ...etwas Aussergewöhnliches. (*something extraordinary* – the correct answer)
- ☐ ...etwas Langweiliges. (*something boring*)
- ☐ ...etwas Normales. (*something normal*)
- ☐ ...etwas, das sie jeden Tag tut. (*something she does every day*)

Piloting the reading task

To avoid ceiling and floor effects, all the tests were piloted with a total of 194 students between May and June 2012: 94 students from Grade 4, 21 from Grade 5 and 79 from Grade 6 completed the tasks either in the school language (n=155, 91 in the German-speaking part, 64 in the French-speaking part), or in the heritage language (n=39). This allowed us to get an idea of the progression between grades as well as the degree of difficulty expected for Grade 4 and Grade 6.

The results of these pilot sessions also determined the choice of the final texts for the reading comprehension task. With this goal in mind, four tests were designed using four different extracts from *Alice in Wonderland*. In the end, two of them were chosen as a result of their comparable scores (78% of correct answers for the German version and 70% for the French version at Grade 6 for Text 1 and 70% of correct answers for the Portuguese version of Text 2). Furthermore, from these results, it can be concluded that the language of the texts was familiar and simple enough to the children, as required by HarmoS.

Descriptive Analyses of the Answers to the Reading Task

The whole sample consists of a total of 508 participants, divided into five different categories (see Table 4.1). For the descriptive analyses in the two next subsections, we will not distinguish between the participants who did and did not attend heritage language courses, due to the latter's low number (n=4 in the German part of Switzerland, n=35 in the French part of Switzerland).

Table 4.1 Whole sample of participants at T1, T2 and T3

Group	*T1*	*T2*	*T3*
French-speaking comparison group	79	77	73
German-speaking comparison group	80	80	75
Portuguese-speaking comparison group	89	91	81
Bilingual group with school language French	119	114	107
Bilingual group with school language German	127	115	116

Note: See Chapter 2 for a discussion of dropout and missing data.

Four reading subskills

As mentioned earlier, the tests were designed in order to measure four main reading subskills forming part of the HarmoS requirements: the retrieval of explicit information, the retrieval of implicit information, the establishment of a global coherence and empathic reading. These four subskills are not observed variables *per se*, but rather latent variables assumed to be covered by a handful of related questions (see Table 4.2).

Measuring the intended reading subskills

As the data are dichotomous (correct vs. incorrect answers to each question), we computed tetrachoric correlations (using the psych package for R; Revelle, 2016) to verify whether the four subskills in Table 4.2 are

Table 4.2 Questions for each subskill for the German/French and Portuguese versions

	German/French	*Portuguese*
Explicit information	Q7: *Why does the rabbit call Alice 'Mary'?* Correct answer: *The rabbit thinks that Alice is Mary* (Line 13)	Q8: *Why is Alice sad when she is walking to the middle of the room?* Correct answer: *Because the rabbit has disappeared* (Lines 10 and 11)
	Q9: *Who does Alice think Marie is?* Correct answer: *The rabbit's maid* (Line 13)	Q9: *Where does Alice find a key?* Correct answer: *On a table* (Lines 12 and 13)
	Q10: *How does Alice found out the name of the rabbit?* Correct answer: *The name of the rabbit is written on the door of the house* (Lines 16 and 17)	Q10: *Why does Alice not see the little door at the beginning?* Correct answer: *Behind a curtain* (Lines 16 and 17)
	Q13: *Where does Alice find what she is looking for?* Correct answer: *In a room* (Line 26)	Q11: *What does Alice find behind the door?* Correct answer: *A corridor* (Lines 19 and 20)
Implicit information	Q5: *Why does Alice decide to help the rabbit?* Correct answer: *Because Alice likes to help other people* (Lines 5 and 6 French, Line 6 German)	Q6: *Why does Alice start to run?* Correct answer: *She wants to catch the rabbit* (Lines 3–5)
	Q8: *How does Alice think the rabbit will react when he will find out that she is not Mary?* Correct answer: *She thinks he is going to be surprised* (Line 13 French, Lines 13 and 14 German)	Q12: *Why can't Alice leave the room?* Correct answer: *Because she is too tall* (Lines 22–24)
	Q14: *Alice finds a small bottle on the table. Who put it there?* Correct answer: *We don't know.*	Q13: *Why does Alice believe that it is possible to go out of the room?* Correct answer: *Because she believes everything is possible* (Lines 26 and 27)
	Q15: *Why does Alice want to drink something?* Correct answer: *She wants to become taller* (Lines 32 and 33 French, Lines 33 and 34 German)	Q15: *Alice finds a small bottle on the table. Who put it there?* Correct answer: *We don't know*

(*Continued*)

Table 4.2 (Continued)

	German/French	*Portuguese*
Global coherence	Q1: *The story takes place* Correct answer: *In a fantasy world*	Q1: *The story takes place* Correct answer: *In a fantasy world*
	Q2: *Who tells the story?* Correct answer: *An unknown narrator*	Q2: *Who tells the story?* Correct answer: *An unknown narrator*
	Q6: *Whom does the narrator speak to when he says: 'but YOU know, nothing were to be found'* [Line 6 French, Lines 6 and 7 German]?	Q14: *Whom does the narrator speak to when he says: 'as YOU should understand'* [Line 25]?
Empathic reading	Q5: *Why does Alice decide to help the rabbit?* Correct answer: *Because Alice likes to help other people* (Lines 5 and 6 French, Line 6 German)	Q6: *Why does Alice begin to run?* Correct answer: *She wants to catch the rabbit* (Lines 3–5)
	Q11: *For Alice, to do a job for the rabbit is…* Correct answer: *Something extraordinary* (Line 20 French; Line 20 German)	Q8: *Why is Alice sad when she is walking to the middle of the room?* correct answer: because the rabbit has disappeared (lines 10 & 11)
	Q15: *Why does Alice want to drink something?* Correct answer: *She wants to become taller* (Lines 32 and 33 French, Lines 33 and 34 German)	Q13: *Why does Alice believe that it is possible to go out of the room?* Correct answer: *Because she believes everything is possible* (Lines 26 and 27)

Note: Lines in which the information can be found in the text are indicated in parentheses.

borne out in our data. Tetrachoric correlation coefficients are typically used to measure the correlation between two dichotomous observed variables representing continuous latent variables (Long *et al.*, 2009). These correlation coefficients indicate the extent to which two or more variables vary together, but also whether these observed variables do measure the same construct or not: the higher the correlation coefficient, the higher the probability of a common dimension (Brown, 2006: 13). However, as shown in the correlation matrices (see Tables A1 through A4 in the Appendices), the coefficients between the items were low, giving a first indication that the items didn't measure the same dimension. Furthermore, very often, the correlation matrix indicates an inconsistency between the values, like, for example, the correlation coefficients between Q14 and Q8 for the construct 'Retrieval of implicit Information' in French: 0.74 for T1, 0.24 for T2 and 0.08 for T3. Looking at tetrachoric correlations is a first step towards the acceptance that a latent construct is built by several variables. A further step would then typically be a confirmatory factor analysis (CFA). Due to the weak correlation values, we abandoned the idea of using a CFA.

Global scores

Reliability

As the four reading subskill dimensions were not confirmed by the tetrachoric correlation analyses, the reading comprehension data were merged into a global score, measuring our participants' reading comprehension competence as a whole. This global score is the sum of all

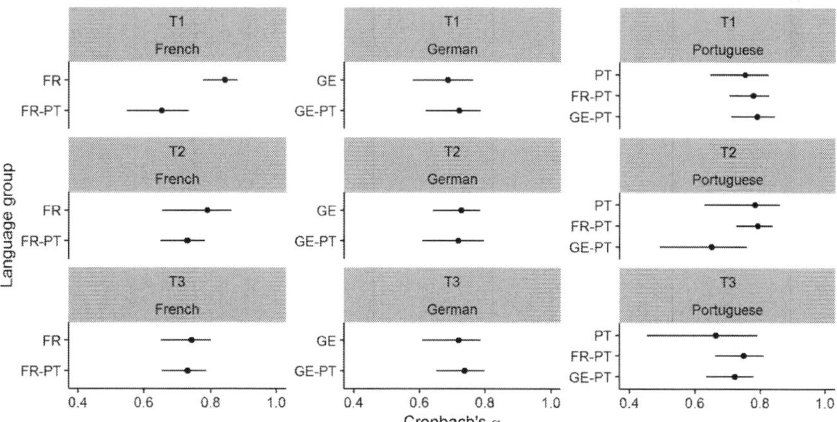

Figure 4.1 Cronbach's alphas for all groups at each data collection points. The error bars show 95% confidence intervals (not corrected for multiple comparisons) (FR: French comparison; FR–PT: French–Portuguese bilinguals; GE: German comparison; GE–PT: German–Portuguese bilinguals; PT: Portuguese comparison)

questions answered by the participants. The final score of 19 points is the sum of 13 single choice questions, one question with two sub-items which were separately coded, and a multiple-choice question where all four sub-items were separately coded. The reported data is the percentage out of these 19 items. It is used as an indicator of how well the participants understood the passage and ultimately as an indicator for their reading competence. Reliability coefficients (Cronbach's alpha; computed using the psych package for R; Revelle 2016) for the global scores are presented in Figure 4.1 and indicate a reasonable internal consistency, with Cronbach's alpha values ranging from 0.65 to 0.84 depending on language tested, participant group and data collection (mean: 0.74).

Developmental patterns

In this section, we describe the results of our participants in terms of progression from T1 to T3. Figure 4.1 shows boxplots summarising the data distributions in all five groups at each data collection point: the bilinguals with French and German as school languages as well as the three control groups (French, German and Portuguese); Table 4.3 shows the corresponding means and standard deviations. The size of the boxes and whiskers (showing the range of the middle 50% and the upper and lower 25% of the data, respectively) is roughly comparable for all of the three languages, for the bilingual and the comparison groups and across all three measurement times, as are the standard deviations reported in Table 4.3. This suggests that these groups perform comparably homogeneously throughout all measurement times. This seems to contradict a common notion that groups

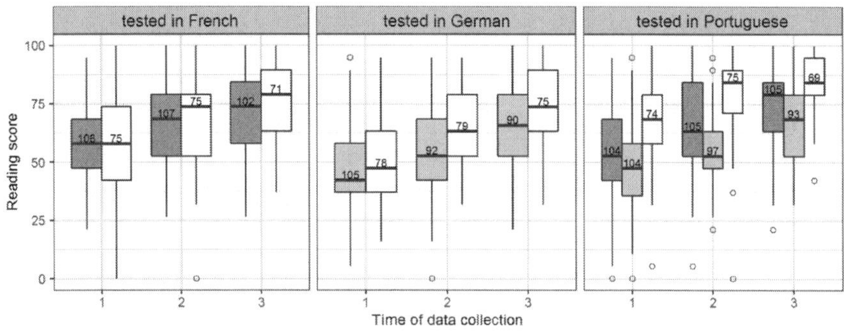

Figure 4.2 Boxplots showing the distribution of the reading scores for each group, in each language, at each data collection. The numbers in the boxes show how many data points there are (The thick horizontal lines show the medians; the boxes cover the middle 50% of the data, and the whiskers the upper and lower 25%. Individual circles show data points relatively far from the bulk of the data)

Table 4.3 Mean and standard deviations for the reading scores for each language, in each group, at each point in time

Language tested	*Group*	*Mean (SD) at T1*	*Mean (SD) at T2*	*Mean (SD) at T3*
French	Bilingual	57.2 (16.8)	65.1 (17.8)	73.0 (17.1)
	Comparison	56.2 (23.8)	68.6 (18.8)	75.9 (16.8)
German	Bilingual	45.0 (17.9)	54.9 (18.2)	65.1 (18.2)
	Comparison	51.1 (17.6)	65.8 (17.8)	73.5 (16.5)
Portuguese	Bilingual French	53.3 (20.1)	65.2 (20.0)	73.8 (17.5)
	Bilingual German	43.6 (20.1)	55.3 (15.8)	66.0 (18.0)
	Comparison	67.9 (17.9)	77.9 (17.4)	83.8 (12.4)

attending heritage classes are linguistically more heterogeneous than groups attending regular schools (e.g. Grosso *et al*., 2011: 18). The exception to the relatively homogeneous distribution of scores seems to be the performance of the comparison group for the heritage language, Portuguese, at the third data collection, which is largely constrained to the upper part of the scale (Figure 4.2).

Figure 4.3 better highlights the average trends in the reading data and the uncertainty about these trends. (The panels in Figure 4.3 were constructed by fitting the reading data in mixed-effects models that specified all combinations of participant group [bilingual French, bilingual German, comparison] and measurement time [T1, T2, T3] using fixed effects and modelled the participant- and class-specific contributions by means of random effects. Separate models were fitted for French, German and Portuguese.) For ease of exposition, we base our further discussion on this figure.

Figure 4.3 Mean reading scores as fitted by mixed-effects models (see main text) and their 95% confidence intervals (dotted lines: French–Portuguese bilinguals; dashed lines: German–Portuguese bilinguals; solid lines: the respective comparison group).

First, across all panels, the progression in the mean reading scores from T1 through T3 seems to be approximately linear (when taking into account the uncertainty about the means) and, moreover, within each language, the different groups progress roughly in parallel.

Second, as for the differences between bilingual and comparison groups in the school language, Figure 4.3 highlights the trends already visible in Figure 4.2. Specifically, the left panel suggests that, on average, bilingual participants in the French-speaking part of Switzerland perform about on par with the French comparison group. The middle panel, however, suggests that, in the German-speaking part of Switzerland, Portuguese children have lower reading skills in German than their peers from the German comparison group. This difference in the performance of French–Portuguese and German–Portuguese bilinguals relative to their comparison groups could be explained by differences in linguistic behaviours between both groups. According to Lüdi *et al.* (2005), only 19% of the Portuguese families speak the local language at home in the German-speaking part of Switzerland, compared to 42% in the French-speaking region. As this more important exposure to the language spoken at school also appears in the answers of our participants' parents in the bio-linguistic questionnaire (see Chapter 3, the self-assessed proficiency of the parents is much higher in French than it is in German), this may explain the lower level of reading comprehension in German than in French.

Third, concerning the heritage language, the Portuguese children hailing from Portugal obtained considerably better average scores than Portuguese children hailing from either French- or German-speaking Switzerland. What is more, the average scores for the Portuguese children from French-speaking Switzerland and German-speaking Switzerland in Portuguese clearly diverge. One possible explanation for this difference could lie in the typological proximity between Portuguese and French compared to Portuguese and German, which may allow for a greater degree of transfer from one language to the other (see also Chapter 6 for inferential analyses of transfer processes). Another explanation could be that the Portuguese participants in the French-speaking part of Switzerland had on average better general reading skills than their peers in the German-speaking part of Switzerland (see results for the reading comprehension task in the language spoken at school). Clearly, these two explanations aren't mutually exclusive.

Summary

The first aim of this chapter was to describe the design of the task, and in particular the attempt to operationalise and measure four reading subskills (understanding of the global coherence of the text, finding explicit information, finding implicit information and empathic reading). The results of tetrachoric correlation analyses suggest that these constructs were not operationalised by our items or that they are not detectable for other reasons in the type of data collected in our study. This doesn't mean that these competences weren't used for solving the tasks or reading the text. Indeed, it is possible that other factors interfered with or were used in parallel in order to find the correct solution, making it difficult or impossible to isolate these constructs with the test format chosen in our study. As a result, a global reading score was used for the further descriptions, and for the inferential analyses of transfer between languages (see Chapter 6 of this book).

The second aim of this chapter was to describe our participants' responses to the reading comprehension task from a developmental perspective. The global analysis of the answers showed that the task was of an appropriate level of difficulty for most groups. We only found some signs of a ceiling effect for the Portuguese comparison group at T3, a group that we weren't able to run a pilot study for. Furthermore, all groups of participants showed a similar, linear progression between T1, T2 and T3.

As regards average differences between bilingual and comparison groups, the global scores showed that in the heritage language, children living in Switzerland have significantly more difficulties in reading comprehension than their monolingual peers in Portugal. Portuguese children living in the French-speaking part of Switzerland are nevertheless more proficient than Portuguese children living in the German-speaking part of Switzerland. In the school language, the bilinguals have lower average scores than the comparison group. In French, Portuguese children and their peers show comparable results.

These better performances, relatively speaking, of the Portuguese children in French-speaking Switzerland in contrast to their peers living in the German-speaking part of Switzerland could be the result of difference between the two groups in terms of exposure to the local language inside the family. As our sociolinguistic data shows (see Chapter 3), Portuguese parents living in the French-speaking part of Switzerland assess their proficiency in the school language at a higher level than Portuguese parents living in German-speaking Switzerland.[4] Similar results were furthermore found in writing performance: Portuguese children living in German-speaking Switzerland showed worse writing skills (in particular in argumentative texts) than their peers from the comparison groups in the school language. Nevertheless, the difference between Portuguese children living in French- and German-speaking Switzerland, respectively, doesn't appear in the heritage language as far as writing is concerned (argumentative and narrative), in contrast to what happens for reading comprehension. Possible conclusions on transfer and other aspects of the multilingual acquisition of reading skills will be drawn in Chapters 6 and 10 of this book.

Notes

(1) É capaz de compreender informação, em textos, ou partes de textos, razoavelmente extensos, seleccionando-a para cumprimento duma tarefa específica.
(2) See also the section 'Piloting the Reading Task' in this chapter.
(3) Excerpt concerned: 'und wollte gerade wieder aus dem Zimmer laufen, als ihr Blick auf ein Fläschchen fiel, das in der Nähe des Spiegels stand. Diesmal war kein Schildchen daran mit der Aufschrift >Trink mich< (*And was about to leave the room when she noticed a small bottle near the mirror. This time it wasn't labeled >drink me<*), Appendix C, lines 28–31.
(4) As this question is part of an ongoing PhD project, it is not further discussed in this book.

References

Aarnoutse, C., Van Leeuwe, J., Voeten, M. and Oud, H. (2001) Development of decoding, reading comprehension, vocabulary and spelling during the elementary school years. *Reading and Writing* 14 (1), 61–89.

Alderson, J.C. (2000) *Assessing Reading*. Cambridge/New York: Cambridge University Press.

Asfaha, Y.M., Beckman, D., Kurvers, J. and Kroon, S. (2009) L2 reading in multilingual Eritrea: The influences of L1 reading and English proficiency. *Journal of Research in Reading* 32 (4), 351–365.

Bernhardt, E.B. (2000) Second-language reading as a case study of reading scholarship in the 20th century. In M.L. Kamil, P.D. Pearson and R. Barr (eds) *Handbook of Reading Research* (pp. 791–811). Mahwah, NJ: Lawrence Erlbaum.

Bérubé, D. and Marinova-Todd, S.H. (2012) The development of language and reading skills in the second and third languages of multilingual children in French immersion. *International Journal of Multilingualism* 9 (3), 272–293. https://doi.org/10.1080/14790718.2011.631708.

Brown, T.A. (2006) *Confirmatory Factor Analysis for Applied Research*. New York: Guilford Press.

Carroll, L. (1979) *Tout Alice*. Paris: Flammarion.

Carroll, L. (1998) *Alice in Wunderland*. Frankfurt am Main: Insel Taschenbuch.

Carroll, L. (2000) *As aventuras de Alice no País das Maravilhas e Alice da Outro Lado do Espelho*. Lisboa: Relógio D'Água.

Catts, H.W. and Weismer, S.E. (2006) Language deficits in poor comprehenders: A case for the simple view of reading. *Journal of Speech Language and Hearing Research* 49 (2), 278. https://doi.org/10.1044/1092-4388(2006/023).

Clarke, M.A. (1980) The short circuit hypothesis of ESL reading—or when language competence interferes with reading performance. *The Modern Language Journal* 64 (2), 203–209.

Da Fontoura, H.A. and Siegel, L.S. (1995) Reading, syntactic, and working memory skills of bilingual Portuguese-English Canadian children. *Reading and Writing* 7 (1), 139–153.

Dreyert, L.G. and Katzt, L. (1992) An examination of 'the simple view of reading'. In C.K. Kinzer and D.J. Leu (eds) *Literacy Research, Theory, and Practice: Views from Many Perspectives. Forty-First Yearbook of the National Reading Conference* (pp. 169–176). Chicago, IL: National Reading Conference.

Geva, E. and Wiener, J. (2015) *Psychological Assessment of Culturally and Linguistically Diverse Children and Adolescents. A Practitioner's Guide*. Berlin: Springer.

Gough, P.B. and Tunmer, W.E. (1986) Decoding, reading, and reading disability. *Remedial and Special Education* 7 (1), 6–10. See https://doi.org/10.1177/074193258600700104.
Grabe, W.P. and Stoller, F.L. (2013) *Teaching and Researching: Reading*. New York: Routledge.
Grosso, M.J., Soares, A., Sousa, F. de and Pascoal, J. (2011) QuaREPE. Quadro de referência para o ensino português no estrangeiro. Documento orientador. See http://d3f5055r2rwsy1.cloudfront.net/images/stories/EPE_incricoes_2011_2012/quarepe/manual_quarepe_orientador_versao_final_janeiro_2012.pdf.
Hoover, W.A. and Tunmer, W.E. (1993) The components of reading. In G.B. Thompson, W.E. Tunmer and T. Nicholson (eds) *Reading Acquisition Processes* (Vol. 4, pp. 1–19). Clevedon: Multilingual Matters. See http://books.google.de/books?hl=fr&lr=&id=I_4G7V76ZFcC&oi=fnd&pg=PA1&dq=the+components+of+reading+hoover+tunmer&ots=OinZTfUCHl&sig=YSEyeAGDBEit7cO20Zfaan9eDRU.
Jeon, E.H. and Yamashita, J. (2014) L2 reading comprehension and its correlates: A meta-analysis. *Language Learning* 64 (1), 160–212.
Koda, K. (2008) Impacts of prior literacy experience on second language learning to read. In K. Koda and A. Zehler (eds) *Learning to Read across Languages: Cross-Linguistic Relationships in First- and Second-Language Literacy Development* (pp. 68–96). New York: Routledge.
Lindauer, T., Bertschi-Kaufmann, A., Furger, J., Knechtel, N. and Schmellentin, C. (2010) *Langue de scolarisation. Rapport scientifique de synthèse et modèle de compétences. Consortium HarmoS Langue de scolarisation. Version provisoire (avant adoption des standards de base)Etat : 2 février 2010*. CDIP: Conférence Suisse des directeurs cantonaux de l'instruction publique.
Long, M.A., Berry, K.J. and Mielke, P.W. (2009) Tetrachoric correlation: A permutation alternative. *Educational and Psychological Measurement* 69 (3), 429–437.
Lüdi, G., Werlen, I. and Colombo, S. (2005) *Sprachenlandschaft in der Schweiz*. Office fédéral de la statistique Neuchâtel. See http://chprojekt.hoppingmad.ch/www/images/docs/02_sprachenlanschaft_schweiz_49_64.pdf.
Lutjeharms, M. (2006) Déchiffrement de textes en langue étrangère. *Babylonia* 3–4, 20–24.
Mckee, S. (2012) Reading comprehension, what we know: A review of research 1995 to 2011. *Language Testing in Asia* 2 (1), 1–14.
Olsen, R. (2011) Das Phänomen „Empathie“ beim Lesen literarischer Texte. *Eine didaktisch-kompetenzorientierte Annäherung. zeitschrift ästhetische bildung, Jg* 3, 1–16.
Proctor, C.P., August, D., Snow, C. and Barr, C.D. (2010) The interdependence continuum: A perspective on the nature of Spanish–English bilingual reading comprehension. *Bilingual Research Journal* 33 (1), 5–20. See https://doi.org/10.1080/15235881003733209.
Revelle, W. (2016) Psych: Procedures for psychological, psychometric, and personality research. R package version 1.6.12. See http://cran.r-project.org/package=psych.
Rosebrock, C. and Nix, D. (2008) *Grundlagen der Lesedidaktik und der systematischen schulischen Leseförderung*. Schneider-Verlag Hohengehren. See http://scholar.google.ch/scholar?q=Grundlagen+der+Lesedidaktik+und+der+systematischen+schulischen+Lesef%C3%B6rderung&btnG=&hl=fr&as_sdt=2005&sciodt=0%2C5&cites=9356677225512443116&scipsc=.
Shiotsu, T. and Weir, C.J. (2007) The relative significance of syntactic knowledge and vocabulary breadth in the prediction of reading comprehension test performance. *Language Testing* 24 (1), 99–128. See https://doi.org/10.1177/0265532207071513.
Verhoeven, L.T. (1994) Transfer in bilingual development: The linguistic interdependence hypothesis revisited. *Language Learning* 44 (3), 381–415. See https://doi.org/10.1111/j.1467-1770.1994.tb01112.x.

Walter, C. (2007) First- to second-language reading comprehension: Not transfer, but access. See http://www.academia.edu/1125834/First-_to_second-language_reading_comprehension_not_transfer_but_access (accessed 23 June 2014).
Yamashita, J. (2001) Transfer of L1 reading ability to L2 reading : An elaboration of the linguistic threshold. *Studies in Language and Culture* 23 (1), 189–200.

Appendices

Table A1 Tetrachoric correlation matrix: Subskill—establishing global coherence

German T1				*German T2*				*German T3*			
	Q1	**Q2**	**Q6**		**Q1**	**Q2**	**Q6**		**Q1**	**Q2**	**Q6**
Q1	1			**Q1**	1			**Q1**	1		
Q2	0.2	1		**Q2**	0.68	1		**Q2**	-0.20	1	
Q6	0.12	0.2	1	**Q6**	0.51	0.44	1	**Q6**	0.2	0.6	1
French T1				*French T2*				*French T3*			
	Q1	**Q2**	**Q6**		**Q1**	**Q2**	**Q6**		**Q1**	**Q2**	**Q6**
Q1	1	1		**Q1**	1			**Q1**	1		
Q2	0.07	1		**Q2**	0.39	1		**Q2**	0.28	1	
Q6	0.56	0.54	1	**Q6**	0.44	0.51	1	**Q6**	0.58	0.51	1
Portuguese T1				*Portuguese T2*				*Portuguese T3*			
	Q1	**Q2**	**Q14**		**Q1**	**Q2**	**Q14**		**Q1**	**Q2**	**Q14**
Q1	1	1		**Q1**	1			**Q1**	1		
Q2	0.25	1		**Q2**	0.31	1		**Q2**	0.49	1	
Q14	0.37	0.56	1	**Q14**	0.46	0.75	1	**Q14**	0.51	0.69	1

Table A2 Tetrachoric correlation matrix: Subskill—empathic reading

German T1				*German T2*				*German T3*			
	Q5	**Q11**	**Q15**		**Q5**	**Q11**	**Q15**		**Q5**	**Q11**	**Q15**
Q5	1			**Q5**	1			**Q5**	1		
Q11	0.28	1		**Q11**	-0.08	1		**Q11**	0.01	1	
Q15	0.24	0.40	1	**Q15**	0.18	0.5	1	**Q15**	0.18	0.1	1
French T1				*French T2*				*French T3*			
	Q5	**Q11**	**Q15**		**Q5**	**Q11**	**Q15**		**Q5**	**Q11**	**Q15**
Q5	1	1		**Q5**	1			**Q5**	1		
Q11	0.15	1		**Q11**	0.01	1		**Q11**	0.26	1	
Q15	0.3	0.56	1	**Q15**	0.06	0.41	1	**Q15**	0.18	0.39	1
Portuguese T1				*Portuguese T2*				*Portuguese T3*			
	Q6	**Q8**	**Q13**		**Q6**	**Q8**	**Q13**		**Q6**	**Q8**	**Q13**
Q6	1			**Q6**	1			**Q6**	1		
Q8	0.25	1		**Q8**	0.3	1		**Q8**	-0.02	1	
Q13	0.32	0.08	1	**Q13**	0.25	0.25	1	**Q13**	-0.16	0.18	1

Table A3 Tetrachoric correlation matrix: Subskill—retrieving implicit information

German T1					*German T2*					*German T3*				
	Q5	**Q8**	**Q14**	**Q15**		**Q5**	**Q8**	**Q14**	**Q15**		**Q5**	**Q8**	**Q14**	**Q15**
Q5	1				**Q5**	1				**Q5**	1			
Q8	0.28	1			**Q8**	0.07	1			**Q8**	0.19	1		
Q14	0.32	0.37	1		**Q14**	0.36	0.14	1		**Q14**	0.19	0.06	1	
Q15	0.24	0.33	0.3	1	**Q15**	0.18	0.22	0.43	1	**Q15**	0.18	0.05	0.52	1
French T1					*French T2*					*French T3*				
	Q5	**Q8**	**Q14**	**Q15**		**Q5**	**Q8**	**Q14**	**Q15**		**Q5**	**Q8**	**Q14**	**Q15**
Q5	1				**Q5**	1				**Q5**	1.00			
Q8	0.42	1			**Q8**	0.38	1			**Q8**	0.03	1		
Q14	0.33	0.53	1		**Q14**	0.25	0.34	1		**Q14**	0.38	-0.01	1	
Q15	0.3	0.49	0.58	1	**Q15**	0.06	0.4	0.41	1	**Q15**	0.18	0.16	0.43	1
Portuguese T1					*Portuguese T2*					*Portuguese T3*				
	Q6	**Q12**	**Q13**	**Q15**		**Q6**	**Q12**	**Q13**	**Q15**		**Q6**	**Q12**	**Q13**	**Q15**
Q6	1				**Q6**	1				**Q6**	1			
Q12	0.38	1			**Q12**	0.29	1			**Q12**	0.15	1		
Q13	0.32	0.40	1		**Q13**	0.25	0.38	1		**Q13**	-0.16	0.28	1	
Q15	0.30	0.48	0.42	1	**Q15**	0.07	0.43	0.23	1	**Q15**	0.24	0.48	0.17	1

Table A4 Tetrachoric correlation matrix: Subskill—retrieving explicit information

German T1					*German T2*					*German T3*				
	Q7	**Q9**	**Q10**	**Q13**		**Q7**	**Q9**	**Q10**	**Q13**		**Q7**	**Q9**	**Q10**	**Q13**
Q7	1				**Q7**	1				**Q7**	1			
Q9	0.39	1			**Q9**	0.3	1			**Q9**	0.56	1		
Q10	0.19	0.29	1		**Q10**	0.33	0.43	1		**Q10**	0.44	0.5	1	
Q13	0.16	0.12	0.37	1	**Q13**	0.08	0.22	0.28	1	**Q13**	0.45	0.47	0.39	1
French T1					*French T2*					*French T3*				
	Q7	**Q9**	**Q10**	**Q13**		**Q7**	**Q9**	**Q10**	**Q13**		**Q7**	**Q9**	**Q10**	**Q13**
Q7	1				**Q7**	1				**Q7**	1			
Q9	0.45	1			**Q9**	0.5	1			**Q9**	0.34	1		
Q10	0.42	0.52	1		**Q10**	0.33	0.7	1		**Q10**	0.43	0.62	1	
Q13	0.46	0.49	0.53	1	**Q13**	0.19	0.54	0.6	1	**Q13**	0.47	0.5	0.52	1
Portuguese T1					*Portuguese T2*					*Portuguese T3*				
	Q8	**Q9**	**Q10**	**Q11**		**Q8**	**Q9**	**Q10**	**Q11**		**Q8**	**Q9**	**Q10**	**Q11**
Q8	1				**Q8**	1				**Q8**	1			
Q9	0.44	1			**Q9**	0.17	1			**Q9**	0.09	1		
Q10	0.23	0.42	1		**Q10**	0.15	0.29	1		**Q10**	0.24	0.42	1	
Q11	0.25	0.29	0.39	1	**Q11**	0.33	0.41	0.40	1	**Q11**	0.11	0.43	0.48	1

Appendix A

Uma sala especial

Ao correr atràs dum coelho, Alice cai num buraco e vai parar a uma sala um pouco estranha.

Alice não estava nada magoada da queda, e, levantando-se imediatamente como uma mola, olhou para cima, mas estava tudo escuro: à sua frente, havia outra longa passagem, e ainda se podia ver o coelho branco a descer por ali abaixo. Não havia um momento a perder: Alice correu como o vento, e chegou mesmo a tempo de ouvir dizer, quando ele desapareceu à esquina:

— Oh, pelas minhas orelhas e pelos meus bigodes, como se faz tarde!

Ela estava mesmo atrás dele quando de repente o coelho desapareceu. Alice viu-se então numa grande sala muito baixa, iluminada por uma fila de candeeiros pendurados no teto.

Havia muitas portas à volta da sala, mas estavam todas fechadas. E, depois de a percorrer de uma ponta à outra, experimentando cada porta, a menina avançou tristemente para o centro a pensar como é que ia sair dali.

De repente, viu á sua frente uma mesa de três pernas, toda em vidro; em cima dela havia apenas uma pequena chave dourada, e o primeiro pensamento de Alice foi que devia pertencer a uma das portas da sala. Mas não: ou as fechaduras eram muito largas, ou era a chave que era muito pequena — de todas as maneiras, não conseguia abrir nenhuma. Mas, da segunda vez que deu a volta, viu uma pequena cortina que não tinha visto antes, e atrás dela estava uma pequena porta de cerca de trinta centímetros de altura: tentou enfiar a chave dourada na fechadura e, para seu grande contentamento, servia!

Alice abriu a porta e descobriu que dava para um corredor, pouco maior que a toca de um rato: ajoelhou-se e quando olhou lá para dentro viu o mais belo jardim que se possa imaginar. Como desejava sair da escura sala, e passear entre aqueles canteiros de flores coloridas e aquelas fontes de água fresca! Mas não conseguia meter a cabeça pela porta, «e ainda que a minha cabeça entrasse», pensou a pobre Alice, «de pouco me serviria pois tenho uns ombros largos. Oh, quem me dera poder encolher-me como um telescópio! Acho que era capaz, se soubesse por onde começar.» É que, como vocês devem compreender, tinham acontecido ultimamente tantas coisas extraordinárias, que Alice começou a pensar que, na realidade, havia muito poucas coisas impossíveis.

Não valia a pena ficar ao pé da pequena porta, pelo que voltou para a mesa, com a esperança de encontrar lá uma outra chave, ou pelo menos um manual de instruções para as pessoas se encolherem como telescópios: desta vez encontrou uma pequena garrafa ('que de certeza não estava aqui antes', pensou Alice) com a palavra 'BEBE-ME' escrita em grandes letras.

Appendix B

Le lapin

En poursuivant un lapin blanc, Alice est tombée dans un trou et se trouve maintenant dans le pays des merveilles.

C'était le lapin Blanc. II revenait au petit trot en jetant autour de lui des regards inquiets, comme s'il avait perdu quelque chose; et Alice l'entendit marmonner : « La Duchesse! La Duchesse! Oh, mes pauvres petites pattes! Oh, ma fourrure et mes moustaches! Elle va me faire exécuter, aussi sûr qu'un furet est un furet! Où ai-je bien pu les laisser tomber, je me le demande ? » Alice devina tout de suite qu'il cherchait son parapluie et sa paire de gants blancs, et, avec son désir habituel de se rendre utile, elle commença à les chercher, elle aussi; mais, savez-vous, ils n'étaient visibles nulle part.

Au bout d'un très court instant le lapin aperçut Alice qui cherchait autour d'elle, et il l'interpella d'une voix courroucée : « Eh bien! Marianne, qu'est-ce que vous faites là ? Courez tout de suite à la maison, et rapportez-moi une paire de gants et un parapluie! Allez, vite! » Alice eut si peur qu'elle partit aussitôt à toutes jambes dans la direction qu'il avait indiquée, sans tenter de lui expliquer son erreur.

« II m'a prise pour sa servante, se disait-elle tout en courant. Quel va être son étonnement lorsqu'il saura qui je suis! Mais il vaut mieux que je lui rapporte son parapluie et ses gants; si, du moins, je peux les trouver. »

Comme elle prononçait ces mots, elle arriva tout à coup devant une coquette petite maison sur la porte de laquelle une étincelante plaque de cuivre portait, gravée, le nom de l›habitant : « J. LAPIN ». Elle entra sans frapper et gravit quatre à quatre l›escalier, redoutant d›y rencontrer la vraie Marianne et de se voir chassée de la demeure avant d›y avoir trouvé le parapluie et les gants. ·

Comme cela semble bizarre, se dit Alice, d'aller faire des commissions pour un lapin! Bientôt, ce sera Dinah la chatte qui me donnera des ordres ! » Et elle se mit à imaginer comment les choses se passeraient alors : « Mademoiselle Alice! Venez, tout de suite, vous préparer pour la promenade! » - « J'arrive dans une minute, nounou! Mais, il me faut d'abord surveiller ce trou jusqu'au retour de Dinah, pour empêcher la souris d'en sortir. » Seulement, poursuivit Alice, je ne pense pas que l'on garderait Dinah à la maison si elle se mettait à donner aux gens des ordres comme cela! »

Cependant, elle était arrivée dans une petite chambre proprette, devant la fenêtre de laquelle on voyait une table et, sur cette table (comme elle l›avait espéré), un parapluie et deux ou trois paires de minuscules gants blancs : elle prit le parapluie et l›une des paires de gants, et elle était en train de quitter la pièce quand son regard tomba sur un petit flacon qui se trouvait a côté du miroir. II n›y avait pas, cette fois, d›étiquette portant les mots« BOIS-MOI», mais elle le déboucha tout de même et le porta à ses lèvres : « Je sais, se dit-elle, que quelque chose d›intéressant se produit toujours dès que je mange ou bois quelque chose : je vais voir un peu l'effet de ce flacon. J'espère bien qu'il me fera grandir de nouveau, car je commence à en avoir assez d'être une si petit chose

Appendix C

Das Kaninchen

Als Alice ein weisses Kaninchen verfolgt, fällt sie in ein Loch und landet in einem Wunderland, wo sie wieder auf das Kaninchen trifft.

Es war das weisse Kaninchen, das da langsam zurückgetrottet kam und dabei ängstlich nach rechts und links Ausschau hielt, als ob es etwas verloren hatte; und Alice hörte, wie es vor sich hin murmelte: „Die Herzogin! Die Herzogin! Ach, meine schönen Pfoten! Mein Pelz und mein Schnurrbart ! Sie wird mich köpfen lassen, oder ein Otter ist kein Otter! Wo kann ich sie nur verloren haben?' Alice hatte im Handumdrehen erraten, dass es den Regenschirm und die weissen Handschuhe suchte, und hilfsbereit, wie sie war, begann auch sie nach ihnen zu suchen, aber, wisst ihr, sie waren nirgends zu finden.

Das Kaninchen wurde sehr bald auf Alice aufmerksam, wie sie da herumsuchte, und rief ihr ärgerlich zu: „Aber Marie! Was hast du denn hier draussen zu suchen? Sogleich läufst du heim und holst mir ein Paar Handschuhe und einen Regenschirm! Und dass du dich beeilst!' Alice war so erschrocken, dass sie sofort in die Richtung lief, in die das Kaninchen gedeutet hatte, und gar nicht erst versuchte, den Irrtum aufzuklären.

„Er hat mich für sein Dienstmädchen gehalten', sagte sie sich, während sie dahinlief. „Der wird aber Augen machen, wenn er merkt, wer ich bin! Aber den Regenschirm und die Handschuhe will ich ihm doch lieber holen - das heisst, wenn ich sie überhaupt finde!' Bei diesen Worten kam sie an ein sauberes kleines Haus mit einem blanken Messingschild an der Tür, auf dem der Name >W.Kaninchen< eingraviert war. Ohne anzuklopfen, trat sie ein und lief schnell die Treppe hinauf, denn sie fürchtete, sie könnte der wirklichen Marie begegnen und aus dem Haus hinaus geworfen werden, bevor sie Regenschirm und Handschuhe gefunden hatte.

„Wie sonderbar das doch ist', sagte Alice zu sich, „für ein Kaninchen etwas zu erledigen! Wahrscheinlich soll ich nächstens für Suse die Katze den Laufburschen machen!' Und gleich stellte sie sich vor, was dann alles passieren würde: „Fräulein Alice! Hierher, wenn ich bitten darf! Es ist Zeit für den Spaziergang!' „Ich bin gleich soweit, Fräulein, ich muss nur noch das Mausloch bewachen, bis Suse zurück ist, damit die Maus nicht inzwischen herausschlüpft. Aber ich glaube kaum', dachte Alice weiter, „dass Suse im Haus bleiben dürfte, wenn sie anfinge, die Leute so herumzukommandieren!'

Mittlerweile war sie in ein sauber aufgeräumtes kleines Zimmer gelangt, mit einem Tisch unter dem Fenster, und darauf lagen (ganz wie sie gehofft hatte) ein Regenschirm und zwei oder drei Paar winzige weisse Handschuhe; den Regenschirm und die Handschuhe nahm sie mit und wollte gerade wieder aus dem Zimmer laufen, als ihr Blick auf ein Fläschchen fiel, das in der Nähe des Spiegels stand. Diesmal war kein Schildchen daran mit der Aufschrift >Trink mich<, aber sie entkorkte es trotzdem und führte es an die Lippen. »Irgendetwas Interessantes passiert ja immer«, sagte sie sich, „sobald ich etwas esse oder trinke; ich will doch einmal sehen, wie diese Flasche hier wirkt. Hoffentlich lässt sie mich wieder grösser werden, denn langsam bin ich es wirklich leid, so winzig klein herumzulaufen.

5 The Development of Argumentative and Narrative Writing Skills in Portuguese Heritage Speakers in Switzerland (HELASCOT Project)

Magalie Desgrippes, Amelia Lambelet and Jan Vanhove

Introduction

Writing coherent and relevant texts is a paramount competence in most school curricula. In Switzerland, it is one of the skills required to succeed in the school language classes, as well as in the foreign languages classes. When assessing heritage language speakers' linguistic development, it is therefore a key competence to investigate. The Heritage Language and School Language: Are Literacy Skills Transferable? (HELASCOT) research project focused on text writing (and reading comprehension, see Chapter 4 of this book) competence in both the school and the heritage language, with the aim of investigating potential transfers from one language to the other (see Chapter 2 of this book for more information on the study design).

The goal of this chapter is first to describe the written production tasks that the participants in the HELASCOT project were asked to do. Second, we discuss the task scores from a developmental perspective. In a nutshell, the participants (aged between 8 and 10) wrote two short essays – a narrative text and an argumentative letter – following instructions based on the Swiss Intercantonal Agreement on Compulsory Education Standards (see below) in their heritage language (Portuguese) and in their school language[1] (French or German). These tasks were designed in order to test the assumed influence of one language of heritage language speakers on the development of their other language(s) (see Chapter 1 of this book for a discussion of the theoretical foundation of the project).

In this chapter, we adopt a developmental perspective and answer the following research questions:

- To what extent do writing skills improve between Grade 3 and Grade 4 in Portuguese heritage speakers living in Switzerland and in their (monolingual) peers in the comparison groups?
- Are there between-group differences in the rate of writing skills development?

To that end, the texts written by the participants were rated by means of evaluation grids described below. This allowed us to show our participants' progression, and to compare this progression among bilingual (Portuguese–French/Portuguese–German) and comparison (French, German, and Portuguese speaking) groups.

Text competence

Most research on writing by monolinguals and bilinguals is related to the very early stages of literacy development with the emergence of phonological and phonemic awareness, the appropriation of letter–sound correspondences (see Chapter 7 for an empirical investigation of the development of these skills), or first reading and writing experiences in both languages. Our study focuses on the subsequent step in writing skills development, namely the development of *text competence*. As a background paradigm, we chose to use text genres theory (Bakhtine, 1984; Bronckart, 1997). This theory is based on the idea that the speech action is to be situated in a social context, and that text genres result from stabilised language practices in a given community. More precisely, language use is construed as embedded in inter-individual contexts (extra-linguistic situations). Context governs the interaction (who says what to whom, how the message is understood and interpreted, etc.), and influences the choice of the text genre most efficient to perform the intended message. Once the text genre is chosen, a second linguistic operation consists of *discursive planning*. Discursive planning precedes the process of actual textualisation and it involves 'the planning of the text on the basis of more or less stereotypical models (genres) related to the context and the anchoring of the text, that is archetypical ways of language functioning that determine, to a certain degree, the envelope of certain linguistic units' (Schneuwly, 1997: 246).

If text genres are conceptualised as (more or less) stereotypical structures, children, in their process of (bi)literacy development, must acquire the model used in their societal environment in order to perform as expected. They must, therefore, learn how to correctly structure a text using appropriate connectors and textual organisers, and use verbal tenses and anaphora adequately to ensure the text's cohesion. These skills are a central part of literacy teaching in school, but they also rely strongly on the language proficiency that children bring from home: to be able to write essays adequately, children need to master the basic characteristics of written language, as well as the ability to construct situated text respecting the rules of cohesion and coherence. Moreover, they must be able to express their intention, take into account the reader, and balance the flow of known and new information. These skills are acquired gradually by the children and, as complex structuration and planning processes, their learning seems to be dependent on the development of working memory capacity (see Chanquoy & Alamargot, 2003).

From the perspective of biliteracy development, adequate text genre production also raises the question of the transversality of these skills between languages: is the production of adequate genre-specific features in texts language-specific or is a text model acquired in one language usable in another (see Figure 1.2 and discussion in Chapter 1)? This question is addressed in Chapters 1, 6 and 10 of this book. In the present chapter, we focus on the description of developmental differences between the groups.

Text competence development

Narrative skills, which are deemed central for language development, emerge in early childhood. Narratives cover a variety of functions, such as the construction of identity, socialisation, experience transmission and organisation of thinking. The development of narrative skills is highly dependent on literacy practices in the family, such as storytelling and book reading, which allow the children to acquire the model (i.e. the knowledge about the narrative schema) as well as the linguistic devices typically pertaining to it. Studies using story grammar showed that children begin producing complete narrative sequences from 6 years of age on, but it is only at age 7–8 that they can produce stories that are goal based, taking into account the mental states of characters and relating several events to one another (Berman & Slobin, 2013; Shapiro & Hudson, 1997).

The development of argumentative skills, too, is dependent on experience with the model. In the field of text genre theory, Schneuwly and colleagues therefore studied the use of temporal and argumentative connectors (for instance, Schneuwly, 1997; Schneuwly & Bronckart, 1986), or verbal density (Schneuwly & Bronckart, 1986) in different types of texts in French (and comparatively in other languages, see Bronckart & Bourdin, 1993). These analyses allowed the authors to specify linguistic items more likely to appear in one or the other text genres (temporal organisers in narrative for instance; Bain *et al.*, 1985), and set an evolution of their use based on their complexity. Following these descriptions of the evolution of text competence, Dolz-Mestre *et al.* (2010) developed an evaluation grid for text production in children. An adapted version of this grid was used for the analyses of the argumentative and narrative texts collected in the current project.

HELASCOT Project: Description of the Writing Tasks

Participants were asked to write two short essays at three different times of data collection (beginning of third grade, end of third grade and end of fourth grade). For the sake of comparability between the three data collections, the exact same instructions were given each time. Portuguese participants living in Switzerland wrote essays in their heritage language as well as in the school language (i.e. either in French or German). Comparison groups did the tasks only in the school language.

Instructions were designed to meet the standards described in the HarmoS concordat (see Table 5.1). As discussed in more detail in Chapter 2, the Swiss cantons have the main authority in educational matters regarding compulsory school. The Swiss Conference of Cantonal Ministers of Education (EDK) agreed in 2004 on overall objectives for

Table 5.1 HarmoS Standards for the 'writing' skill for Grades 2 and 6

Grades	*HarmoS Standards (our translation)*
2	The students can: Introduce one to three arguments in an argumentative text when the instruction requires it explicitly and add the beginning of a sentence to illustrate the task. Express a simple opinion, initiated by a verb like 'I prefer...' Present a coherent (understandable) argumentation (with one to three arguments) underlying the opinion when the beginning of the sentence is given in the instruction:' I prefer to go...'.
6	The students can: Use language models, text features, simple linguistic means; use materials or proposed examples. Use text models and simple writing conventions when the instruction requires it explicitly. Start using autonomously the necessary means to ensure text coherence (use of specific words, thematic development, text structure), if the instructions are clear and well-structured for narrative and argumentative tasks.

compulsory education. Based on this agreement, national standards were developed for the end of Grades 2, 6 and 9 in mathematics, natural sciences, local language and foreign languages (another national language and English).

The HarmoS concordat describes the skill 'writing' as follows:

> The 'writing' skill is made up of abilities and knowledge domains, such as correctly writing words and sentences, using an adequate register, and knowing certain text genres. World knowledge and diverse cognitive aptitudes, such as the ability to control the writing process, are also part of the writing skill. Social skills such as *changing perspective* and *anticipating the reader's reaction* are also necessary to express a thought understandable by everyone even if it is removed from the concrete situation and the writer's perspective. (Our translation[2])

On the basis of this definition of writing skills, descriptors were developed for Grades 2 and 6 (see Table 5.1). Those descriptors also guided the design of our study's two writing tasks (instructions and analyses grids).[3]

More precisely, participants were asked to

- Write a letter to their aunt (godmother in the heritage language version) in which they communicate their choice between two options for going on holidays with her (to the sea or to the mountains in the Portuguese version [see (i) in the Appendix]; travelling by plane or by car in the French/German versions [see (ii) and (iii), respectively, in the Appendix]).
- Narrate in some detail a specific day (last school run in the French/German version, day of last holidays in the Portuguese version [see (iv)–(vi), respectively, in the Appendix]).

Analysis grids

For each text genre, a grid comprising seven axes of evaluation was used for the analyses: general presentation, thematic content, planning (text structuration), taking account of the receiver, textualisation mechanisms (connectives, cohesion), affective aspects and transversal elements (punctuation, syntax, capital letters). The number of grammatical inconsistencies in terms of gender, number, conjugation and case was also elicited. Portuguese and French productions were evaluated by the same (Portuguese–French bilingual) rater, and German texts were evaluated by a German native speaker under close supervision of the first rater (Table 5.2).

Table 5.2 Description of the grids used for the analyses of the narrative and argumentative texts

	Narrative	*Type*	*Argumentation*	*Type*
General presentation	Are the expected linguistic devices (title/ signature) present?	ord. (0–2)	Are the expected linguistic devices (place/date/ addressing/greetings/signature) present?	ord. (0–5)
Thematic content	Is the thematic content (narration of a particular day) present?	dichot. (0/1)	Are the expected thematic elements (choice between sea and mountain / plane and car) present?	dichot. (0/1)
	How many thematic units are present?	nb of thematic units	Are the three arguments present?	ord. (0–3)
Planning			Are the various parts of the argumentation (addressing – choice and arguments – conclusive paragraph) well-articulated?	ord. (0-3)
Taking the receiver into account	Is the receiver explicitly addressed?	dichot. (0/1)	Is the receiver explicitly addressed?	dichot. (0/1)
Textualisation	Is the story temporally anchored?	ord. (0–2)	Are textual (simple[a] and/or complex) connectives used?	ord. (0–3)
	Is there a temporal progression in the story?	nb of temporal organisers	Are the verbal tenses correctly used?	Not used
	Is the story spatially anchored?	ord. (0–2)		
	Are the verbal tenses correctly used?	Not used		

Affective aspects	Is the story exposed neutrally, or does the child express his/her feelings about what happened?	nom.	Does the child use any affective pragmatic tool to influence the receiver's decision?	nom.
Transversal elements	Does the child use punctuation adequately?	ord. (0–2)	Does the child use punctuation adequately?	ord. (0–2)
	Does the child make correct use of capital letters?	ord. (0–2)	Does the child make correct use of capital letters?	ord. (0–2)
	Does the child produce syntactically correct sentences?	ord. (0–4)	Does the child produce syntactically correct sentences?	ord. (0–4)
	Morphology	nb of errors	Morphology	nb of errors

[a] 'and'/'because' are considered simple connectives; other connectives are categorised as complex.

Descriptive Analyses of the Two Writing Tasks

The sample consists of five different groups of participants (see Table 5.3). In the next sections, we will descriptively analyse the progression of the different groups in the total score, an aggregation of the six principal dimensions assessed in the grids. The affective aspects in the grid are not quantified and therefore not considered in the score, neither are the morphological errors or the number of thematic units in the narrative texts. Another category not taken into account is verbal cohesion, as the chosen way to elicit a score was not usable for German. The maximum total score is 24 for argumentative texts and 17 for narrative texts.

Total scores

Narrative writing

Table 5.4 shows the means and standard deviations for each group at the three data collections for the total scores for the narrative task. Readers interested in the distribution underlying these summary statistics are referred to Chapter 6 (Figure 6.4). For the average trends in the narration total scores as well as the uncertainty about these trends, we here refer to Figure 5.1. The panels in Figure 5.1 were constructed by fitting the narration total scores in mixed-effects models that specified all combinations of participant group (bilingual French, bilingual German, comparison) and

Table 5.3 Number of participants at each data collection time

Language	*Group*	*Genre*	*T1*	*T2*	*T3*
French	Bilingual	Narrative	85	94	100
		Argumentative	102	102	102
	Comparison	Narrative	43	67	63
		Argumentative	76	76	70
German	Bilingual	Narrative	97	82	88
		Argumentative	104	92	88
	Comparison	Narrative	72	77	74
		Argumentative	79	79	75
Portuguese	Bilingual French	Narrative	87	95	98
		Argumentative	102	104	99
	Bilingual German	Narrative	84	80	80
		Argumentative	99	93	92
	Comparison	Narrative	73	69	68
		Argumentative	73	75	72

Note: Separate numbers are given for the narrative and argumentative essays in the school language (SL) and in the heritage language (HL). The variation between the data collections is due to drop-outs and absentees.

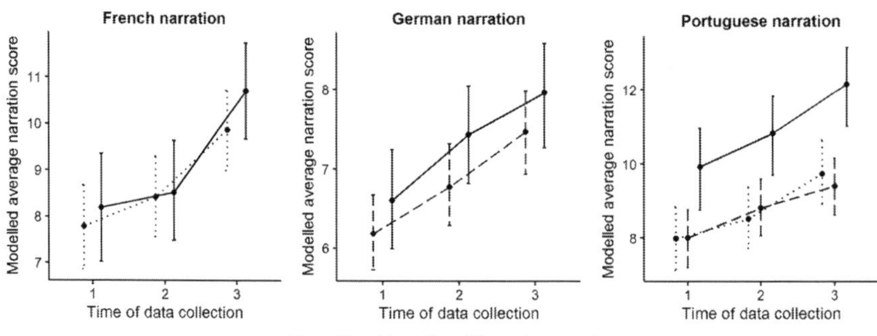

Figure 5.1 Mean narration scores as fitted by mixed-effects models (see main text) and their 95% confidence intervals (dotted lines: French–Portuguese bilinguals; dashed lines: German–Portuguese bilinguals; solid lines: the respective comparison group). The *y*-axes in the three panels cover different ranges.

Table 5.4 Means and standard deviations for the narration total scores

Language tested	*Group*	*Mean (SD) at T1*	*Mean (SD) at T2*	*Mean (SD) at T3*
French (SL)	Bilinguals	7.6 (2.0)	8.3 (2.7)	9.7 (2.7)
	Comparison	8.1 (2.8)	8.5 (2.6)	10.8 (2.6)
German (SL)	Bilinguals	6.1 (2.2)	6.7 (2.0)	7.4 (2.3)
	Comparison	6.7 (1.7)	7.5 (2.2)	8.0 (2.2)
Portuguese (HL)	Bilinguals (French)	7.8 (2.1)	8.3 (2.3)	9.6 (2.8)
	Bilinguals (German)	8.0 (1.9)	8.8 (2.3)	9.4 (2.2)
	Comparison	9.9 (2.0)	10.8 (2.0)	12.1 (2.6)

measurement time (T1, T2, T3) using fixed effects and modelled the participant- and class-specific contributions by means of random effects. Separate models were fitted for French, German and Portuguese. For ease of exposition, we base our further discussion on this figure.

As can be seen in the first panel, Portuguese heritage speakers and their peers from the comparison group show a parallel development of their narrative skills in French (the school language). In both groups, the progression appears to be non-linear, with a rather low improvement between T1 and T2, and an increase in scores between T2 and T3. We don't have explanations for this unexpected pattern.

In German, the progression seems roughly linear, and parallel between Portuguese heritage speakers and children from the comparison group. The bilinguals' average score at T2 and T3 is about equal to the comparison group's at T1 and T2, respectively, suggesting that the bilinguals lag about a year behind the comparison group in the development of their narration skills. That said, at each point in time, the confidence intervals for the bilinguals and the comparison group overlap considerably.

In Portuguese, the progression between T1 and T3 is roughly linear in the three groups (Portuguese heritage speakers in French- and German-speaking Switzerland, Portuguese comparison group in Portugal). Nevertheless, both bilingual groups lag behind the Portuguese comparison group at all times of data collection. Between the two bilingual groups, no mean differences appear at any time of data collection.

Argumentative writing

Table 5.5 shows the means and standard deviations for each group at the three data collections for the total scores for the argumentative task. Readers interested in the distribution underlying these summary statistics

Table 5.5 Means and standard deviations for the argumentation total scores

Language tested	*Group*	*Mean (SD) at T1*	*Mean (SD) at T2*	*Mean (SD) at T3*
French (SL)	Bilinguals	10.9 (3.8)	12.5 (4.1)	15.5 (4.3)
	Comparison	11.4 (4.7)	14.1 (4.6)	17.4 (3.9)
German (SL)	Bilinguals	8.8 (3.2)	10.9 (3.3)	12.2 (3.5)
	Comparison	10.4 (3.2)	13.7 (3.2)	14.2 (3.7)
Portuguese (HL)	Bilinguals (French)	10.7 (4.4)	11.9 (4.7)	15.1 (4.3)
	Bilinguals (German)	9.6 (3.9)	11.8 (3.9)	14.7 (4.4)
	Comparison	15.0 (3.4)	17.3 (3.2)	18.9 (3.9)

are referred to Chapter 6 (Figure 6.7). For the average trends in the narration total scores as well as the uncertainty about these trends, we here refer to Figure 5.2, which was constructed in the same fashion as Figure 5.1.

The development of the argumentative skills in school language French seems more linear and more pronounced than the development of the narrative skills for both bilingual and comparison groups. Bilinguals may lag behind the comparison group somewhat at T2 and T3.

For German, there is an approximately parallel development between heritage speakers and their peers from the comparison group, though the bilinguals lag behind the comparison group at all three times. For both groups, the progression is more evident between T1 and T2 than between T2 to T3.

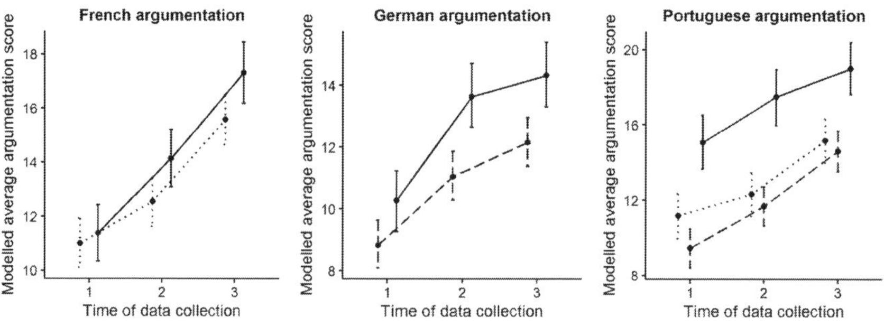

Figure 5.2 Mean argumentation scores as fitted by mixed-effects models (see main text) and their 95% confidence intervals (dotted lines: French–Portuguese bilinguals; dashed lines: German–Portuguese bilinguals; solid lines: the respective comparison group). The *y*-axes in the three panels cover different ranges.

In Portuguese, a similar pattern of differences appears in the argumentation data as in the narration data: the heritage speakers from both French- and German-speaking Switzerland lag considerably behind the Portuguese comparison group, but the differences between both heritage language groups are relatively small.

Summary

The descriptive analyses of participants' responses to the writing tasks show a progression for all groups and all text genres. The progression is nevertheless more pronounced in argumentative than narrative texts. A possible explanation for the more important progression in argumentative compared to narrative writing is that there is more training in argumentative writing in school than in narrative skills. However, this cannot be verified based on the evidence gathered in our project.

An interesting result is that, in French-speaking Switzerland, bilingual children don't lag behind their peers from the comparison groups in the school language at several times of data collection (at least in narrative skills). In German-speaking Switzerland, the differences between Portuguese children and comparison groups are larger, particularly in the case of the argumentative texts. This difference between Portuguese children living in French- and German-speaking Switzerland can be linked to similar results found for the reading task (see Chapter 4 for details): Portuguese children have results close to their peers from the French comparison groups, whereas their performances on average lie below those of their peers from the German comparison groups. This pattern of results may be linked to the lower self-evaluated level of proficiency in the school language of Portuguese parents living in German-speaking Switzerland compared to their peers living in French-speaking Switzerland (see Chapter 3 of this book). The relationship between such environmental factors and the participants' language skills is the focus of Magalie Desgrippes' ongoing PhD project and will not be further discussed in this volume.

In Portuguese, as is the case for reading, Portuguese children living in Switzerland are less proficient than their monolingual peers living in Portugal. There is no notable difference between Portuguese living in French- and German-speaking Switzerland; however, both groups are comparable in terms of the quality of their argumentative and narrative written productions. This result contrasts with the analyses of the reading tasks: as Chapter 4 details, Portuguese children living in German-speaking Switzerland have worse reading skills in their heritage language than their peers living in French-speaking Switzerland.

The relationship between writing skills development in the heritage and school languages, specifically regarding transfer and interdependence, is further addressed in Chapter 6 of this book.

Notes

(1) School language only for comparison groups: French or German in Switzerland, Portuguese in Portugal.

(2) La compétence «écrire» se compose d'aptitudes et de domaines de savoir tels qu'écrire correctement mots et phrases, trouver un style de langue adéquat, connaître certains genres de textes. La connaissance du monde et diverses aptitudes cognitives comme diriger et contrôler l'écriture font également partie intégrante de la compétence écrire. A cela s'ajoutent les compétences sociales comme *changer de perspective* et *anticiper la situation du lecteur* pour exprimer par écrit une pensée qui puisse être comprise de tous bien qu'effectivement éloignés de la situation concrète et de la perspective du narrateur.

(3) We chose to follow the HarmoS concordat after consulting the Portuguese as Heritage Language curriculum (QuaREPE; Grosso *et al.*, 2011) which uses the Common European Framework of Reference for Languages, as its descriptors for the writing skills were not precise enough for our study. They nevertheless are not in contradiction with HarmoS standards.

References

Bain, D., Bronckart, J.-P. and Schneuwly, B. (1985) Typologie du texte français contemporain. *Bulletin CILA* (41), 7–43.

Bakhtine, M. (1984) Les genres du discours. *Esthétique de la création verbale*, 263–308.

Berman, R.A. and Slobin, D.I. (2013) *Relating Events in Narrative: A Crosslinguistic Developmental Study*. New York: Psychology Press. See https://books.google.ch/books?hl=fr&lr=&id=UGwwQ2Edo6gC&oi=fnd&pg=PP1&dq=Relating+events+in+narrative:+A+crosslinguistic+developmental+study&ots=fvQIf_rTfm&sig=N-SKnC1cRE_pkl60TSenI4kluLI.

Bronckart, J.-P. (1997) Activité langagière, textes et discours. Pour un interactionisme socio-discursif. See http://archive-ouverte.unige.ch/unige:37758.

Bronckart, J.-P. and Bourdin, B. (1993) l'Acquisition des valeurs des temps des verbes: Etude comparative de l'allemand, du basque, du catalan, du français et de l'italien. *Langue française* 97, 102–124.

Chanquoy, L. and Alamargot, D. (2003) Mise en place et développement des traitements rédactionnels: le rôle de la mémoire de travail. *Le langage et l'homme* 37 (2), 171–190.

Dolz-Mestre, J., Gagnon, R. and Decandio, F.R. (2010) Produção escrita e dificuldades de aprendizagem. See http://archive-ouverte.unige.ch/unige:22675.

Grosso, M. J., Soares, A., de Sousa, F., & Pascoal, J. (2011). *QuaREPE-Quadro de Referência para o Ensino Português no Estrangeiro–documento orientador.* Lisboa: Ministério da Educaçao e Ciência/Direçao Geral de Inovaçao e Desenvolvimento Curricular.

Schneuwly, B. (1997) Textual organizers and text types: Ontogenetic aspects in writing. In J. Costermans and M. Fayol (eds) *Processing Interclausal Relationships. Studies in the Production and Comprehension of Text* (pp. 245–263). Hove: Psychology Press.

Schneuwly, B. and Bronckart, J.-P. (1986) Connexion et cohésion dans quatre types de textes d'enfants. *Cahiers de linguistique française* 7, 279–294.

Shapiro, L.R. and Hudson, J.A. (1997) Coherence and cohesion in children's stories. In J. Costermans and M. Fayol (eds) *Processing Interclausal Relationships: Studies in the Production and Comprehension of Text* (pp. 23–48). Hove: Psychology Press.

Appendix

(i) **Preferes passar as tuas férias no mar ou na montanha?**

A tua madrinha convidou-te para passar as férias com ela. Ela ainda não decidiu onde vai passar as férias e quer saber a tua opinião.

Preferes passar as tuas férias no mar ou na montanha?

Escreve uma carta à tua madrinha na qual tu lhe explicas a tua escolha. Não te esqueças de lhe dar **ao menos três razões** pelas quais tu preferes passar as férias no mar ou na montanha.

Tenta convencê-la!

(ii) **Préfères-tu voyager en voiture ou en avion?**

Ta tante t'a invité pour passer les vacances avec elle. Elle n'a pas encore décidé du moyen de transport et veut savoir ton opinion.

Préfères-tu voyager en voiture ou en avion?

Ecris une lettre à ta tante où tu lui expliques ce que tu préfères. N'oublie pas de lui donner **au moins trois raisons** pour lesquelles tu préfères l'avion ou la voiture. **Essaie de la convaincre!**

(iii) **Reist du lieber mit dem Auto oder mit dem Flugzeug?**

Deine Tante hat dich eingeladen, mit ihr Ferien zu verbringen. Sie hat sich noch nicht entschieden, welches Transportmittel ihr benützen werdet. Sie möchte deine Meinung wissen:

Reist du lieber mit dem Auto oder mit dem Flugzeug, wenn du in die Ferien gehst?

Schreibe deiner Tante einen Brief, wo du ihr erzählst, was du lieber hast. Vergiss nicht deiner Tante **mindestens drei Gründe** anzugeben, weshalb du lieber das Auto oder das Flugzeug nimmst. **Versuche sie zu überzeugen.**

(iv) **Ta dernière course d'école**

Le prochain numéro d'un magazine pour enfants sera consacré aux courses d'école. Tu vas écrire un article pour ce magazine pour y raconter ta dernière course d'école.

Repense à ta dernière course d'école : Où es-tu allé ? Qu'est-ce qui s'est passé ? Qu'as-tu fait pendant cette sortie de classe depuis le début jusqu'à la fin de la journée?

Raconte aux lecteurs du magazine le plus possible de détails sur cette journée.

(v) **Deine letzte Schulreise**

Die nächste Nummer einer Jugendzeitschrift handelt von Schulreisen. Du sollst nun ein Artikel für diese Zeitschrift schreiben, wo du von deiner letzten Schulreise berichtest.

Denke an deine letzte Schulreise zurück : Wo bist du hingegangen ? Was ist dort alles passiert ? Was hast du von morgens bis abends gemacht ?

Erzähle den Lesern dieser Jugendzeitschrift so viel wie möglich über diese Reise.

(vi) **Um dia de férias**

O próximo número de uma revista para crianças será dedicado às férias. Vais escrever um artigo para esta revista onde falas de um dia de tuas férias. **Pensa num dia das tuas últimas férias: Onde é que foste? O que aconteceu? O que fizeste durante esse dia desde o início até ao fim**?

Conta esse dia aos leitores da revista com o máximo de detalhes possível.

6 Testing the Interdependence of Languages (HELASCOT Project)

Jan Vanhove and Raphael Berthele

Introduction

In this chapter, we analyse the reading and writing data collected in the Heritage Language and School Language: Are Literacy Skills Transferable? (HELASCOT) project to which Chapters 2 through 5 of this volume are also devoted. The goal of the analysis is to establish whether the Portuguese–French and Portuguese–German bilinguals transferred their literacy skills from one language to the other. To put the analyses and the following discussion in context, we start by providing a brief overview of how such questions are commonly tackled in what we will call 'interdependence studies'. We then introduce three predictions derived from the interdependence hypothesis, i.e. three kinds of patterns that we'd expect to find in the present data if our participants' languages were indeed interdependent. In the next section, we briefly summarise the key aspects of this study (participants and method). In the three following sections, the reading and writing data are analysed both descriptively and with an eye to testing these three predictions. Lastly, we critically discuss these results, identifying key methodological concerns for interdependence studies along the way.

Chapter 3 discusses sociolinguistic factors that are known to shape the development of language and literacy skills in mono- and multilinguals. As the focus of our chapter lies on putting the interdependence of the languages in the multicompetent individual to the test, we do not account for these external factors in the following analyses.[1]

Research designs in interdependence studies

Interdependence theories, even in strong formulations regarding the role of the first language (L1), are often considered uncontroversial in language policy documents, as this quote illustrates:

> For school-age bilingual children or children with a different native language, it is essential to have a good grasp of the first language in order to successfully acquire the local national language and other languages. Withholding support to the first language can lead to learning difficulties and to a loss of skills in the two languages […]. (CDIP 1998; our translation)[2]

When interdependence is considered to be so self-evidently true, testing it empirically may not seem necessary. However, in the scholarly literature, interdependence theories are much more a matter of debate than the quote above would suggest. For instance, interdependence theories are criticised for their lack of sociolinguistic realism (Sagasta Errasti, 2003; Troike, 1984), and if such theories are furnished with proficiency thresholds that govern whether skill transfer can occur, some scholars even consider them to be 'paradoxical and […] virtually impossible to support in a meaningful manner' (Takakuwa, 2005: 2230). Moreover, if not-so-uncontroversial interdependence theories are to guide curricular reforms, it would be vital not only to know *if* interdependence theories are at all supported empirically, but also to what *extent* interdependence affects the languages in learners' repertoires (see discussion in Chapter 10).

As Chapters 7 through 9 in this volume show, however, interdependence may be seen less as an indisputable fact than as a scientific theory from which testable predictions can be derived. One such prediction is that if languages in participants' repertoires are interdependent, then participants' performance in their languages should be found to be correlated at any given time (examples for such cross-sectional correlational studies are da Fontoura & Siegel [1995] and Proctor *et al.* [2010]). However, positively correlated L1 and second language (L2) test results aren't, in and by themselves, convincing evidence for L1–L2 interdependence. The reason is that alternative factors, such as the participants' motivation, form on the day, testwiseness, etc., can't be ruled out as more mundane explanations of correlated test scores. As the phrase goes, correlation doesn't imply causation.

There are two types of research designs that may allow stronger claims about causality when investigating interdependence: experimental designs and longitudinal observational studies. Experimental designs that test interdependence claims typically take the form of intervention studies in which instructors try to impart language skills to learners in one of their languages and then assess whether these learners subsequently show progress in the same skill in their other language compared to an uninstructed control group (e.g. Moser *et al.*, 2010). Overall, such intervention studies have found little evidence that developing skills in one language positively affects those same skills in the other language (see Chapter 7 of this volume). In addition, the practical challenges involved in conducting such intervention studies are vast.

In light of these practical challenges, the HELASCOT project adopted the second kind of research design, i.e. a longitudinal observational design. This design can be used regardless of whether the skill in question is language-neutral and only needs to be applied in the individual languages or whether it is language-specific but can somehow be 'transferred' to the other language (see Chapter 1 for discussion). The key prediction for longitudinal studies of interdependence is that skills in one language (typically the one that participants are more proficient in) somehow, and after a certain time lag, spill over to or can be deployed in the other language.

When planning a longitudinal study, one key decision concerns the number of measurement points and, crucially, the time interval between them. These choices can fundamentally affect the study's conclusions and are, ideally, based on solid theorising (see Collins, 2006; Collins & Graham, 2002). Curiously, when we combed through longitudinal interdependence studies, we didn't find any *theoretical* justifications for the time intervals used, even though theories such as the Dynamic Model of Multilingualism (Herdina & Jessner, 2002) and related approaches (e.g. de Bot *et al.*, 2007) postulate rapid, non-linear changes in language proficiency and would call for a high temporal resolution in data collection. (The practical downside of repeated testing at short intervals, however, is that the changes observed may be due to the participants' adapting to the tests rather than to genuine language development.) Like other longitudinal interdependence studies, however, the interval used in our study – approximately 1 year each between T1, T2 and T3 – rests exclusively on practical considerations: the goal was to have as long an interval between T1 and T3 and as many data points as possible without exhausting the patience of pupils, parents and teachers – and without running out of funds. That said, it is ultimately unsatisfactory to let an important design feature of a study be determined by such practical considerations, and the fact that this applies to most or even all other studies on the topic, too, is little consolation.

Three research questions and predictions

The present project assesses three predictions that can be derived from the interdependence hypothesis and that can be tested in a longitudinal study. These predictions are tested in this chapter for three dependent variables (reading comprehension, narrative writing and argumentative writing) in identical analyses and are formulated as follows.

(1) Crosslinguistic longitudinal effects: To what extent does an individual's score at time T predict their score in the same skill in the other language at time T+1?

If languages are interdependent, we expect to find that good (weak) readers/writers in the heritage language (HL) at one point in time will be relatively good (weak) readers/writers in the school language (SL) at a later point in time. Similarly, good readers/writers in the SL are expected to be relatively good readers/writers in the HL at a later point in time. Crucially, readers'/writers' performance in a given language at time T+1 can be predicted from their performance in the *same* language at time T, and such within-language effects also need to be taken into account. The crucial question, then, is: 'To what extent does an individual's score at time T predict their score in the same skill in the other language at time T+1 after taking into account their score in the same skill in the other language at time T?' The interdependence-based prediction is that positive crosslinguistic longitudinal effects exist even after taking into account within-language effects.

(2) Different crosslinguistic longitudinal effects from the HL to the SL vs. from the SL to the HL: To what extent does the fact that literacy training takes place predominantly in the SL affect crosslinguistic effects?
Our participants receive most of their literacy education in the SL – though many participants also took HL courses (see Chapter 2). The interdependence-related expectation would therefore be that literacy skills developed in the SL will be put to use in the HL, in which less literacy training is received. We therefore expect crosslinguistic longitudinal effects to be stronger from the SL to the HL than from the HL to the SL.

(3) Effects of typology: To what extent does language typology affect crosslinguistic effects?
Two SLs are involved in the present study: French and German. French is a Romance language that is genealogically closely related to the participants' HL (Portuguese). German, on the other hand, is a Germanic language and more distantly related to the HL. The greater formal (lexical and morphosyntactic) similarities between French and Portuguese are expected to be more conducive to positive crosslinguistic effects, and hence stronger crosslinguistic longitudinal effects are expected between French and Portuguese than between German and Portuguese.

Method Recap

For ease of reference, we briefly summarise the most methodological aspects of the study here. Chapters 3 through 5 provide full-fledged accounts.

Participants

The participants were children with Portuguese as a HL living in Switzerland. In total, 114 of these children lived in the French-speaking part of Switzerland and had French as their SL; 119 lived in the German-speaking part of Switzerland and had Standard German as their SL.[3] Additionally, 3 groups of participants without Portuguese as a HL served as comparison groups: 78 in French-speaking Switzerland, 80 in German-speaking Switzerland and 91 in Portugal. The average age of the participants at the first data collection was 8 years and 8 months. For further details about the participants and their availability, see Chapters 2 and 3.

Language tests

The participants were given three kinds of tasks: reading comprehension, narrative writing and argumentative writing. For further details about the reading comprehension task, see Chapter 4. For details about the writing tasks, see Chapter 5.

Procedure

The language tests were administered three times: at the beginning of third grade (average age 8;8), at the end of third grade (9;3) and at the end of fourth grade (10;3). Participants with Portuguese as a HL were tested in both Portuguese and their SL (French or German); comparison participants were tested only in French, German or Portuguese. Within each language, participants were given the same tasks at each data collection. For further details, see Chapters 4 and 5.

Reading Comprehension

Data description

Figure 6.1 shows boxplots for the reading task scores. The boxplots show that the bilinguals' scores in French and German tend to be lower at T2 and T3 compared to the comparison groups (visible in the lower medians and central box containing the middle 50% of the data points). Note that the French, German and Portuguese reading tests were not calibrated on the same scale. It is therefore not possible to directly compare, say, the scores in French to those in German. Consequently, the relatively low scores in German by bilinguals and comparison participants alike should not be taken to suggest that participants based in German-speaking Switzerland had lower literacy levels than those in French-speaking Switzerland (see Chapter 4 for further details).

To help the reader get a sense of how performance in the reading task differs between groups, we computed so-called 'common-language effect sizes' (CLES; McGraw & Wong, 1992). This statistic expresses the probability that a bilingual participant selected at random from the sample

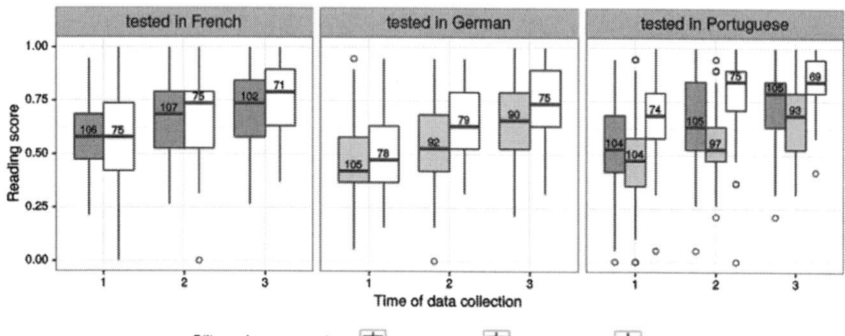

Figure 6.1 Reading comprehension scores of participants with Portuguese as a heritage language in French- (dark grey) and German-speaking Switzerland (light grey) and of natively French-, German- and Portuguese-speaking children (white) at data collections 1, 2 and 3. The numbers of participants are given in the boxplots.

has an equal or higher test score than a participant randomly selected from the relevant comparison sample.[4] For instance, the CLESs for the French reading scores vary between 48% and 54% between T1–T3, meaning that if you took one random Portuguese–French bilingual and one child from the French-speaking comparison group, there is about a one-in-two chance that the bilingual's reading score is at least equal to the comparison child's. This suggests that there is no noteworthy difference between French–Portuguese bilinguals and French-speaking comparison children: if there was no difference, one would expect that randomly sampled bilinguals would perform better than randomly sampled comparison participants 50% of the time and worse the other 50% of the time. For German, the CLESs are somewhat lower (between 37% and 45%), which is also visible in the boxplots in Figure 6.1. As for Portuguese, CLESs are lowest for Portuguese–German bilinguals (between 18% and 25%) and higher for Portuguese–French bilinguals (between 33% and 38%). Possible reasons for this difference are discussed in Chapter 4.

Figure 6.2 shows how the bilinguals' French, German and Portuguese reading skills at T2 and T3 correlate with their Portuguese reading skills from the previous year (T1 and T2, respectively). As expected, the Portuguese–Portuguese correlations are positive: relatively good readers in Portuguese tend to be relatively good readers in Portuguese one year later. In addition, the across-language correlations are also positive: relatively good readers in Portuguese tend to be relatively good readers in French or German one year later. These correlations are weaker for cross-language effects: both French and German reading skills are less well predicted by Portuguese reading skills at T1. These across-language relationships going from the HL to the SLs are somewhat stronger in the second time interval tested.

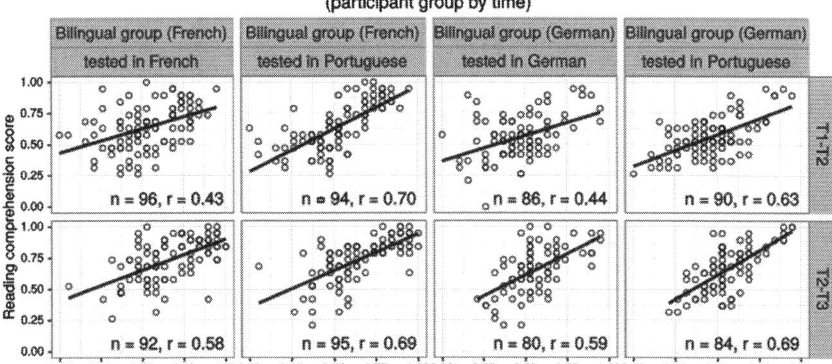

Figure 6.2 Relationship between reading comprehension scores in Portuguese at one data collection and reading comprehension scores in French, German and Portuguese at the next data collection for participants with Portuguese as a heritage language. Upper row: Portuguese at T1 and both languages at T2; bottom row: Portuguese at T2 and both languages at T3.

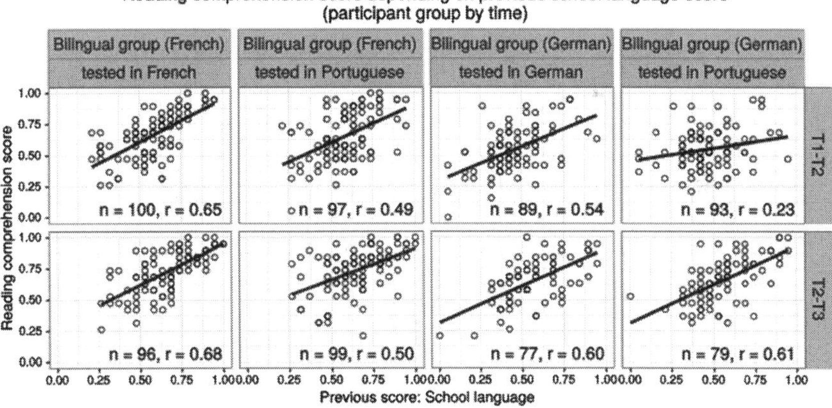

Figure 6.3 Relationship between reading comprehension scores in the school language at one data collection and reading comprehension scores in French, German and Portuguese at the next data collection for participants with Portuguese as a heritage language. Upper row: school language at T1 and both languages at T2; bottom row: school language at T2 and both languages at T3.

Figure 6.3 shows how the bilinguals' French, German and Portuguese reading skills at T2 and T3 correlate with their French or German reading skills at the previous data collection (T1 and T2, respectively). Most striking is the weak relationship between German and Portuguese between T1 and T2 (upper right panel) that seems to be considerably stronger between T2 and T3 (bottom right panel).

After this description of some key aspects of the reading comprehension data, we put three predictions derived from the interdependence assumption to the test in the following sections.

Crosslinguistic longitudinal effects

The first prediction involves estimating participants' reading scores in a particular language (SL or HL) at a given point in time using their reading scores in the other language from the year before. Clearly, we can more accurately estimate their reading scores in a given language when we know their reading scores in the *same* language from the year before than when we don't; the question addressed here is whether *additionally* knowing their previous score in the other language permits more accurate estimates still. If the answer is yes, this wouldn't necessarily vindicate the interdependence hypothesis, as alternative explanations are possible (see the 'Discussion' section). If, however, the answer is no, there would be no evidence for the interdependence hypothesis.

To address this question, we analysed the data in mixed-effects models using the lme4 package (Bates *et al.*, 2016) for R (R Core Team, 2016). We briefly describe the structure of these models here, but readers interested in the finer details are referred to the online datasets and R code (http://dx.doi.org/10.17605/OSF.IO/JH4U8), whereas readers less interested in the technicalities may want to skip to the next paragraph. Mixed-effects models model an outcome variable in terms of fixed-effect predictors and random effects. In this case, the outcome variable consisted of the bilingual participants' reading scores at T2 and T3 in both of their languages. The fixed-effect predictors included several variables that specified the study's design. These are not of primary interest here, but we deemed it necessary to include these variables to reflect the study's design in the analyses. These fixed-effect predictors were (a) the time of data collection (T2 vs. T3); (b) the language tested (SL vs. HL); (c) the language region (French- vs. German-speaking Switzerland); as well as (d) an interaction term between the language tested and language region in order to allow for the possibility that French–Portuguese bilinguals attained different scores from German–Portuguese bilinguals in either of their languages. Additionally, a fixed-effect predictor modelled the linear effect of the participants' previous scores in the same language ('previous same'): if the outcome variable contained a T2 observation in French, the corresponding predictor value was the participant's

T1 score in French; if the outcome variable contained a T3 observation in Portuguese, the corresponding predictor value was the participant's T2 score in Portuguese. To these fixed effects, we added a predictor that modelled the linear effect of the participants' previous scores in the *other* language ('previous other'): if the outcome variable contained a T2 observation in French, the corresponding predictor value was the participant's T1 score in Portuguese; if the outcome variable contained a T3 observation in Portuguese and the participant resided in German-speaking Switzerland, the corresponding predictor value was the participant's T2 score in German. This is the predictor that is of chief interest. Lastly, the models contained random effects that allowed scores to vary between participants (by-participant random intercept) and between classes (by-class random intercept), as well as random effects that allowed the effects of the time of data collection, the language tested and the participants' previous scores in the same and other language to differ from class to class (by-class random slopes). These random effects were included to account for the clustered nature of the data (multiple observations per participant; participants nested in classes).

The question is whether a model with the participants' previous scores in both languages yields more accurate estimates than one with the participants' previous scores in the same language only – or in other words, whether the fixed-effect predictor for 'previous other' in the model described above is significant. A likelihood-ratio test suggests that this is the case ($\chi^2_{\text{LRT}}(1)=10.7$, $p=0.001$), i.e. that there is indeed an added value in modelling the participants' previous scores in both languages when estimating their scores in a particular language a year later. The estimated (non-standardised) coefficient for 'previous other' was 0.16 ± 0.04 ($\hat{\beta} \pm SE$) compared to 0.47 ± 0.04 for 'previous same', indicating that 'previous same' is nonetheless the stronger predictor.

Heritage language to school language vs. school language to heritage language

In the second analysis, we investigate whether the crosslinguistic effect found above is stronger from the HL to the SL or from the SL to the HL. To this end, we included an interaction between 'previous other' and the language tested (HL vs. SL) in the model. However, this interaction was not significant ($\chi^2_{\text{LRT}}(1)=0.6$, $p=0.42$). Thus, the prediction that crosslinguistic effects are stronger from the SL to the HL wasn't borne out.

Effects of relatedness

In this third step, we investigate whether crosslinguistic effects are stronger between genealogically more closely related languages (French and Portuguese) than between more distantly related languages (German and Portuguese). If literacy in French benefits more from literacy experience in Portuguese (or vice versa) than does literacy in German, we'd expect an interaction between 'previous other' and language region (French- vs. German-speaking Switzerland). However, this interaction was not significant ($\chi^2_{\text{LRT}}(1)=0.01$, $p=0.93$).

In sum, we find no evidence for a difference between the effects between Portuguese on the one hand and French vs. German on the other hand. This is an unexpected finding as we had assumed that the genealogical proximity would be more helpful to children with French as their SL. However, a closer examination of Figure 6.3 suggest that the absence of such a difference could be due to differences in this effect between T1–T2 and T2–T3. Specifically, Figure 6.3 shows that the crosslinguistic effects between German and Portuguese may be stronger from T2 to T3 than from T1 to T2, and that an effect of typology may yet be present at T1–T2.

In order to further explore this possibility, we modelled the three-way interaction between 'previous other', language region and time of data collection (T2 vs. T3). Compared to a model without this three-way interaction but with the lower-order interactions between 'previous other' and language region, 'previous other' and time, and language region and time, the model with the three-way interaction provided a better fit to the data ($\chi^2_{\text{LRT}}(1)=10.2$, $p=0.001$). The pattern suggested by this interaction is that the slope between 'previous other' and French is steeper between T1–T2 than the one between 'previous other' and German, but that between T2–T3, the opposite is true. In the aggregate, these effects cancelled each other out, yielding the null result reported above.

This result has to be interpreted with caution, however. First, the three-way interaction was not in our initial analysis plan: we had not hypothesised any genealogical effects on HL–SL relationships to be variable across the data collections. This analysis was thus contingent on patterns we observed in the data (on the perils of taking data-contingent analyses at face value, see Gelman & Loken [2013] and Simmons *et al.* [2011]), and any theorising about the finding is speculation after the fact (see Kerr, 1998) and should be tested on new, independent data. For the time being, in fact, we are unable to come up with a coherent account of this three-way interaction and prefer to offer it as a possibly interesting result of an exploratory analysis in want of both explanation and replication.

Narrative Writing

Data description

We now turn to the first of two writing tasks: writing a narrative text. Figure 6.4 shows the boxplots of the group comparisons. Overall, the plots suggest that there is a rather modest increase in narrative skills over time

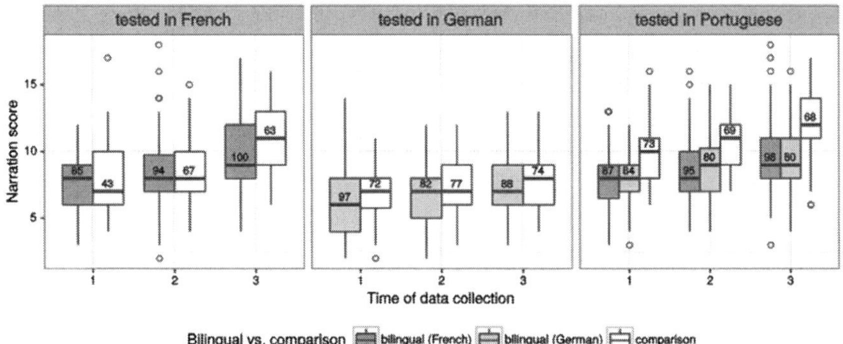

Figure 6.4 Narration scores of participants with Portuguese as a heritage language in French- (dark grey) and German-speaking Switzerland (light grey) and of natively French-, German- and Portuguese-speaking children (white) at data collections 1, 2 and 3.

in the bilingual groups. More pronounced increases can be seen in the French- and Portuguese-speaking comparison groups. The bilingual groups as a whole have either similar or lower scores compared to the comparison groups.

The CLESs show a similar picture for the reading comprehension task. The CLESs for the French narration scores vary between 44% and 53%, suggesting again that there is no noteworthy difference between the Portuguese children in French-speaking Switzerland and the French-speaking comparison group. The CLES for the German scores are similar (between 46% and 50%). For narrative writing in Portuguese, the CLESs are comparable for the subgroups in German- and French-speaking Switzerland (between 24% and 29% in the French-speaking area and between 24% and 32% in the German-speaking area). We do not have an explanation for the relatively low central tendency in the Francophone comparison group at T1.

Figure 6.5 shows how the bilinguals' French, German and Portuguese narration scores at T2 and T3 correlate with their Portuguese narration scores a year before (T1 and T2, respectively). Interestingly, the correlations are roughly comparable in strength within each language group, though they may be different between the language groups (around 0.45 for the Portuguese–French bilinguals and around 0.25 for the Portuguese–German bilinguals). Unlike for the reading comprehension data, the relationship between participants' scores in Portuguese and their French and German scores a year later does not seem to have grown stronger with time.

Figure 6.6 shows how the bilinguals' French, German and Portuguese narration at T2 and T3 correlate with their French or German narration scores at the previous data collection (T1 and T2, respectively). In the

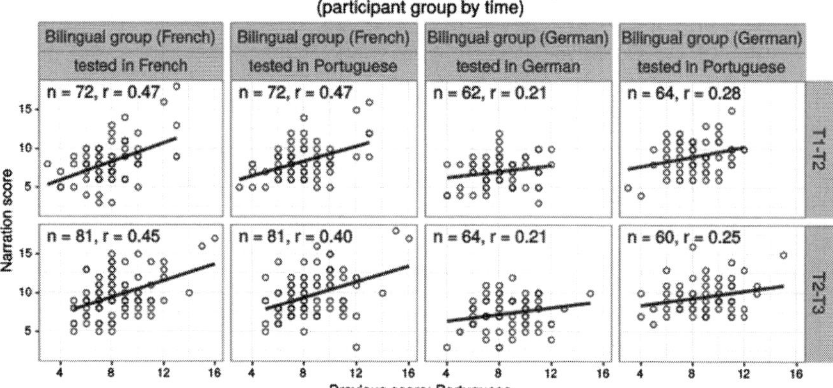

Figure 6.5 Relationship between narration scores in Portuguese at one data collection and narration scores in French, German and Portuguese at the next data collection for participants with Portuguese as a heritage language. Upper row: Portuguese at T1 and both languages at T2; bottom row: Portuguese at T2 and both languages at T3.

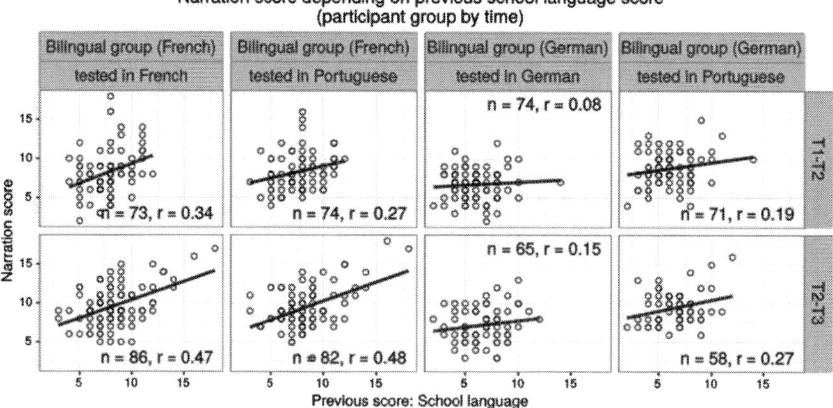

Figure 6.6 Relationship between narration scores in the participants' school language at one data collection and narration scores in French, German and Portuguese at the next data collection for participants with Portuguese as a heritage language. Upper row: school language at T1 and both languages at T2; bottom row: school language at T2 and both languages at T3.

Portuguese–French group, the SL–HL and SL–SL correlations are similar at each point in time, and furthermore, the correlations seem to be stronger in the Portuguese–French group than in the Portuguese–German group. In fact, the Portuguese–German bilinguals' narration scores in German at T2 don't seem to be correlated with their German narration scores from the year before.

In the next steps, we proceed along the lines of the analyses shown in the preceding section in order to put predictions based on the interdependence assumption to the test. Here, too, we use linear mixed models, this time with the scores obtained in the narrative writing task as the outcome variable.

Crosslinguistic longitudinal effects

First, we investigate whether we can more accurately estimate the narration scores in a particular language (SL or HL) at a given point in time by taking into account the previous scores in both languages than by only considering that same language. Again, a positive finding would be consistent with – but not proof of – the interdependence hypothesis, whereas a negative one would be difficult to reconcile with this hypothesis.

The question again is whether a model with the participants' previous scores in both languages yields better estimates than one with the participants' previous scores in the same language only – or in other words, whether the fixed-effect predictor for 'previous other' in the model described above is significant. A likelihood-ratio test suggests that this is the case ($\chi^2_{\text{LRT}}(1)=7.2$, $p=0.01$), i.e. that there is indeed an added value in modelling the participants' previous scores in both languages when estimating their narration scores in a particular language a year later. The estimated (non-standardised) coefficient for 'previous other' was 0.21 ± 0.07 ($\hat{\beta}\pm$SE); for 'previous same', it was 0.19 ± 0.06, indicating that 'previous same' and 'previous other' are roughly equally strong predictors. We do not have an explanation for why this should be the case; for the reading data, the effect of 'previous same' was about three times stronger than that of 'previous other'.

Heritage language to school language vs. school language to heritage language

In the second analysis, we investigate whether the crosslinguistic effect found above is stronger from the HL to the SL or from the SL to the HL. To this end, we included an interaction between 'previous other' and the language tested (SL vs. HL) in the model. This interaction was not significant ($\chi^2_{\text{LRT}}(1)=0.04$, $p=0.83$). Again, the prediction that literacy instruction in the L2 would be reflected in stronger SL-to-HL crosslinguistic longitudinal effects wasn't borne out.

Effects of relatedness

In this third step, we investigate whether crosslinguistic effects are stronger between genealogically more closely related languages (French and Portuguese) than between more distantly related languages (German and Portuguese). This would be reflected in an interaction between 'previous other' and language region (French- vs. German-speaking Switzerland). However, as for the reading data, this interaction wasn't significant ($\chi^2_{LRT}(1)=0.8$, $p=0.36$). This is again unexpected as we had predicted the genealogical proximity to result in stronger crosslinguistic relationships in production, too.

Like before for the reading data, we don't find a significant two-way interaction between 'previous other' and language region. This time, however, the three-way interaction between 'previous other', language region and time of data collection wasn't significant ($\chi^2_{LRT}(1)=0.03$, $p=0.86$). It is thus not the case that a moderating effect of language typology at one point in time got lost in the aggregate. In fact, the narration data do not lend any support to the prediction that across-language relationships are affected by language typology.

Argumentative Writing

Data description

The second of the two writing tasks was to compose an argumentative text (see Chapter 5 for details about the task and the scoring procedure). Figure 6.7 shows the boxplots of the group comparisons.

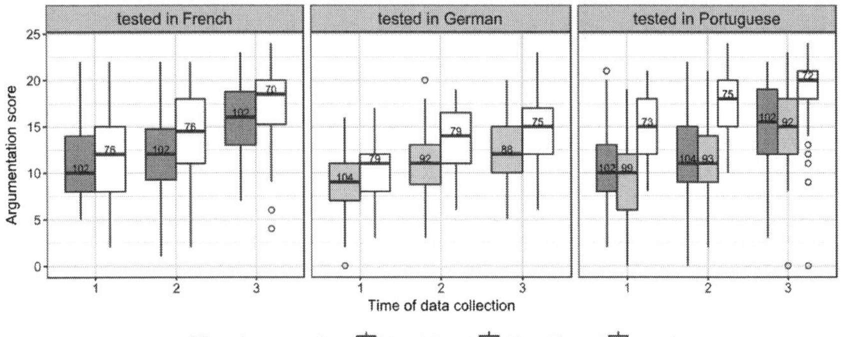

Figure 6.7 Argumentation scores of participants with Portuguese as a heritage language in French- (dark grey) and German-speaking Switzerland (light grey) and of natively French-, German- and Portuguese-speaking children (white) at data collections 1, 2 and 3.

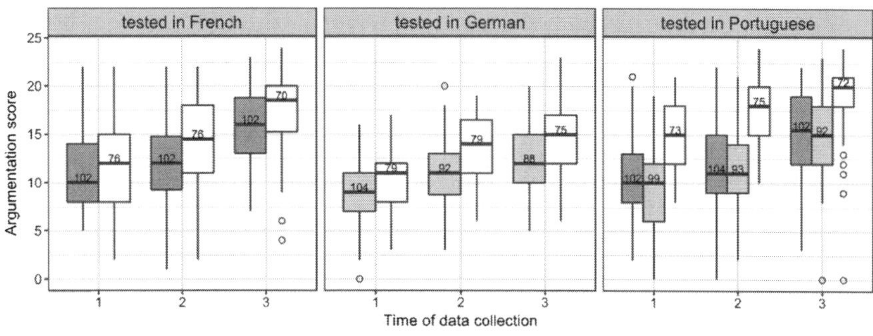

Figure 6.8 Relationship between argumentation scores in Portuguese at one data collection and argumentation scores in French, German and Portuguese at the next data collection for participants with Portuguese as a heritage language. Upper row: Portuguese at T1 and both languages at T2; bottom row: Portuguese at T2 and both languages at T3.

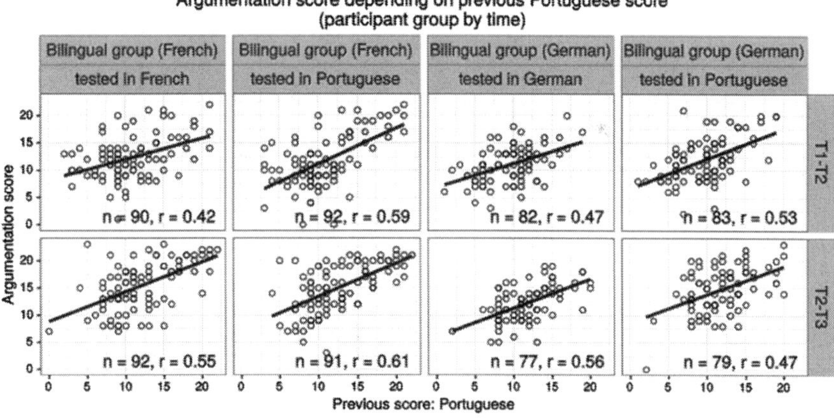

Figure 6.9 Relationship between argumentation scores in the participants' school language at one data collection and argumentation scores in French, German and Portuguese at the next data collection for participants with Portuguese as a heritage language. Upper row: school language at T1 and both languages at T2; bottom row: school language at T2 and both languages at T3.

The common-language effect sizes show a similar pattern as for the two previous tasks. The CLESs for French vary between 40% and 50%, suggesting a somewhat lower performance for the Portuguese children compared to the French-speaking comparison group. This tendency is more pronounced in the CLESs for German (between 32% and 41%). For narrative writing in Portuguese, the CLESs are comparable for the subgroups in French- and German-speaking Switzerland (between 20% and 26% in the French-speaking area and between 16% and 24% in the German-speaking area).

Figures 6.8 and 6.9 show the relationships between participants' argumentation scores at T2 and T3 and their Portuguese (Figure 6.8) and SL (Figure 6.9) scores on the argumentation task a year earlier. The overall picture is one of rather strong, positive within- and across-language correlations with little obvious systematic variation in the strength of the correlation coefficients or the slopes of the regression lines. In the next steps, we proceed along the lines as in the previous two sections. This time, the scores obtained in the argumentative production task serve as the outcome variable.

Crosslinguistic longitudinal effects

First, we investigate whether we can more accurately estimate the argumentation scores in a particular language (SL or HL) at a given point in time by taking into account the previous scores in both languages than by only considering that same language. Again, a positive finding would be consistent with – but not proof of – the interdependence hypothesis, whereas a negative one would be difficult to reconcile with this hypothesis.

The question again is whether the fixed-effect predictor for 'previous other' in the model described above is significant. A likelihood-ratio test suggests that this is the case ($\chi^2_{\text{LRT}}(1)=14.6$, $p<0.001$), i.e. for the third time confirming that there is added value in taking into account the participants' previous scores in both languages when estimating their scores in a particular language a year later. The estimated (non-standardised) coefficient for 'previous other' was 0.25±0.06 ($\hat{\beta}\pm$SE); for 'previous same', it was 0.35±0.04, suggesting, as one would expect, that 'previous same' is the stronger predictor.

Heritage language to school language vs. school language to heritage language

In the second step, we investigate whether the crosslinguistic effect found above is stronger from the HL to the SL or from the SL to the HL, which would be reflected in an interaction between 'previous other' and the language tested (SL vs. HL). This interaction wasn't significant ($\chi^2_{\text{LRT}}(1)=1.1$, $p=0.29$). For the third time, the prediction that literacy instruction in the L2 would be reflected in stronger L2-to-L1 crosslinguistic longitudinal effects wasn't borne out.

Effects of relatedness

Third, we investigate whether crosslinguistic effects are stronger between genealogically more closely related languages (French and Portuguese) than between more distantly related languages (German and Portuguese). However, as for the reading and narration data, the interaction between 'previous other' and language region was not significant ($\chi^2_{LRT}(1)=0.7$, $p=0.39$). This, again, runs counter to our expectations. Like for the narration data, the three-way interaction between 'previous other', language region and time of data collection wasn't significant either ($\chi^2_{LRT}(1)=0.4$, $p=0.55$). The argumentation data, then, don't lend any support to the prediction that across-language relationships are affected by language typology either.

Discussion

We identify four general patterns from the three preceding sections. First, there is a substantial degree of overlap between the Portuguese children's reading and writing skills in French or German and the reading and writing skills of the comparison groups. This degree of overlap is somewhat higher for Portuguese–French bilinguals than for Portuguese–German bilinguals. In Portuguese, however, both Portuguese–French and Portuguese–German bilinguals have weaker reading and writing skills than Portuguese-speaking comparisons, though Portuguese readings skills seem to be better developed in bilinguals hailing from French-speaking Switzerland than in those hailing from German-speaking Switzerland. These descriptive findings are not directly relevant to the predictions set out in the introduction to this chapter, but will be discussed in more detail in Chapter 10 (see also Chapters 3 through 5).

Second, descriptive results suggest that participants' performance in a given language at a given point in time can be estimated from their HL and SL scores from the year before. Furthermore, the regression models suggest that participants' scores in a given language can more accurately be predicted if their earlier scores in their other language are taken into account in addition to their previous scores in the same language. This finding corroborates the first prediction that we derived from the interdependence hypothesis (i.e. crosslinguistic longitudinal effects), but – as we will discuss below – it doesn't vindicate the assumption of interdependence.

Third, we didn't find any evidence whatsoever that the participants' SL (French or German) contributes more to later literacy skills in their HL (Portuguese) than vice versa. Interpreting null results is always a challenge – after all, we cannot rule out that more fine-grained measures of literacy skills or a larger sample might have produced more favourable results. But the finding that crosslinguistic longitudinal effects aren't clearly affected by the fact that the participants received most of their literacy training in their SL does instil scepticism about the assumption of interdependence.

Fourth, the evidence for typological influences on crosslinguistic longitudinal effects is, at best, inconsistent. Specifically, we didn't find stronger crosslinguistic effects between French and Portuguese than between German and Portuguese across the board. What we did find is a difficult-to-explain pattern which suggests that crosslinguistic effects in reading are relatively strong between French and Portuguese at the onset but are weaker a year later, whereas these effects start out weak between German and Portuguese but grow stronger within a year. Perhaps it would be possible to come up with an explanation which assumes that Portuguese–French bilinguals had reached a lower threshold for more extensive HL–SL influence at T1–T2 but had reached an upper threshold by T2–T3, whereas Portuguese–German bilinguals had yet to reach the lower threshold at T1–T2. However, on conceptual grounds alone, we consider such an explanation problematic: without external theoretical justification, one can posit arbitrary double thresholds to salvage just about any prediction (see also Takakuwa, 2005). In addition to specifying where these thresholds lie precisely and why they exist, such a theoretical justification would also need to account for the absence of the three-way interaction for the other variables. In the meantime, we conclude that language genealogy does not exert a measurable influence on crosslinguistic longitudinal effects.

What are we to make of these results? We see two possible explanations:

(1) The crosslinguistic longitudinal effects show that Portuguese on the one hand and German or French on the other are interdependent, but HL vs. SL status and language genealogy don't affect interdependence.
(2) The absence of effects of HL vs. SL status and language genealogy casts doubt on the usefulness of the interdependence notion as a scientific framework, and the crosslinguistic longitudinal effects found can be explained in a different way.

At present, we lean towards the second explanation for the following reasons. First, assuming that the bilinguals' languages are interdependent and that literacy skills acquired in one language may be applied in another, the prediction that the application of literacy skills flows from the language in which these are predominantly acquired to the other language seems obvious. Similarly, it seems evident that it is easier to apply a set of skills in a similar context (i.e. in a closely related language; see Chapter 1). Barring gross theoretical oversights on our part, two clear predictions based on the assumption of interdependence weren't borne out, casting doubt on the tenability of this assumption itself.

Second, as we pointed to in the introduction, the time lag between the different measurement times in this study, as well as all other studies we are aware of, was chosen for practical but theoretically arbitrary reasons. However, this time lag must be factored in when interpreting the results (see also Selig & Little, 2012). If we take the significant crosslinguistic longitudinal effects at face value, then the interpretation must be that, at time T, Portuguese–French and Portuguese–German bilinguals applied some of their literacy subskills in Portuguese that they didn't yet apply in French or German but that they did apply in French or German one year later. Similarly, these bilinguals also applied some literacy subskills in French or German at time T that they didn't apply in Portuguese until a year later. To us, such a face-value interpretation raises a number of questions: (1) What are the subskills that are applied in Portuguese but not in French/German? (2) What are the subskills that are applied in French/German but not in Portuguese? (3) Why do both kinds of subskills happen to be roughly equally important in reading and writing (as suggested by the lack of HL vs. SL effects)? (4) Why weren't these subskills applied immediately (at time T) in the other language, seeing as they were useful at T+1? (5) What, in the course of this one year, triggered the participants to apply these subskills in the other language?

These are five tough questions, but we suggest that the issue is with interpreting the crosslinguistic longitudinal effects for an arbitrary time lag at face value rather than with identifying some unspecified literacy-related subskills. This brings us to the third reason why we favour explanation (2) above: the crosslinguistic longitudinal effects can be accounted for, at least in part, without assuming interdependence. Specifically, Brunner and Austin (2009) and Westfall and Yarkoni (2016), among others, show that when two variables are correlated but imperfectly measured and only one of them is actually causally related to a third variable, then measurement error will increase the probability that a significant effect is found between the unpredictive and the third variable. This description sounds eerily familiar: Portuguese and French/German skills at a given point in time are likely to be correlated, and they are certain to be measured with error. As Portuguese skills at time T are causally predictive of Portuguese skills at time T+1, measurement error causes the causal relationship between French/German at time T and Portuguese at time T+1 to be overstated – *even after accounting for Portuguese at time T.* This does not exclude the possibility that French/German at time T and Portuguese at time T+1 really are causally related, but Brunner and Austin's (2009) and Westfall and Yarkoni's (2016) results compellingly show that these effects are at least overstated.[5]

Conclusions

In conclusion, the fact that neither the 'HL–SL vs. SL–HL' nor the 'language genealogy' prediction was borne out in combination with a plausible alternative explanation for the confirmation of the 'crosslinguistic longitudinal effects' prediction suggests that the interdependence of languages *sensu* Cummins hasn't affected the current results. Moreover, these results cast doubt on the interdependence hypothesis more generally and seem to warrant a re-evaluation of previous longitudinal results. Lastly, as the ramifications of arbitrary time lags and measurement error only became clear to us after the fact, we suggest that researchers working on this topic try to decide on the temporal design of their studies based more on theoretical considerations rather than practical considerations and fully consider the effects that measurement error may have on the results.

Notes

(1) To the extent that these external factors correlate with the participants' literacy skills at the second and third data collection (see the main text), they will be similarly correlated with these skills at earlier data collections. Thus, the effect of such external factors on the participants' literacy skills at a later point in time is largely mediated by the more direct effect of the participants' literacy skills at an earlier point in time. As we discuss in the main text, we already take into account this more direct effect. Consequently, there is little added value in considering factors that affect the participants' skills at both later and earlier points in time.

(2) 'Pour les enfants bilingues ou de langue étrangère, en âge de scolarité, une bonne maîtrise de leur langue première est une condition indispensable pour acquérir avec succès la langue nationale locale et d'autres langues; renoncer au soutien de la langue première peut conduire à des difficultés d'apprentissage et à un appauvrissement des compétences dans les deux langues [...]'. (Section 4)

(3) The exact number of data points varies due to the unavailability of certain pupils at the test times; see Chapter 4: Table 4.1 and Chapter 5: Table 5.3 for more details.

(4) In principle, the samples are assumed to be drawn from normal distributions with comparable variances, and the CLES is calculated from the sample means and standard deviations. As this assumption may not be justified in this case, we also estimated the CLESs by sampling 10,000 random pairs of bilingual and comparison participants and noting how often the bilingual performed at least on par with the comparison participant. It is these percentages that are reported in the text, though CLESs calculated from the sample means and standard deviations paint the same picture.

(5) Both Brunner and Austin (2009) and Westfall and Yarkoni (2016) suggest that researchers incorporate measurement errors in their statistical models, e.g. using structural equation modelling (SEM). Such models have been used in interdependence studies and related research (e.g. Gebauer *et al.*, 2013; Schoonen *et al.*, 2010; Verhoeven, 1994) but typically require multiple indicators for each construct, which the present project doesn't have. Additionally, even when multiple indicators per construct are available, the causal relationships in SEMs may still be overstated: in longitudinal interdependence studies, the measurement errors are likely to be correlated both across languages and across different points in time inasmuch as the same or similar tasks are used. As Reddy (1992) demonstrates, ignoring such correlations may also cause the causal relationships in the SEM to be overstated. Unfortunately, estimating all these additional parameters would quickly exhaust the data available. In sum, we don't see any quick solutions to establishing whether crosslinguistic longitudinal effects are

due to interdependence (or another structural factor) or simply a by-product of measurement error. Resolving this issue is a clear desideratum for future studies.

References

Bates, D., Maechler, M., Bolker, B. and Walker, S. (2016) lme4: Linear mixed-effects models using 'Eigen' and S4. R package, version 1.1-12. See http://cran.r-project.org/package=lme4.

Brunner, J. and Austin, P.C. (2009) Inflation of Type I error rate in multiple regression when independent variables are measured with error. *Canadian Journal of Statistics* 37, 33–46.

CDIP (=Conférence suisse des directeurs cantonaux de l'instruction publique) (1998) *Quelles langues apprendre en Suisse pendant la scolarité obligatoire?* Bern: CDIP.

Collins, L.M. (2006) Analysis of longitudinal data: The integration of theoretical model, temporal design, and statistical model. *Annual Review of Psychology* 57, 505–528.

Collins, L.M. and Graham, J.W. (2002) The effect of the timing and spacing of observations in longitudinal studies of tobacco and other drug use: Temporal design considerations. *Drug and Alcohol Dependence* 68, 85–96.

Da Fontoura, H.A. and Siegel, L.S. (1995) Reading, syntactic, and working memory skills of bilingual Portuguese-English Canadian children. *Reading and Writing* 7, 139–153.

De Bot, K., Lowie, W. and Verspoor, M. (2007) A Dynamic Systems Theory approach to second language acquisition. *Bilingualism: Language and Cognition* 10, 7–21.

Gebauer, S.K., Zaunbauer, A.C.M. and Möller, J. (2013) Cross-language transfer in English immersion programs in Germany: Reading comprehension and reading fluency. *Contemporary Educational Psychology* 38, 64–74.

Gelman, A. and Loken, E. (2013) The garden of forking paths: Why multiple comparisons can be a problem, even when there is no 'fishing expedition' or 'p-hacking' and the research hypothesis was posited ahead of time. Unpublished manuscript. See http://www.stat.columbia.edu/~gelman/research/unpublished/p_hacking.pdf.

Herdina, P. and Jessner, U. (2002) *A Dynamic Model of Multilingualism: Perspectives of Changes in Psycholinguistics*. Clevedon: Multilingual Matters.

Kerr, N.L. (1998) HARKing: Hypothesizing after the results are known. *Personality and Social Psychology Review* 2, 196–217.

McGraw, K.O. and Wong, S.P. (1992) A common language effect size statistic. *Psychological Bulletin* 111, 361–365.

Moser, U., Bayer, N. and Tunger, V. (2010) Erstsprachförderung bei Migrantenkinder in Kindergärten: Wirkungen auf phonologische Bewusstheit, Wortschatz sowie Buchstabenkenntnis und erstes Lesen in der Erst- und Zweitsprache. *Zeitschrift für Erziehungswissenschaften* 13, 631–648.

Proctor, C.P., August, D., Snow, C. and Barr, C. D. (2010) The interdependence continuum: A perspective on the nature of Spanish-English bilingual reading comprehension. *Bilingual Research Journal* 33 (1), 5–20.

R Core Team (2016) R: A language and environment for statistical computing. Software, version 3.3.0. See http://r-project.org.

Reddy, S.K. (1992) Effects of ignoring correlated measurement error in structural equation models. *Educational and Psychological Measurement* 52, 549–570.

Sagasta Errasti, M.P. (2003) Acquiring writing skills in a third language: The positive effects of bilingualism. *International Journal of Bilingualism* 7 (1), 27–42.

Schoonen, R., van Gelderen, A., Stoel, R.D., Hulstijn, J. and de Glopper, K. (2011) Modeling the development of L1 and EFL writing proficiency of secondary school students. *Language Learning* 61, 31–79.

Selig, J.P. and Little, T.D. (2012) Autoregressive and cross-lagged panel analysis for longitudinal data. In B. Laursen, T.D. Little and N.A. Card (eds) *Handbook of Developmental Research Methods* (pp. 265–278). New York: Guilford.

Simmons, J.P., Nelson, L.D. and Simonsohn, U. (2011) False-positive psychology: Undisclosed flexibility in data collection and analysis allows presenting anything as significant. *Psychological Science* 22, 1359–1366.

Takakuwa, M. (2005) Lessons from a paradoxical hypothesis: A methodological critique of the threshold hypothesis. In J. Cohen, K.T. McAlister, K. Rolstad and J. MacSwan (eds) *ISB4: Proceedings of the 4th International Symposium on Bilingualism* (pp. 2222–2232). Somerville, MA: Cascadilla.

Troike, R.C. (1984) SCALP: Social and cultural aspects of language proficiency. In C. Rivera (ed.) *Language Proficiency and Academic Achievement* (pp. 44–54). Clevedon: Multilingual Matters.

Verhoeven, L.T. (1994) Transfer in bilingual development: The linguistic interdependence hypothesis revisited. *Language Learning* 44, 381–415.

Westfall, J. and Yarkoni, T. (2016) Statistically controlling for confounding constructs is harder than you think. *PLOS ONE* 11 (3), e0152719. doi:10.1371/journal.pone.0152719.

7 Language Skill Transfer Effects: Moving from Heritage Language to School Language in Kindergarten[1]

Urs Moser, Nicole Bayer and Martin J. Tomasik

Introduction

Children with immigrant backgrounds often grow up bilingually, as their heritage language is usually different from the majority language, and the language spoken at school. Due to the increasing number of children with an immigrant background, bilingualism is becoming more common worldwide. Data from Switzerland, for instance, suggest that the number of children speaking a minority language at home is approximately one-third of the population (BFS, 2016).

There is a strong relationship between immigrant background and socio-economic status within Switzerland (Moser, 2013). This might be a reason why children with immigrant backgrounds often cannot gain the cognitive and academic benefits of bilingualism.

> Bilingualism can have certain cognitive advantages. Several studies have shown that bilingual children GENERALLY perform better than monolingual children on executive control tasks, working memory, metalinguistic awareness, abstract and symbolic representation skills, and spatial perspective taking .... Despite the cognitive advantages of bilingualism, most bilingual children with an immigrant background generally score lower on standardized reading and math assessments. (Prevoo *et al.*, 2016: 237–238)

Accordingly, studies from Germany and Switzerland show that the language competencies of immigrant children with German as a second language (L2) are significantly less developed upon entry into kindergarten compared to children who grow up in a monolingual environment. This finding primarily applies to immigrant children from socio-economically disadvantaged families (Bayer & Moser, 2009; Dubowy *et al.*, 2008).

Having a good command of the language of instruction is decisive for success in school (Gogolin, 2009). However, growing up in a bilingual context often precipitates language acquisition where children can master their heritage language better than the school or majority language (Chapter 2, this volume; see also Bayer & Moser, 2009; Kielhöfer & Jonekeit, 1995). The resulting discrepancy between these children's competencies and the requirements at school can become an issue for their educational success (Rösch, 2001: 23f.). Together with other risk factors, such as limited support in their family environment (Maaz *et al.*, 2007), dwelling in disadvantaged neighbourhoods (Angelone & Moser, 2011) and lower parental educational aspirations (Paulus & Blossfeld, 2007), school language deficits are one of the reasons why immigrant children fail in school more often than natives (Baumert & Schümer, 2001; Moser, 2002; Müller, 1997).

Education authorities and schools have been trying to respond to this challenge by launching targeted intervention programmes (Ahrenholz, 2008; Gomolla, 2005; Stamm *et al.*, 2009). However, none of the interventions aimed at promoting language competencies in children with language deficits manifested before they enter primary school have proved successful to date (Bayer & Moser, 2009; List, 2005; Schründer-Lenzen & Merkens, 2006).

A widely cited contribution to language acquisition is Cummins' theory of linguistic interdependence between heritage (L1) and school (L2) language proficiency. This interdependence is supposed to affect the cognitive and educational development of bilingual children. The central proposition of this theory is that bilingualism can be beneficial for cognitive and educational development if children have developed sufficient proficiency in their heritage language:

> The developmental interdependence hypothesis proposes that the level of L2 competence which a bilingual child attains is partially a function of the type of competence the child has developed in L1 at the time when intensive exposure to L2 begins. (Cummins, 1979: 223)

According to the interdependence hypothesis, the development of competencies in the school language depends on competencies in the heritage language. The heritage language relates positively to the school language because a part of the school language does not have to be acquired from scratch. As competencies in the school language are in part rooted in competencies in the heritage language, both languages should to be encouraged and promoted equally (Bialystok, 2001; Cummins, 1984).

This theory has been criticised (e.g. Tracy, 2005) and empirical support for Cummins' proposition is unclear (see also Chapters 1 and 10 of this book for a discussion of the empirical investigation of interdependence). Several studies point to the mastery of the heritage language as a necessary condition for the successful acquisition of a school language (Baker & De Kanter, 1983; Baker & Prys Jones, 1998; Baur & Meder, 1992; Preibusch & Kröner, 1987; Reich & Roth, 2002; Romaine, 1994). Other studies report contrasting results that question the positive effect of competencies in a heritage language on the competencies of a school language (Esser, 2006; Hopf, 2005; Söhn, 2005).

The degree of interdependence between L1 and L2 also seems to differ between the various aspects of language competencies. For phonological awareness, in particular, strong positive correlations between competencies in the two languages have been observed. Contrastingly, competencies in other aspects, such as grammar or spelling, correlate only weakly (Bialystok *et al.*, 2005; Branum-Martin *et al.*, 2006; Proctor *et al.*, 2006; Wang *et al.*, 2006).

Findings on the importance of competencies in the heritage language, and success in school language acquisition, have thus far been mainly based on studies in Anglo-American or Asiatic languages. In Europe, and especially in the German-speaking world, no overview studies are available on the relationship between dual language acquisition for immigrant children and their success in school. To date, there are only a few regionally and thematically narrow studies. Evidence from these studies ranges from no interdependence between heritage and school language at all, to moderately positive associations (Reich & Roth, 2002; Rosenberg *et al.*, 2003).

Against this backdrop, we designed an intervention aimed at promoting competencies in the heritage language that were supposed to transfer to competencies in the school language. The intervention lasted 2 years, and was carried out with children who entered kindergarten in the city of Zurich in the summer of 2006. We evaluated the effects of this intervention in terms of both heritage and school language competencies against a control group that did not receive this treatment. Our hypothesis was that the treatment group would perform better in language tests in both the heritage (Hypothesis 1) and the school language (Hypothesis 2). Furthermore, we hypothesised that the development of language competencies in the heritage and the school language would be interrelated across time (Hypothesis 3).

Interventions for Language Promotion

Generally, there are at least five categories of preschool and school programmes aimed at supporting children with an immigrant background (Limbird & Stanat, 2006; Reich & Roth, 2002). These programmes differ based on whether or not their educational goal is *additive bilingualism*, where learners become active users of the school language while maintaining or expanding their heritage language competencies, or *subtractive bilingualism*, where only the school language is trained, often at the expense of the heritage language (Siegel, 2003: 193).

A subtractive bilingualism intervention widely applied in German-speaking countries is the training of the school language outside the regular school curriculum. A central advantage of this model is that it can be implemented quite easily because the additional language teaching takes place primarily outside of regular school hours.

Also common in German-speaking countries are models of structured immersion, where teachers adapt their instruction to the language competencies of the student. Teachers are usually bilinguals, or at least trained in teaching the school language to children with a different heritage language. Children with insufficient competencies in the school language are prepared for education in regular school classes. Integration into regular school classes is supported by additional training in the school language in addition to the regular school programme.

Less prevalent are the three kinds of additive bilingual models, in which the heritage language is trained in a systematic way. Transitional bilingual models start instruction in both languages and later switch to the school language. Bilingual maintenance programmes aim at maintaining heritage language competencies, while providing instruction in both the heritage and the school language. In bilingual two-way programmes, both native and immigrant children are instructed in their own language and in the language of the other group. This method is only feasible if there is one predominant group of immigrant children that comprises at least half of the class population (Siegel, 2003: 194). As the number of heritage languages is usually large, all three additive bilingual programmes are much more difficult to implement compared to the subtractive bilingual ones.

Methods

Sample

A quasi-experimental, longitudinal study was conducted with 181 children, from four school districts in the city of Zurich. The heritage languages of these children were Albanian, Bosnian/Croatian/Serbian, Portuguese, Spanish and Tamil. Of these children, 63 were assigned to the treatment group and 118 to the control group. The criterion for assignment to the treatment group was whether a special teacher with an appropriate first language and knowledge of first language acquisition was available at the school or not. The control group children were supported in their regular

Table 7.1 Sample by experimental group and language

	Albanian	*Bosnian /Croatian/ Serbian*	*Portuguese*	*Spanish*	*Tamil*	*Total*
Treatment group	25	5	16	0	17	63
Control group	28	32	25	16	17	118
Total	55	37	41	16	34	181

lessons exclusively in the German language, following the subtractive bilingual approach. Details on the study participants by heritage language are presented in Table 7.1.

To ensure comparability between the two groups, the age, gender and general basic cognitive skills of the children were assessed, with the highest level of education of their parents as an indicator of socio-economic status. Parental education and the general basic cognitive skills were transformed into an index with a mean of M=0 and a standard deviation of SD=1. Cognitive skills were measured with 24 non-verbal items from the 'similarities' and 'matrices' subscales of the Culture Fair Test-1 (CFT-1) by Weiss *et al.* (1997). The internal consistency of the scale was $\alpha=0.81$ and was therefore very satisfactory. Intercorrelation between the CFT-1 overall score and HAWIK was $r=0.66$ for non-verbal intelligence and $r=0.48$ for verbal intelligence (Weiss *et al.*, 1997).

The two groups did not statistically differ with respect to gender. The proportion of boys was 52% in the experimental group compared to 49% in the control group ($\chi^2_{(1)}=-0.62$, $p=0.54$).

Table 7.2 provides an overview of the means and standard deviations of age, general basic cognitive skills and the index of parental education of the treatment and control groups. Age: $t_{(179)}=-1.63$, $p=0.11$; general basic cognitive skills: $t_{(179)}=1.80$, $p=0.07$; and parental education: $t_{(179)}=-0.81$, $p=0.42$, did not statistically differ between the two groups.

Table 7.2 Age, cognitive skills and parental education by experimental group

	Treatment group		*Control group*	
	M	*SD*	*M*	*SD*
Age (years)	4.86	0.34	4.94	0.27
Basic cognitive skills	0.181	0.939	−0.098	1.022
Highest level of parents education	−0.068	0.944	0.055	0.996

Intervention

Our intervention followed the bilingual maintenance approach, and relied on findings on the cognitive advantages that bilingualism can have (Prevoo *et al.*, 2016: 238). Specifically, we assumed that an optimal promotion of bilingual language acquisition would be achieved with combined and coordinated measures to promote learning of the heritage language and the school language (Cummins, 1984; Reich & Roth, 2002). These coordinated measures were set up both within kindergarten as well as between kindergarten and the children's homes. For the promotion of language in kindergarten, the same learning content was taught in both the heritage language and in the school language, so that the children could expand their vocabulary and global knowledge in both. However, language acquisition also takes place outside the kindergarten and involves various factors including those located in the children's homes (Ritterfeld, 2000: 435f.). For instance, family access to books or reading habits at home is known to shape linguistic development (Böhme-Dürr, 2000: 447; Reich & Roth, 2002: 35; Retelsdorf & Möller, 2008: 232ff.). We therefore assumed that coordinating the promotion of the two languages, by providing families with reading material on the topic that was taught in kindergarten, would have positive effects on language acquisition (Codina *et al.*, 1999).

With these considerations, the intervention followed three complementary approaches:

(1) Promotion of the heritage language in kindergarten for two lessons per week.
(2) Coordinated language promotion in the heritage and the school language.
(3) Support of parents in the promotion of the heritage language within the family.

The promotion of the heritage language in kindergarten was implemented by special teaching staff, who had personal roots in the respective countries of origin of the children, and knew the heritage culture well. Instruction took place two hours per week in the heritage language only, and was integrated into the regular class schedule of the kindergarten so that children attending these lessons did not have to come to kindergarten outside of the regular hours. In these heritage language lessons, content-related sequences from regular lessons were consolidated, new aspects of a topic were addressed and cultural similarities and differences were pointed out. Instruction took place individually or in small groups. Children with the same first language were taught in the same small group. The remaining students were taught by the class teacher.

For the coordinated language promotion, four 12-week phases were selected over a period of two years. In these phases, at least two topics from the regular instruction were addressed and consolidated in the heritage language. Additionally, in each of the four intervention phases, a fictional story was introduced to the children both in the school language during regular instruction and in their heritage language during the heritage language lessons described above. This was meant to activate the children's existing vocabulary and global knowledge in their heritage language, to strengthen their language skills and to promote the acquisition of the school language.

Parents were supported in the promotion of the heritage language within the family jointly by the heritage language teachers and the regular kindergarten teachers. The cooperation of the parents was encouraged through parent–teacher meetings before the start of each of the four intervention phases. These meetings were chaired by the heritage language teaching staff. The aim was to thoroughly establish cooperation between school and home, so that the parents recognised their role in their child's learning. Parents were deliberately included in the linguistic development of their children, and were requested to read aloud to their children for 15 minutes, three times per week in their heritage language, or to play audio books in their presence. Moreover, parents received advice on how they could support linguistic development in everyday situations. During the intervention phase, at least one meeting took place between the heritage language teacher and the parents, to uphold the importance of promoting language and to discuss questions.

Longitudinal design

Table 7.3 shows the longitudinal design with the test times and intervention phases. Language competencies in the heritage and school languages of both children of the treatment and control groups were assessed four times over two years: shortly after the transition to kindergarten, after half a year in kindergarten, at the end of the first year and shortly before entering school.

Instruments for language assessment

For the documentation of linguistic competencies in German, the language part of the standardised test, 'wortgewandt & zahlenstark', was used (Moser & Berweger, 2007). This test is a diagnostic instrument for assessing the linguistic and mathematical skills of children from 4 to 6 years of age. The test was standardised to roughly 1000 randomly sampled children in German-speaking Switzerland, including children with a heritage language other than the school language. The language part of the test comprises measures on phonological awareness, vocabulary, alphabetic understanding and elementary reading, and is conducted as an individual assessment.

Table 7.3 Longitudinal design with test times and intervention periods

	Treatment group with intervention (EG)	*Control group without intervention (CG)*
Assessment of language competencies T1 (September 2006)	X	X
Intervention period 1 (October 2006–January 2007, 12 weeks)	X	
Assessment of language competencies T2 (February 2007)	X	X
Intervention period 2 (March–May 2007, 12 weeks)	X	
Assessment of language competencies T3 (June 2007)	X	X
Intervention period 3 (October 2007–January 2008, 12 weeks)	X	
Intervention period 4 (March–May 2008, 12 weeks)	X	
Assessment of language competencies T4 (June 2008)	X	X

To assess the linguistic competencies in the heritage languages of immigrant children, the language component of the test, 'wortgewandt & zahlenstark', was adopted into the five languages of the target group. As a large number of the tasks of the test in the German language assessed linguistic abilities with regards to sounds, syllables, rhymes and letters, a direct translation into the five other languages was not possible. Instead of translating the language test, an adaptation was designed. The aim was to create equivalent test versions in the five target languages that corresponded with the German version of the test in relative scope, content and difficulty. Whenever possible, concepts and internal structure were maintained as per the German version. If an item was not relevant in one of the target languages (for example, because the linguistic phenomenon assessed did not exist or was peripheral), we tried to find a solution that was equivalent to the original version.

Comparison of the test versions

The adaptation of linguistic testing material into another language raises the question of functional and measurement equivalence. To ensure that the different versions of the test were as equivalent as possible to the original version, tests were adapted by experts who had a linguistic educational background, knowledge of the structure of both languages, knowledge of first language acquisition and an understanding of the composition and purpose of the original test material. These adaptations were then scrutinised for measurement equivalence using item response theory (IRT; cf. Rost, 2004: 115). Thus, we could empirically establish whether the different test versions assessed the same linguistic competencies, so that children with equivalent skills would solve the test items with the same likelihood, independent of the test version.

The assumptions of the Rasch model are fundamental to the development of a single test for the assessment of linguistic competencies in six languages. This includes item homogeneity and person homogeneity as a component of specific objectivity (Rost, 2004: 40). First, the difficulties of the test tasks must be the same for all children, and all test tasks must address the same latent variables in terms of the competence measured (Rost, 2004: 100). Second, competence must be measured independently of the selection of tasks for each person. This means that all children tested should take the test based on the same competencies (Rost, 2004: 347ff.).

Items that fulfil the assumptions of IRT can be compared as per their difficulty on the same metric scale. Differences in task difficulties between the different test versions indicate differential item functioning (DIF; Wu *et al.*, 1998: 76), which means that they measure a different ability or the same ability at a different level of difficulty. If, for example, an item is difficult in the German version but easy in the Albanian one, one can assume that the linguistic structure differs between the two languages, or that the children react culturally in different ways to the task. Inconsistencies in the adaptation of the original material could also occur.

A comparison of all six test versions (Albanian, German, Bosnian/Croatian/Serbian, Portuguese, Spanish and Tamil) resulted in a low number of tasks with the same difficulty. Thus, the adapted test versions were compared separately with the original German version. Additionally, the Spanish test version was omitted due to its small sample size.

The comparison of the four test versions with the original German version resulted in a satisfactory outcome. Figure 7.1 shows an example of the correspondence and statistically insignificant divergence of difficulty parameters for the tasks for phonological awareness between the German and Albanian versions. The figure includes a graphical model test, with which the sample independence and Rasch homogeneity between the German and Albanian tests may be examined. The closer the difficulty parameters come to the main diagonal, the greater the sample independence and the higher the Rasch homogeneity (Amelang & Schmidt-Atzert, 2006: 77). The difficulty parameters presented in Figure 7.2 are close to the main diagonal and do not deviate from one another to a statistically significant degree.

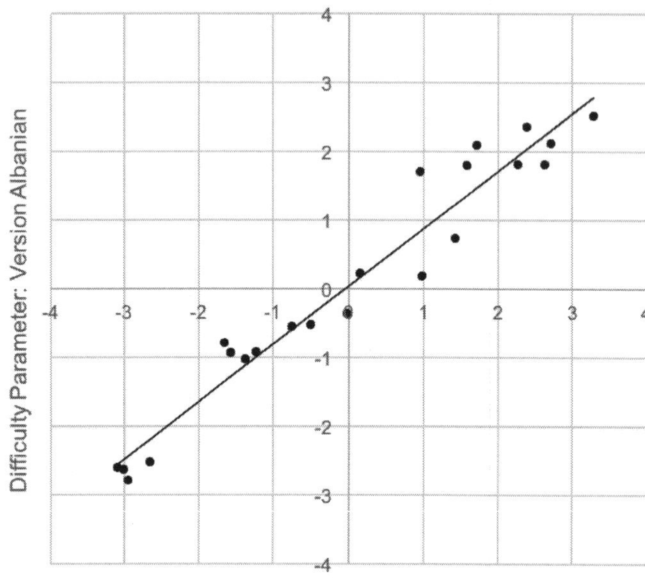

Figure 7.1 Graphical representation of differential item functioning (DIF): Phonological awareness: Original German version and adopted Albanian version (link items only)

The separate matching of the adopted test versions with the original German version revealed that the equivalence of difficulty differed between the three domains of competence investigated. For the domains of alphabetic understanding and elementary reading and phonological equivalence, it was relatively easy to define test versions with the same difficulty. Depending on the test version, 47–89 (i.e. 35%–81%) of the original items proved equivalently difficult. In the domain of vocabulary, however, establishing equivalent difficulty was more challenging. Here, only 27%–42% of the original items were useful.

Table 7.4 indicates the strength of concordance between the respective adaptations and the original German version in the different domains of competence. The second column in Table 7.4 contains the number of tasks without significantly different difficulty parameters. The third column contains the number of all tasks in the original German version that could be adapted. The fourth column contains the correlation coefficients between the difficulty parameters of the adapted test versions and the original German version.

Depending on the language and competence area, the number of items with the same difficulty was occasionally too small for a valid assessment of linguistic competencies. In these cases, tasks with identical difficulty

Table 7.4 Concordance of translated test versions with the original test in German

Domain of competence	*Number of items with same difficulty: Link items*	*Number of items in total: Original items*	*Correlation r: Item parameters original test (German: second language) and test versions (first language link items)*
Phonological awareness			
Albanian	22	58	0.97
Portuguese	25	58	0.96
Bosnian/ Croatian/Serbian	35	58	0.96
Tamil	15	43	0.98
Alphabetic understanding and elementary reading			
Albanian	59	66	0.96
Portuguese	44	66	0.87
Bosnian/ Croatian/Serbian	41	66	0.89
Tamil	31	66	0.86
Vocabulary			
Albanian	12	33	0.94
Portuguese	13	33	0.92
Bosnian/ Croatian/Serbian	11	33	0.94
Tamil	9	33	0.84

parameters were used as 'link items'. The estimation of children's linguistic competencies was, respectively, fixed to the difficulty parameters of the link items, and the remaining tasks were used variably (Kolen & Brennan, 2004: 278; Wright & Stone, 1979: 97ff.). By connecting the test versions with the link items, all tasks of the test versions that were Rasch-compliant could be used.

For scaling, the difficulty parameters of the standardised test 'wortgewandt & zahlenstark' (Moser & Berweger, 2007) were imported. The scale was standardised at a mean of M=500 points and a standard deviation of SD=100 points.

Methods of analysis

Taking into account the hierarchical structure of the longitudinal data, analyses were conducted with Hierarchical Linear Modelling (HLM) by

Raudenbush and Bryk (2002). The longitudinal study was designed such that from the outset, the sampling units were individual students, not entire classes; hence, two-level models could be applied. In doing so, the dependence of the data was considered and appropriate standard errors were calculated.

As learning progress and development is not necessarily linear in nature, the results were calculated using quadratic growth models (Langer, 2009: 241ff.).[2] Based on these models, we analysed whether the mean values (intercepts) and gradients (slopes) of the two groups statistically differed. Furthermore, we estimated the effect of the learning preconditions (age, gender, general basic cognitive abilities and parental education) on both the intercept and the slope of language proficiency, and used these variables as covariates in all growth models. Thus, all parameters for learning progress were statistically controlled for these learning pre-conditions. For analysing the correlation between heritage and school language, a longitudinal cross-lagged panel design (Reinecke, 2005: 74ff.) was specified. Data from all students, including treatment and control groups, have been used for analysis.

Results

Learning progress in the heritage language

Table 7.5 shows the results of the hierarchical regression analysis for the heritage language. The intercepts of the two groups are significantly different for phonological awareness. With 462 points, the intercept of the treatment group was 39 points higher than the intercept of the control group. The mean value in the domain of vocabulary differed by 48 points in the same direction. The intercept for alphabetic understanding and elementary reading, however, was not significantly different in the two groups.

The linear slope of the control group increased by 5 points slower per month than that of the treatment group, in all three domains of language functioning. However, the differences between the two groups were not statistically significant. The negative values of the treatment group for the quadratic component of phonological awareness and vocabulary indicate an attenuating effect. Over the course of kindergarten schooling, the growth of language competence tends to slow down. For the children in the control group, this attenuation is less pronounced than for the children in the treatment condition, although this difference is not statistically significant. For the domain of alphabetic understanding and elementary reading, children in the control group show somewhat greater learning progress, which, however, does not significantly differ from the learning progress of the treatment group.

Table 7.5 First language (phonological awareness, vocabulary, alphabetic understanding and elementary reading): Fixed effects and variable effects

Fixed effects	*Phonological awareness First language*		*Vocabulary First language*		*Alphabetic understanding and elementary reading First language*	
Intercept β0	*Coefficient*	*SE*	*Coefficient*	*SE*	*Coefficient*	*SE*
Treatment group	461.66***	8.69	523.04***	11.45	445.70***	28.56
Control group	−38.67***	10.97	−48.20***	12.89	−14.44	28.36
Age (in years)	37.38	22.83	3.44	23.26	−3.79	72.78
Sex (boy as reference)	20.43	11.39	8.63	12.62	27.12	29.10
Cognitive skills (*z*-scores)	8.76	6.30	1.41	7.47	16.01	15.44
Highest level of parental education (*z*-scores)	6.62	7.43	11.85	6.74	26.87	14.98
Slope β1 months						
Treatment group	24.01***	2.57	12.32***	2.74	7.25	6.39
Control group	−5.32	2.94	−5.24	3.15	4.66	5.89
Age (in years)	−0.73	5.20	2.53	5.53	−0.93	15.05
Sex (boy as reference)	−2.71	2.76	−1.24	2.85	−3.15	5.98
Cognitive skills (*z*-scores)	2.17	1.64	0.70	1.60	1.92	3.40
Highest level of parental education (*z*-scores)	4.35*	1.64	1.18	1.31	1.08	2.87
Slope β2 months squared						
Treatment group	−0.60***	0.13	−0.34*	0.13	0.24	0.27
Control group	0.14	0.13	0.09	0.15	−0.40	0.24
Age (in years)	0.03	0.25	−0.10	0.25	0.10	0.60
Sex (boy as reference)	0.19	0.13	0.10	0.12	0.21	0.25
Cognitive skills (*z*-scores)	−0.07	0.08	−0.02	0.07	−0.03	0.15
Highest level of parental education (*z*-scores)	−0.16*	0.07	−0.04	0.05	−0.06	0.11

Variable effects	*Variance components*	*Variance components*	*Variance components*
Intercept	2679.62***	4668.57***	13540.03***
Slope months	87.24**	132.14***	390.28***
Slope months squared	0.17**	0.15***	0.54***
Level 1	2777.15	2075.73	4276.96

*$p<0.05$; **$p<0.01$; ***$p<0.001$, SE=robust standard error.

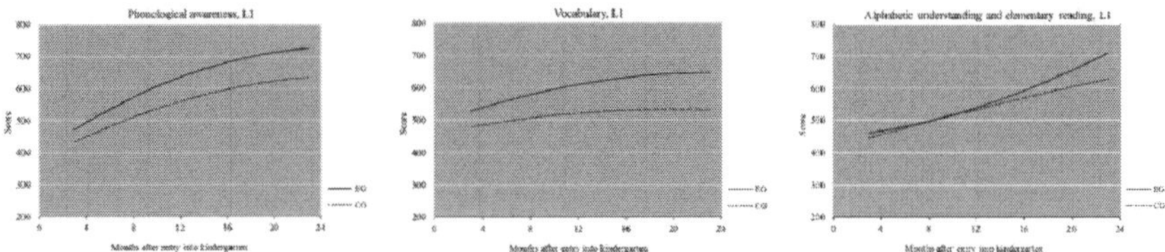

Figure 7.2 Treatment and control group: Mean differences in first language

Figure 7.2 summarises the results described above, and shows that on a descriptive level both groups become increasingly dissimilar. The difference increases for phonological awareness from 39 to 91 points (d=0.75), for vocabulary from 48 to 115 points (d=1.33) and for alphabetic understanding and elementary reading from 15 to 82 points (d=0.50). These differences represent moderate to strong effects.

Learning progress in German as a school language

Table 7.6 shows the results of the hierarchical regression analysis for German as the school language. Generally, school language competencies were much lower than heritage language competencies. Both the intercepts and slopes for all three domains significantly differed between children in the treatment and control groups. In comparison to the results for the heritage language, the mean values and learning progress from all four testing instances were very close to one another. Overall, statistically significant attenuation effects were evident for phonological awareness and vocabulary.

Individual learning conditions had a partial impact on the intercept at the time of testing, but not on learning progress. Gender and cognitive skills were significantly correlated with the intercept of phonological awareness, where girls scored 32 points higher than boys, and one standard deviation in cognitive skills implied an intercept that was 47 points higher. In the domain of vocabulary, cognitive skills (21 points higher per standard

Table 7.6 Second language (phonological awareness, vocabulary, alphabetic understanding and elementary reading): Fixed effects and variable effects

Fixed effects	*Phonological awareness Second language*		*Vocabulary Second language*		*Alphabetic understanding and elementary reading Second language*	
Intercept β0	*Coefficient*	*SE*	*Coefficient*	*SE*	*Coefficient*	*SE*
Treatment group	391.86***	13.29	328.09***	12.74	420.50***	25.07
Control group	−0.38	15.88	17.48	15.61	8.40	28.54
Age (in years)	48.09	27.75	14.32	23.00	−0.37	56.38
Sex (boy as reference)	31.71*	15.19	13.39	13.40	24.20	35.60
Cognitive skills (*z*-scores)	47.27***	8.96	21.49**	8.00	15.18	15.58
Highest level of parental education (*z*-scores)	7.09	7.29	21.83***	6.39	9.60	14.80
Slope β1 months						
Treatment group	17.19***	2.45	15.70***	2.01	3.22	5.17
Control group	2.26	3.16	−1.87	2.81	2.56	6.29
Age (in years)	−2.47	4.55	0.62	3.95	6.79	12.65
Sex (boy as reference)	−1.52	3.13	−1.90	2.32	−1.57	7.46
Cognitive skills (*z*-scores)	−3.06	1.78	0.18	1.28	−0.37	3.55
Highest level of parental education (*z*-scores)	2.73	1.44	−0.06	1.12	2.55	2.91
Slope β2 months squared (quadratic growth curve model)						
Treatment group	−0.35***	0.10	−0.38***	0.09	0.28	0.21
Control group	−0.10	0.13	0.08	0.12	−0.22	0.26

Age (in years)	0.06	0.20	−0.05	0.18	−0.26	0.51
Sex (boy as reference)	0.07	0.14	0.06	0.11	0.13	0.30
Cognitive skills (*z*-scores)	0.13	0.08	0.02	0.06	0.08	0.15
Highest level of parental education (*z*-scores)	−0.12	0.07	−0.01	0.05	−0.10	0.12
Variable effects	*Variance components*		*Variance components*		*Variance components*	
Intercept	6452.74***		5048.31***		10982.66***	
Slope months	138.93***		22.15*		327.34***	
Slope months squared	0.21***		0.03		0.44*	
Level 1	2005.51		1489.31		6179.19	

**p*<0.05; ***p*<0.01; ****p*<0.001, SE=robust standard error.

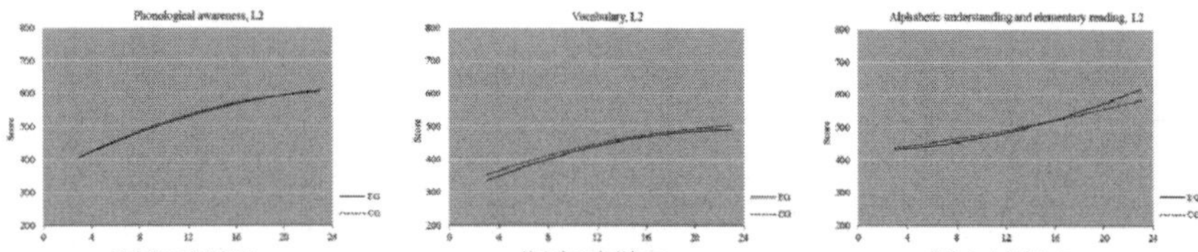

Figure 7.3 Treatment and control group: Mean differences in second language

deviation) and parental education (22 points higher per standard deviation) were significantly correlated with the intercept. Figure 7.3 summarises these results and shows virtually no differences between the two groups. The trajectories are almost overlapping.

Associations between heritage and school language development

Figure 7.4 presents the path model testing cross-lagged effects between competencies in heritage and school language. The model fit was good for both phonological awareness (PA: χ^2=16.953, df=10, p=0.075, CFI=0.990, RMSEA=0.072) and alphabetic understanding and elementary reading (UR: χ^2=14.144, df=12, p=0.292, CFI=0.996, RMSEA=0.043).

The results of the cross-lagged panel analyses for phonological awareness showed a relatively strong predictability of the competencies

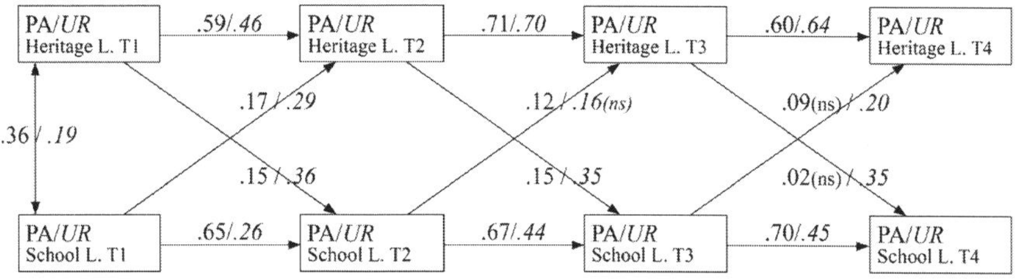

Figure 7.4 Path model representing the association between first and second language competencies (phonological awareness PB and alphabetic understanding and elementary reading BL): standardised coefficients (without covariance between residuals)

in heritage and school language by the competencies of the previous test time (PA heritage languages: $p_{T1T2}=0.59$, $p_{T2T3}=0.71$, $p_{T3T4}=0.60$; PA school languages: $p_{T1T2}=0.65$, $p_{T2T3}=0.67$, $p_{T3T4}=0.70$). However, the hypothesis concerning a correlation between the competencies in the heritage and the school language had to be rejected. The cross-lagged path coefficients showed only small, albeit mostly significant, effects of the competencies in one language for the competencies in the other (PA effect heritage language on school language: $p_{T1T2}=0.15$, $p_{T2T3}=0.15$, $p_{T3T4}=0.02$ [ns]; PA effect school language on heritage language: $p_{T1T2}=0.17$, $p_{T2T3}=0.12$, $p_{T3T4}=0.09$ [ns]).

The results of the cross-lagged panel analysis for alphabetic understanding and elementary reading showed a weaker predictability of the competencies in heritage and school language by the respective competencies measured on the previous occasion (UR heritage language: $p_{T1T2}=0.46$, $p_{T2T3}=0.70$, $p_{T3T4}=0.64$; UR school language: $p_{T1T2}=0.26$, $p_{T2T3}=0.44$, $p_{T3T4}=0.45$). The dependences remained stable up to the school test time. The cross-lagged path coefficients, too, were mostly significant, but small in size (UR effect of heritage language on school language: $p_{T1T2}=0.36$, $p_{T2T3}=0.35$, $p_{T3T4}=0.35$; UR effect of school language on heritage language: $p_{T1T2}=0.29$, $p_{T2T3}=0.16$[ns], $p_{T3T4}=0.20$).

Discussion

Overall, the intervention based on linguistic theory did not have a statistically significant positive effect on the development of linguistic competencies, neither in the heritage nor the school language. Thus, the combination of training in the heritage language in kindergarten, with coordinated training in both the heritage and the school language, combined with parental support in training of the heritage language, had no significant effect on language competencies. However, this conclusion only holds good for those aspects of language acquisition that were assessed with our instrument, and does not detect all aspects of linguistic development. Furthermore, we are unable to comment on long-term effects, as we had no available follow-up data on, for instance, language development in primary school.

The hypothesised effects of the competencies in the heritage language on the competencies in the school language according to Cummins' (1984) interdependence hypothesis, however, received at least some empirical support. Small to medium effects of the competencies in the heritage language on the competencies in the school language were found for alphabetic understanding and elementary reading. The effects were not consistent across all measurement points, and were typically stronger in younger children. Generally, the effects were also stronger for alphabetic understanding compared with phonological awareness. Again, it is possible that these effects would have been stronger had we measured other aspects of linguistic development in our instrument. It is also possible that the effects would have been stronger if children had started learning the school language at a younger age. However, we could not have carried out the intervention at an earlier age, as kindergarten entry age is regulated by law in Switzerland.

The intervention did not have a clear effect despite being conducted for a two-year period; there could be several theoretical reasons for this finding. First, Cummins' hypothesis about the linguistic interdependence of heritage- and school-language proficiency is not specifically related to the bilingual language acquisition of children with an immigration background. Depending on their family context, a considerable proportion of these children may be deprived of opportunities for interaction with native speakers, thus experiencing less language exposure in a natural social environment, a fact that may compromise their ability to acquire the school-language. In other words, although growing up bilingually is considered to be an asset, one could argue that children with immigrant backgrounds and low socio-economic status do not actually grow up bilingually. Opportunities to learn the school language are few, and the quality of the communication with natives is too low to provoke transfer effects from the heritage language to the school language (Reich, 2008). Furthermore, our intervention was part of the regular time spent for language education at kindergarten. No additional hours were spent to improve language competencies, except maybe at home where some parents presumably spent some more time with their children on language-related activities.

The duration and intensity of bilingual language acquisition could also be the reason why the intervention effects did not emerge more clearly in this study. The immigrant children in our study had grown up largely monolingual before they entered kindergarten. The bilingual language instruction of immigrant children likely began only upon entry into kindergarten. In order for bilingual language instruction to provide added value for both languages, a coordinated promotion of greater duration would be necessary. Furthermore, rigorous bilingual models (immersion), or models that offer encouragement of the origin language and increasingly segue into the school language (transition models), are far more successful than models in which the language of origin is taught as a separate subject (language maintenance; Gogolin, 2005; Reich & Roth, 2002; Zurer, 2007). However, we could not revert to these approaches for organisational and financial reasons. Also, parental involvement might have been insufficient and not binding enough. Nevertheless, kindergarten teachers emphasised as part of a final survey that parents highly appreciated the bilingual education, and that the intervention had a positive effect on parent–school cooperation.

Immersion is a successful model for promoting language, and is a necessary condition outside school for bilingual language acquisition and the integration of immigrant children. A linguistically stimulating environment in school is practically impossible to achieve through educational policy measures alone. The segregation of the population by educational and ethnic characteristics has advanced so far that the natural context for bilingual language acquisition or for acquiring German as a school language is extremely unfavourable for many immigrant children at school. Additionally, ethnic concentrations in residential areas significantly hamper the acquisition of the local language (Esser, 2006: 42ff.). These unfavourable constellations are retained in school, as the ethno-linguistic and social composition of the school scarcely differs from that of residential areas.

The intervention carried out cannot rectify the insufficient linguistic competencies in German as a school language of immigrant children. For this purpose, long-term measures, and those which more intensely include the parents or families of the children and their general living situation, seem necessary.

Notes

(1) This chapter is a revised version of an article that was originally published by Moser, U., Bayer, N. and Tunger, V. (2010) Erstsprachförderung bei Migrantenkindern in Kindergärten. *Zeitschrift für Erziehungswissenschaft* 13, 631–648.

(2) With four measurement occasions, linear, quadratic and cubic models can be calculated. The review of the three models showed that the quadratic model fit the data best.

References

Ahrenholz, B. (2008) Einleitung. In B. Ahrenholz (ed.) *Deutsch als Zweitsprache. Voraussetzungen und Konzepte für die Förderung von Kindern und Jugendlichen mit Migrationshintergrund* (pp. 7–16). Freiburg im Breisgau: Fillibach Verlag.

Amelang, M. and Schmidt-Atzert, L. (2006) *Psychologische Diagnostik und Intervention* (4. vollständig überarbeitete und erweiterte Aufl.). Heidelberg: Springer.

Angelone, D. and Moser, U. (2011) Die Bedeutung der Klassenzusammensetzung. In U. Moser, A. Buff, D. Angelone and J. Hollenweger (eds) *Nach sechs Jahren Primarschule. Deutsch, Mathematik und motivational-emotionales Befinden am Ende der 6. Klasse* (pp. 50–62). Zürich: Bildungsdirektion Kanton Zürich.

Baker, C. and Prys Jones, S. (1998) *Encyclopedia of Bilingualism and Bilingual Education*. Clevedon: Multilingual Matters.

Baker, K.A. and De Kanter, A.A. (1983) *Bilingual Education*. Lexington MA: Lexington Books.

Baumert, J. and Schümer, G. (2001) Familiäre Lebensverhältnisse, Bildungsbeteiligung und Kompetenzerwerb. In J. Baumert, E. Klieme, M. Neubrand, M. Prenzel, U. Schiefele, W. Schneider, P. Stanat, K.-J. Tillmann and M. Weiss (eds) *PISA 2000. Basiskompetenzen von Schülerinnen und Schülern im internationalen Vergleich* (pp. 323–409). Opladen: Leske+Budrich.

Baur, R.S. and Meder, G. (1992) Zur Interdependenz von Muttersprache und Zweitsprache bei jugoslawischen Migrantenkindern. In R.S. Baur, G. Meder and V. Previšic (eds) *Interkulturelle Erziehung und Zweisprachigkeit* (pp. 109–140). Baltmannsweiler: Schneider Hohengehren.

Bayer, N. and Moser, U. (2009) Wirkungen unterschiedlicher Modelle der Schuleingangsstufe auf den Lern- und Entwicklungsstand: Erste Ergebnisse einer Längsschnittstudie. *Zeitschrift für Grundschulforschung* 2 (1), 20–34.

BFS (2016) See https://www.bfs.admin.ch/bfs/de/home/statistiken/bildung-wissenschaft/personen-ausbildung.assetdetail.333514.html.

Bialystok, E. (2001) *Bilingualism in Development: Language, Literacy, and Cognition*. Cambridge: Cambridge University Press.

Bialystok, E., McBride-Chang, C. and Luk, G. (2005) Bilingualism, language proficiency, and learning to read in two writing systems. *Journal of Educational Psychology* 97 (4), 580–590.

Böhme-Dürr, K. (2000) Einfluss von Medien auf den Sprachlernprozess. In H. Grimm (ed.) *Enzyklopädie der Psychologie, Band 3, Sprachentwicklung* (pp. 433–459). Göttingen: Hogrefe.

Branum-Martin, L., Mehta, P., Fletcher, J.M., Carlson, C.D., Ortiz, A., Carlo, M. and Francis, D.J. (2006) Bilingual phonological awareness: Multilevel construct validation among Spanish-speaking kindergarteners in transitional bilingual education classrooms. *Journal of Educational Psychology* 98 (1), 170–181.

Codina, E., Westerbeek, K. and de Wit, Y. (1999) Van eerste naar tweede taal. Een onderzoek naar de opbrengsten van het OET-programma Trias. Unpublished manuscript, Rotterdam.

Cummins, J. (1979) Linguistic interdependence and the educational development of bilingual children. *Review of Educational Research* 49, 222–251.

Cummins, J. (1984) *Bilingualism and Special Education: Issues in Assessment and Pedagogy*. Clevedon: Multilingual Matters

Dubowy, M., Ebert, S., von Maurice, J. and Weinert, S. (2008) Sprachlich-kognitive Kompetenzen beim Eintritt in den Kindergarten. Ein Vergleich von Kindern mit und ohne Migrationshintergrund. *Zeitschrift für Entwicklungspsychologie und Pädagogische Psychologie* 40 (3), 124–134.

Esser, H. (2006) *Migration, Sprache und Integration* (AKI-Forschungsbilanz 4). Berlin: Arbeitsstelle Interkulturelle Konflikte und gesellschaftliche Integration (AKI), Wissenschafts-Zentrum Berlin für Sozialforschung.

Gogolin, I. (2005) Erziehungsziel Mehrsprachigkeit. In C. Röhner (ed.) *Erziehungsziel Mehrsprachigkeit. Diagnose von Sprachentwicklung und Förderung von Deutsch als Zweitsprache* (pp. 13–24). Weinhein: Juventa Verlag.

Gogolin, I. (2009) Streitfall Zweisprachigkeit: The bilingualism controversy: Les Préludes. In I. Gogolin and U. Neumann (eds) *Streitfall Zweisprachigkeit: The Bilingualism Controversy* (pp. 15–30). Wiesbaden: VS Verlag.

Gomolla, M. (2005) *Schulentwicklung in der Einwanderungsgesellschaft. Strategien gegen institutionelle Diskriminierung in England, Deutschland und in der Schweiz.* Münster: Waxmann.

Hopf, D. (2005) Zweisprachigkeit und Schulleistung bei Migrantenkindern. *Zeitschrift für Pädagogik* 51 (2), 236–251.

Kielhöfer, B. and Jonekeit, S. (1995) *Zweisprachige Kindererziehung.* Tübingen: Stauffenburg.

Kolen, M.J. and Brennan, R.L. (2004) *Test Equating, Scaling, and Linking. Methods and Practices* (2nd edn). New York: Springer.

Langer, W. (2009) *Mehrebenenanalyse. Eine Einführung für Forschung und Praxis* (2. Aufl.). Wiesbaden: VS Verlag für Sozialwissenschaften.

List, G. (2005) Zur Anbahnung mehr- und quersprachiger Kompetenzen in vorschulischen Bildungseinrichtungen. In K. Jampert, P. Best, A. Guadatiello, D. Holler and A. Zehnbauer (eds) *Schlüsselkompetenz Sprache* (pp. 29–32). Weimar: Verlag das Netz.

Limbird, Ch. and Stanat, P. (2006) Sprachförderung bei Schülerinnen und Schülern mit Migrationshintergrund: Ansätze und Wirksamkeit. In J. Baumert, P. Stanat and R. Watermann (eds) *Herkunftsbedingte Disparitäten im Bildungswesen. Vertiefende Analysen im Rahmen von PISA 2000* (pp. 257–307). Wiesbaden: VS Verlag.

Maaz, K., Watermann, R. and Baumert, J. (2007) Familiärer Hintergrund, Kompetenzentwicklung und Selektionsentscheidungen in gegliederten Schulsystemen im internationalen Vergleich. Eine vertiefende Analyse von PISA-Daten. *Zeitschrift für Pädagogik* 53 (4), 444–461.

Moser, U. (2002) *Kulturelle Vielfalt in der Schule: Herausforderung und Chance.* In A. Meyer (ed.) *Für das Leben gerüstet? Die Grundkompetenzen der Jugendlichen. Bern und Neuenburg: Schweizerische Konferenz der kantonalen Erziehungsdirektoren und Bundesamt für Statistik* (pp. 113–135). Bern und Neuenburg: Schweizerische Konferenz der kantonalen Erziehungsdirektoren und Bundesamt für Statistik.

Moser, U. (2013) Bildungsarmut in der Schweiz. In C. Schweiz (ed.) *Caritas Sozialalmanach, Schwerpunkt Bildung gegen Armut* (pp. 77–91). Luzern: Caritas-Verlag.

Moser, U. and Berweger, S. (2007) *wortgewandt & zahlenstark: Lern- und Entwicklungsstand bei 4- bis 6-Jährigen.* St. Gallen und Zürich: Interkantonale Lehrmittelzentrale, Lehrmittelverlage der Kantone St. Gallen und Zürich.

Müller, R. (1997) *Sozialpsychologische Grundlagen des schulischen Zweitspracherwerbs bei MigrantenschülerInnen.* Aarau: Sauerländer.

Paulus, W. and Blossfeld, H.-P. (2007) Schichtspezifische Präferenzen oder sozioökonomisches Entscheidungskalkül? Zur Rolle elterlicher Bildungsaspirationen im Entscheidungsprozess beim Übergang von der Grundschule in die Sekundarstufe. *Zeitschrift für Pädagogik* 53 (4), 491–508.

Preibusch, W. and Kröner, B. (1987) Deutsch-türkische Sprachenbalance bei türkischen Fünftklässlern. *Deutsch lernen* 13 (4), 19–29.

Prevoo, M.J.L., Malda, M., Mesman, J. and Ijzendoorn, M.H. (2016) Within- and cross-language relations between oral language proficiency and school outcomes in bilingual children with an immigrant background: A meta-analytical study. *Review of Educational Research* 86 (1), 237–276.

Proctor, C.P., August, D., Carlo, M.S. and Snow, C. (2006) The intriguing role of Spanish language vocabulary knowledge in predicting English reading comprehension. *Journal of Educational Psychology* 98 (1), 159–169.

Raudenbush, S.W. and Bryk, A.S. (2002). *Hierarchical Linear Models. Applications and Data Analysis Methods*. Thousand Oaks, CA: Sage.

Reich, H.H. (2008) Die Sprachaneignung von Kindern in Situationen der Zwei- und Mehrsprachigkeit. In K. Ehlich, U. Bredel and H.H. Reich (eds) *Referenzrahmen zur altersspezifischen Sprachaneignung* (pp. 163–169). Berlin: Bundesministerium für Bildung und Forschung.

Reich, H.H. and Roth, H.J. (2002) *Spracherwerb zweisprachig aufwachsender Kinder und Jugendlicher. Ein Überblick über den Stand der nationalen und internationalen Forschung*. Hamburg: Behörde für Bildung und Sport.

Reinecke, J. (2005) *Strukturgleichungsmodelle in den Sozialwissenschaften*. München: Oldenbourg.

Retelsdorf, J. and Möller, J. (2008) Familiäre Bedingungen und individuelle Prädiktoren der Lesekompetenz von Schülerinnen und Schülern. *Psychologie in Erziehung und Unterricht* 55, 227–237.

Ritterfeld, U. (2000) Welchen und wie viel Input braucht das Kind? In H. Grimm (ed.) *Enzyklopädie der Psychologie, Band 3, Sprachentwicklung* (pp. 433–459). Göttingen: Hogrefe.

Romaine, S. (1994) *Bilingualism*. Oxford: Blackwell Publishers.

Rösch, H. (2001) Zweisprachige Erziehung in Berlin im Elementar- und Primarbereich. *Essener Linguistische Skripte – elektronisch* 1 (1), 23–44.

Rosenberg, S., Lischer, R., Kronig, W., Nicolet, M., Bürli, A., Schmid, P. and Bühlmann, R. (2003) *Schul- und Bildungslaufbahn von immigrierten „leistungsschwachen" Schülerinnen und Schülern: Schlussbericht CONVEGNO 2002* (Studien und Berichte 19A). Bern: EDK.

Rost, J. (2004) *Lehrbuch Testtheorie – Testkonstruktion*. Bern: Hans Huber.

Schründer-Lenzen, A. and Merkens, H. (2006) Differenzen schriftsprachlicher Kompetenzentwicklung bei Kindern mit und ohne Migrationshintergrund. In A. Schründer-Lenzen (ed.) *Risikofaktoren kindlicher Entwicklung. Migration, Leistungsangst und Schulübergang* (pp. 15–44). Wiesbaden: SV Verlag für Sozialwissenschaften.

Siegel, J. (2003) Social context. In C.J. Doughty and M.H. Long (eds) *The Handbook of Second Language Acquisition* (pp. 178–223). Oxford: Blackwell.

Söhn, J. (2005) *Zweisprachiger Schulunterricht für Migrantenkinder* (AKI-Forschungsbilanz 2). Berlin: WZB Berlin.

Stamm, M., Reinwand, V., Burger, K., Schmid, K., Viehhauser, M. and Muheim, V. (2009) *Frühkindliche Bildung in der Schweiz – ein Bericht im Auftrag der Schweizerischen UNESCO-Kommission*. Bern: Schweizerische UNESCO-Kommission.

Tracy, R. (2005) Spracherwerb bei vier- bis achtjährigen Kindern. In T. Guldimann and B. Hauser (eds) *Bildung 4- bis 8-jähriger Kinder* (pp. 59–75). Münster: Waxmann.

Wang, M., Park, Y. and Rang Lee, K. (2006) Korean-English biliteracy acquisition: Cross-language phonological and orthographic transfer. *Journal of Educational Psychology* 98 (1), 148–158.

Weiss, R.H., Cattell, R.B. and Osterland, J. (1997) *CFT 1. Grundintelligenztest Skala 1*. Göttingen: Hogrefe.

Wright, B.D. and Stone, M.H. (1979) *Best Test Design. Rasch Measurement*. Chicago, IL: Mesa Press.

Wu, M.L., Adams, R.J. and Wilson, M.R. (1998) *ACER ConQuest: Generalised Item Response Modelling Software Manual*. Melbourne: Australian Council for Educational Research.

Zurer, P.B. (2007) Social factors in childhood bilingualism in the United States. *Applied Psycholinguistics* 28, 399–410.

8 Promoting Multilingualism Through Heritage Language Courses: New Perspectives on the Transfer Effect

Edina Krompàk

Introduction

In the last decade, many research projects on language development in the German-speaking world have focused on the transfer effects of heritage or first languages[1] on German as a second language (Baur & Meder, 1992; Caprez-Krompàk, 2010; Dollmann & Kristen, 2010; Moser *et al.*, 2008) or on third languages (Maluch *et al.*, 2014; Rauch *et al.*, 2010). Two sets of issues constitute the background to these projects. On the one hand, *superdiverse societies* (Creese & Blackledge, 2010; Vertovec, 2007) manifest themselves in linguistically heterogeneous school classes. From this perspective, multilingualism and linguistic diversity are considered a resource and a form of enrichment for the learning environment. Research from this angle concentrates on the benefits of multilingualism and aims to investigate the (accepted positive) effect of multilingualism, more precisely the transfer effects of first languages on second languages (see Chapter 1). On the other hand, the results of several studies show that students with immigrant backgrounds are less successful in school than natives (OECD, 2010; Stanat & Christensen, 2006). Moreover, students with immigrant backgrounds are under-represented at schools with extended offers (such as secondary school) and over-represented at schools for children with special needs (Kronig, 2003, 2007; Kronig *et al.*, 2000). This perspective raises several questions about the determinants of school success of plurilingual students with immigrant backgrounds. Different theoretical and empirical approaches which incorporate the interaction of several systemic factors seek to capture the complexity of these determinants (Allemann-Ghionda, 2006; Diefenbach, 2007; Stanat, 2006). Without doubt, language competence in the language of instruction at school plays an important role in academic achievement. Nevertheless, competence in a second language is not the only key factor for school success (Allemann-Ghionda, 2006; Caprez-Krompàk, 2010; Krompàk, 2015). Based on these two perspectives (linguistic diversity and school success), the studies mentioned above investigate transfer effects and their implications for educational practice, most of them – like the present study – drawing on Cummins' (1981) interdependence hypothesis. For this reason, it is important to draw attention to the hypothesis and its empirical testability.

Cummins' interdependence hypothesis implies reciprocal positive influence between languages:

> To the extent that instruction in Lx is effective in promoting proficiency in Lx, transfer of this proficiency to Ly will occur provided there is adequate exposure to Ly (either in school or environment) and adequate motivation to learn Ly. (Cummins, 1981: 29)

The main benefit of the hypothesis is that it spotlights the language development of children with immigrant backgrounds and allows a differentiated view of competence in the first and second language. However, several challenges confront the empirical verification of the hypothesis. First, the hypothesis is premised on the same adequate exposure to both languages. If the first language is a minority language, it does not receive institutional language promotion. To compensate for this and to support the learning of minority languages, members of language groups or embassies sometimes establish heritage language courses (see Chapter 3 of this volume; Caprez-Krompàk, 2010; Liu *et al.*, 2011). In most European countries, heritage language courses generally take place for only a limited period, typically once a week. Due to the fact that heritage language courses are generally optional, motivation to attend them can vary from one year to the next. It follows that there is a lack of equivalent exposure to both languages that is assumed in the interdependence hypothesis. Second, to verify the hypothesis, important control variables, such as the socio-economic status (SES) of the families and the motivation for language learning, have to be considered. Third, the quality and quantity of the language classes (both in the first and second language) exert a major influence on the language performance, factors which also have to be empirically tested in the hypothesis. These considerations combine to challenge the empirical testability of the interdependence hypothesis (Caprez-Krompàk, 2010: 66–67).

In this chapter, I concentrate on the central result of the study 'Development of first and second language in intercultural contexts', and discuss the relevance of the results from the perspective of linguistics and educational policy. I begin by describing the design of the mixed-methods longitudinal study. This is followed by the research question, which focuses on the impact of heritage language courses on first and second language development. I then describe the groups of participants, present the method and explain the development of the c-test scores for Albanian, Turkish and German for bi- and multilingual children with an immigrant background. C-tests represent a main research instrument for exploring language competence in the first and second language. The results of our participants who took the c-tests indicate that heritage language courses have a positive impact on first language proficiency but not on second language proficiency. They also show differences in the development of language competences. In the conclusion, some strengths and limitations of the present study are discussed. In addition, I indicate implications for a multilingual approach to heritage language courses that aims to transform our presently monolingual education system.

The research project 'Development of first and second language in intercultural contexts'[2]

The longitudinal research study 'Development of first and second language in intercultural contexts' was carried out at the University of Zurich between 2005 and 2007. It investigated heritage language courses in German-speaking Switzerland, especially their relevance to the language development of Albanian-Swiss and Turkish-Swiss fifth and sixth graders with an immigrant background. The study aimed to close several research gaps in the field of language diagnostics in the exploration of the state of the art of heritage language courses. To date, there are still hardly any test instruments which take into consideration the bilingualism and multilingualism of children with immigrant backgrounds. With the German, Albanian and Turkish c-tests applied in this project, an instrument was developed which reliably measures the global language competence of bilingual children. Although heritage language courses in Switzerland, particularly the Italian heritage language courses,[3] look back on a long history, they were discovered as a research field rather late. In addition, the investigation of heritage language courses has been predominantly confined to qualitative studies (see Allemann-Ghionda, 2002; Häusler, 1999; Schuler, 2002) with only a few quantitative studies (Haenni Hoti & Schader, 2005/2006; Moser *et al.*, 2008).

To cope with the complexity of heritage language courses as a research field, a multi-method approach was applied which combined quantitative and qualitative methods. Quantitative instruments were used to analyse individual learning abilities (language tests), and the family and school environments (questionnaire of the parents and the heritage language course teachers). The qualitative instruments (interviews with two Albanian language teachers and 90 minutes of video recordings of their lessons) were developed to analyse important aspects of the subject more deeply. This chapter focuses on the quantitative part of the investigation; accordingly, the following sections refer solely to the effect of heritage language courses on the development of first and second language acquisition.

Research question and hypothesis

Regarding the effect of heritage language courses, the study explores the following question:

> How do heritage language courses impact on first and second language development? What are the differences in the first (Albanian and Turkish) and second language (German) at T1 and T2 between children who attend heritage language classes (treatment group) and children who do not (control group)?

Related to the first research question, we postulate that the attendance of heritage language classes has a positive impact on first and second language acquisition (Hypothesis 1).

We also expect that language development in the first and second languages is higher among children who attend heritage language classes than among those who do not (Hypothesis 2).

Method

Participants

The effectiveness of heritage language courses was investigated by means of a longitudinal quasi-experimental design that included a treatment and a control group. The pupils in the treatment group attended the optional Albanian and Turkish heritage language courses; the control group did not. Data were collected from 10- to 12-year-old pupils in Switzerland in the Canton of Zurich, in two waves, in 2005 and 2006. In the first wave, language tests and questionnaires were used. After one year, the same language tests were used to analyse the effect of heritage language classes. There were 126 pupils in the treatment group and 55 pupils in the control group in the first wave, and 80 and 46 pupils in the second wave, respectively. On average, pupils in the treatment group attended an optional heritage language course for 2 years and 4 months in contrast to the control group, which never attended such courses. The sample consisted of two subsamples: 81 Albanian-speaking pupils and 45 Turkish-speaking pupils in the treatment group, and 45 Albanian-speaking pupils and 10 Turkish-speaking pupils in the control group. Because the heritage language courses were optional, the subsamples of the pupils at the second wave reduced by more than 30%. The already small sample of Turkish-speaking pupils

Table 8.1 Sample of the Albanian- and Turkish-speaking pupils

	Treatment group		*Control group*	
	T1	*T2*	*T1*	*T2*
Albanian	81	51	45	41
Turkish	45	29	10	5
Total	126	80	55	46

Source: Caprez-Krompàk (2010: 115).

in the control group shrunk so dramatically (from 10 in the first wave to 5 in the second), that the sample could not be used for further inferential statistical analyses (Table 8.1).

Measures

German, Albanian and Turkish language achievement

Language performance was assessed using c-tests. The c-test is an integrative written test of general language proficiency (Grotjahn, 1987, 1997, 2002). It consists of 5–6 short authentic texts with 20–25 blanks each, which students have to fill in. The c-test has to be adapted to the language competence and the age of the students. Based on the 'rule of two' principle, the second part of every second word is deleted, starting with the second sentence (Grotjahn, 2002). A precondition to applying the c-test is that adults can solve it 100% (Raatz & Klein-Braley, 2001). An expert team of linguists and heritage language teachers compiled the German, Albanian and Turkish c-test. The test designers had to cope with several challenges. First, the selection of adequate and authentic texts in the particular language represented some difficulties, because of the specific linguistic background of the participant children. As the available German c-test by Raatz and Klein-Braley (2001) was too difficult for our pilot group, it was rejected. For this reason, we developed a German c-test for multilingual children which considers the immigrant background and also the culture-specific elements of the language (see Figure 8.1). We also reduced the c-test in every language to 4 texts with 20 blanks each.

The Albanian c-test provided a further challenge. Due to the spoken but not written dialectal varieties of Albanian (Schader, 2006), we also had to consider the dialectal solution for the c-test (Figure 8.2). This decision was essential for the analysis of the control group, which commanded none or very little written Albanian (Caprez-Krompàk & Selimi, 2006). Besides, official written Albanian was only defined in 1972 (Gjinari & Shkurtaj, 2000, Hetzer, 1995).

Unsichtbare Tinte[4]

Um eine unsichtbare Nachricht zu schreiben, braucht man nur eine Zitrone! Man g*ibt/giesst* (1) etwas Zitr*onensaft/*Zitr*one* (2) auf e*in* (3) Wattestäbchen u*nd* (4) schreibt da*mit*/da*nn* (5) auf ein wei*sses* (6) Blatt. Die Schr*ift* (7) bleibt unsich*tbar* (8). Wird d*as* (9) Blatt gefu*nden* (10), weiss niem*and* (11), dass ei*ne* (12) geheime Botsch*aft* (13) darauf ste*ht* (14). Ma*n* (15) nimmt da*nn* (16) ein war*mes* (17) Bügeleisen und büg*elt* (18) das Bl*att* (19) wie e*in* (20) Taschentuch. Die Nachricht erscheint wie durch Zauberei!

Translation

Invisible ink

To write an invisible message, one only needs a lemon! You pour some lemon on a cotton bud and (then) write with it on a white sheet. The writing remains invisible. If the sheet is found, no one knows that a secret message is written on it. You then take a warm iron and iron the sheet like a handkerchief. The message appears like a magic!

Figure 8.1 Example: German c-test, text 1 with solution in italics and translation[4]

Pranvera u sjell njerëzve gëzim dhe kohë të mirë. Qielli ësh*të* (ësh*te*, ësh*t*)[6] (1) i kal*tërt* (kal*tërtë*, kal*tër*, kal*tert*, kal*ter*, kal*terë*) (2). Dielli ndriçon (ndriçonë, ndriçontë, ndri*qon*, ndri*shon*, ndri*shonë*, ndri*shoj*, ndri*set*, ndri*shet*, ndri*ti*, ndri*t*, ndri*ten*, ndri*te*, ndri*të*, ndri*ton*, ndri*tën*, ndri*n*, ndri*ën*, ndri*të*) (3). Pamja e naty*rës* (naty*res*, natyës) (4) është e bu*kur* (bu*kurë*, bu*ker*) (5). Në ve*rë* *(verrë, vere, ver, vend) (6)* bën va*pë* *(vape, vap, vapi, vapa, vabë) (7)*. Rallë fr*yn* *(frym, fryen, frynë, fryne,* früne, früma, *fryni, fryehn, freskon, fra) (8)* një erë e leh*të* *(lehte, leht, lehter,* lehët, leh*më*, leh*ntë*, leh*n) (9)*. Ditët ja*në* *(jane, jan, jann) (10)* të gja*ta* *(gjatë, gjatha) (11)* e të bu*kura* *(bukra) (12)*, netët janë të shk*urtra* *(shkurta, shkurt, shkurtë, shkurte, shkurtura, shkurtera) (13)*. Pushimet ver*ore* *(verorë, veror) (14)* fillojnë. Njerë*zit* *(*njerë*zitë*, njerë*sitë*, njerë*sit*, njerës, njerë*ne*, njerë*në vit) (15)* shkojnë në det, ku push*ojnë* *(*push*ojne*, push*ojn*, push*ojm) (16)* e këna*qen* *(*këna*qën*, këna*çën*, këna*çen*, këna*tqen) (17)*. Në vjes*htë* *(*vje*shte*, vje*sht)* (18) pemët janë plot me fru*ta* *(*fru*tta*, fru*te*, fru*kta*, fru*tat*, fru*chta*, fr*yta*, fr*yte) (19)*: mollë, dar*dha* *(*dar*dhatë*, dar*dhë*, dar*dh*, dar*dhma) (20)*, ftonj dhe kumbulla. Dimrit bie borë. Fëmijët rrëshqasin me saja, veçanërisht gjatë pushimeve.

Translation:

The seasons

Spring brings people joy and good weather. The sky is blue. The sun shines. Nature is beautiful. In summer it is hot. Seldom does a light wind blow. The days are long and beautiful, the nights are short. The summer holidays begin. The people go to the sea, where they have holidays and fun. In autumn the trees are full of fruits: apples, pears, quinces, and plums. In winter snow falls. The children go sledging, especially in the holidays.

Figure 8.2 Example: Albanian c-test, text 1 with solution in italics and translation[5,6]

The construction of the Turkish c-test, which was developed in close cooperation with the linguist Mesut Gönç, constituted yet another challenge. Because of the specific linguistic structure of Turkish, deleting the second half of the word hindered completion or made it impossible. For this reason, we developed a new deletion principle for the Turkish c-test which allowed the construction of a reliable test (Caprez-Krompàk & Gönç, 2006). According to the 'first-suffix principle', which takes into account the agglutinin structure of Turkish, the first suffix after the root of the word was deleted instead of the second half of the whole word as Grotjahn (2002) proposed for German. The Turkish c-test with the 'first-suffix principle' was piloted with 10- to 12-year-old children in Turkey (Caprez-Krompàk & Gönç, 2006) as well as with Turkish-speaking children in Switzerland. Based on these pilot trials, we developed a reliable Turkish c-test for the main analysis (Figure 8.3).

The German, Albanian and Turkish c-tests were developed especially for 10- to 12-year-old minority children in Switzerland. After a pilot run with adults and pupils, the Albanian and Turkish c-tests were applied to the treatment group in two waves. Each c-test showed a satisfactory to high internal consistency (Caprez-Krompàk, 2010: 130-143): Albanian c-test T1: alpha=0.88 (n=81) T2: alpha=0.91 (n=51); Turkish c-test T1: alpha=0.94 (n=45) T2: alpha=0.87 (n=29). To analyse the reliability of the German c-test, data from both groups were included. The German c-test also showed satisfactory internal consistency T1: alpha=0.88 (n=180) T2: alpha=0.89 (n=127). The sample was ad hoc; accordingly, there is no claim of representativeness. Nevertheless, we succeeded in devising reliable and valid language tests to assess the language competence of multilingual children with immigrant backgrounds.[8]

Bal satan ihtiyar bir adam vardı. Herkes o*na (1)* Balcı Dede der*di (2)*. Tatlı dil*li (3)*, güler yüzl*üy*dü *(4)*. Sesini duy*an*/duy*sa*/duy*unca (5)* çocuklar, yanına *(6)* gider, o*nu (7)* seyrederdi. O da çocuk*ları (8)* çok sev*er*di *(9)*. Balı ç*ok (10)* uzaklardan, arıl*ar*ın *(11)* ülkesinden getir*ir*di *(12)*. Sattığı b*al(13)* çok iyi bal*dı (14)*. Balcı Dede bal gi*bi (15)* tatlı sev*im*li *(16)* mi sev*im*liydi *(17)* doğrusu. O bal değ*il (18)* zehir bi*le (19)* satsa, alıp yer*ler*di *(20)*. Balcı Dede bal satarak geçinirdi. Herkes tarafından çok sevildiği için çok bal satardı.

Translation

The grandfather who sells honey

Once upon a time there was an old man who sold honey. Everybody called him grandfather who sells honey. He was funny and kind. The children who heard his voice went to him and looked at him. He liked the children very much too. He brought the honey from afar, from Honeyland. His honey was very good. The grandfather who sells honey was honey-sweet and really very kind. Even if he had sold poison, the people would have bought and eaten it. He earned his money selling honey. Because he was very popular with everyone, he sold such a lot of honey.

Figure 8.3 Example: Turkish c-test, text 1 with solution in italics and translation[7]

Control measures

To analyse the effect of heritage language courses on language development, we controlled for motivation, SES, parental support and parental orientation related to learning languages.

Motivation for first and second languages was measured with a questionnaire based on Deci and Ryan's (1985, 1993) self-determination theory. According to the self-determination theory of Deci and Ryan (1985, 1993), there are four types of extrinsic motivation from the lowest to the highest level of self-determination. External regulation is defined as those activities that are determined by sources external to the person, such as earning a (external) reward or avoiding punishment. Introjected regulation refers to performance associated with the feeling of pressure to avoid negative emotions like guilt or anxiety (Ryan & Deci, 2000: 62). A third type of extrinsic motivation which is more self-determined is identified regulation. Individuals invest energy in an activity because of personally relevant reasons. The most self-determined form of extrinsic motivation is integrative regulation, which is very close to intrinsic motivation. Integrative regulation is the result of the integration of goals, norms and strategies into the self-concept. Intrinsic motivation refers to the motivation to engage in an activity because it is enjoyable. Two scales were chosen to evaluate motivational variation for the first (17 items) and the second language (17 items). The 17 items applied measured four types of extrinsic motivation (external, introjected, identified and integrative regulation) and intrinsic motivation. Some of the items were adapted from Noels *et al.*'s (2003) Language Learning Orientations Scale (LLOS-IEA), and the scale proposed by Stöckli (2004). To derive a distinctive and reliable subscale for each motivation subtype, exploratory factor analyses and reliability analyses were conducted. The analysis strategy involved an iterative process, whereby any item that did not contribute appreciably to the solution (with loadings <0.30 or that cross-loaded on other factors) was eliminated, and the correlation matrix was reanalysed. Finally, the factor analysis with varimax-rotation showed two specificities: intrinsic motivation and external regulation for first and second languages. The Cronbach's alpha index of internal consistency was acceptable for the subscales 'intrinsic motivation' and 'external regulation' in the first language, varying between 0.76 (intrinsic motivation) and 0.72 (external regulation), and in the second language, varying between 0.71 (intrinsic motivation) and 0.60 (external regulation), (Caprez-Krompàk, 2010: 150).

To determine the SES indicator, we used the number of books at home as a proxy variable. This was included in the questionnaire for the parents. Parents could choose between five scales: (a) none; (b) 1–5; (c) 6–10; (d) 11–50; and (e) more than 50 books in the first and second language. According to the analysis with the *t*-test, there were no significant differences between the treatment group and the control group with respect to the control measure number of books at home (number of Albanian books at home in the treatment group: *n*=23, M=3.39, SD=1.158, in the control group: *n*=35, M=3.11, SD=1.078, n.s.; number of German books in the treatment group: *n*=23, M=3.22, SD=1.085, in the control group: *n*=35, M=3.09; SD=1.067, n.s.), (Caprez-Krompàk, 2010: 119).

Finally, to control for *parental support* for language learning and *parental orientation* to language learning, questionnaires were administered to the parents. Parental support was assessed with seven items, which build a single dimension in the factor analysis. The reported reliability (internal consistency) for this dimension was high at 0.86 (parental support by father) and 0.95 (parental support by mother), (Caprez-Krompàk, 2010: 156). To measure parental orientation to language learning, eight items were applied in the questionnaire. Corresponding to the factor analysis, two factors were identified: identity, and language and cultural orientation. In this case, the Cronbach's alpha index of internal consistency was satisfactory between 0.77 (identity) and 0.78 (language and cultural orientation), (Caprez-Krompàk, 2010: 159).

Results

Development of Albanian language proficiency

In order to investigate the differences related to Albanian language proficiency between the treatment and control groups, we conducted a repeated measure analysis of variance (ANOVA) with Albanian language assessment as the dependent variable and 'time' and 'group' as independent variables (Figure 8.4).

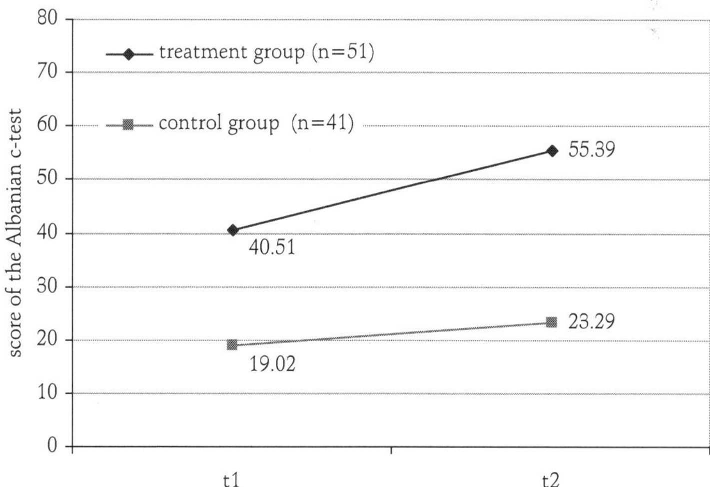

Figure 8.4 Development of Albanian language proficiency (Caprez-Krompàk, 2010: 177)

There was a significant difference between the two groups with respect to the factor time, F (1, 90)=77.3, $p<0.001$, eta^2=0.46, and the factor group, F (1, 90)=72.9, $p<0.001$, eta^2=0.45, and also a significant interaction between the two factors, F (1, 90)=23.8, $p<0.001$, eta^2=0.21. We also found a significant difference with the univariate post-hoc test in the development of language proficiency of the treatment group from T1 (M=40.5, SD=14.4) to T2 (M=55.3, SD=14.7, t(50)=–10.7, $p<0.001$) compared to the control group at T1 (M=19.0, SD=17.3) and T2 (M=23.2, SD=17.2, t(40)=–2.5, $p<0.016$). The development of Albanian language competence by the treatment group differs significantly from the language development by the control group (Figure 8.4). As a result of the variance analysis, we conclude that the heritage language courses improved language performance in the first language (Caprez-Krompàk, 2010: 176).

In the next step, we used regression analysis to examine the main predictor for language achievement in Albanian at T2. In Model 1, we included the following control variables: language achievement at T1; SES (number of books); parental support for language learning; attendance of heritage language courses; and intrinsic motivation regarding the first language (see Table 8.2). In the sequential regression, based on theoretical considerations, we used forced entry as a method of entering predictors. Altogether, Model 1 explained approximately 85% of the variance, with the strongest predictor being language achievement at T1 ($F_{(1; 40)}=110.6, p<0.001$). Thus, the attendance of heritage language courses, although entered after the predictors SES and parental support, explained a larger amount, namely 5.5% ($F_{(1; 37)}=12.4$, $p<0.01$), of the variance. Parental support for language learning emerged as the third strongest predictor in Model 1, explaining 3.6% ($F_{(1; 38)}=6.1$, $p<0.05$) of the variance.

Model 2 additionally includes the predictor 'language orientation of parents' to test to what extent this predictor reduces the effect of heritage language courses. The reason for this is the consideration that the language orientation of the parents has an impact on the motivation of the children to attend the heritage language courses. Nevertheless, in Model 2, the attendance of heritage language courses still remained significant (R^2=4.5%, $F_{(1; 25)}=6.8$, $p<0.05$). Beyond that, parental support, entered as the third predictor in the analysis of variance, showed a significant effect on language achievement (R^2=3.6%, $F_{(1; 27)}=4.4$, $p<0.05$).

In summary, our results indicate a positive effect of heritage language courses and parental support on the development of Albanian language proficiency. Therefore, heritage language courses almost certainly enhance language achievement in Albanian (Caprez-Krompàk, 2010: 180–182).

Table 8.2 Sequential regression model explaining Albanian language achievement

	n	*R*	*Model 1 R^2 (p)*	*Model 2 R^2 (p)*
Language achievement in L2 at T1	92	0.86***	73.4% ($p<0.001$)	73.4% ($p<0.001$)
SES	59	0.29*	0.9% (n.s.)	0.9% (n.s.)
Parental support for language learning	44	n.s.	3.6% ($p<0.05$)	3.6% ($p<0.05$)
Language orientation of parents	47	0.40**	–	1.1% (n.s.)
Attendance of heritage language course	92	0.71***	5.5% ($p<0.01$)	4.5% ($p<0.05$)
Intrinsic motivation regarding first language	86	0.39***	1.1% (n.s.)	1.3% (n.s.)
R^2 total			84.5%	84.8%
R^2 total corrected			82.4%	81.0%

Note: SES=socioeconomic status; r=bivariate correlation with the criteria.

***$p<0.001$, **$p<0.01$, *$p<0.05$; n.s.=no significance.

Development of Turkish language proficiency

Other results showed the repeated measures ANOVA by testing the effect of heritage language courses on Turkish language proficiency. As before, we applied the achievement in the Turkish c-test as the dependent variable, while 'time' and 'group' served as dependent variables (Figure 8.5).

Although the factor time had a significant effect, (1, 32)=25.7, $p<0.001$, the factor group had no significance, F (1, 32)=3.1, $p<0.088$, and there was no significant interaction between the two factors, F (1, 32)=0.4, $p<0.53$. Analogously to the treatment group, the analysis also revealed significant growth in language achievement by the control group. The reason could be the specific character of the control group. Even though the children in the control group did not attend the heritage language courses, they achieved nearly the same mean value in the Turkish c-test at the second data collection (T2) as the children who did attend heritage language courses. On account of this, we did not conduct further analyses with this specific subgroup (Caprez-Krompàk, 2010: 177–178).

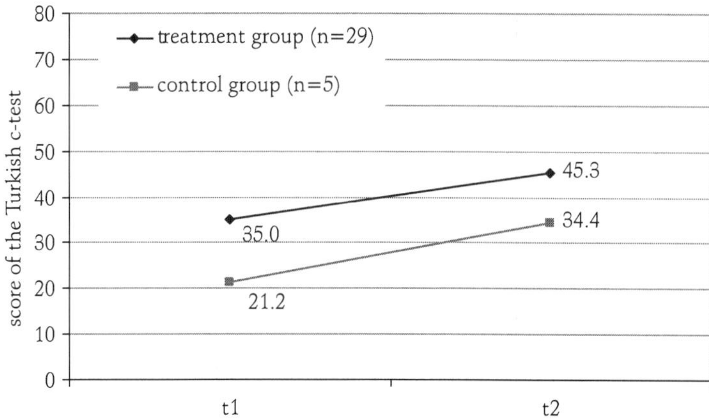

Figure 8.5 Development of Turkish language proficiency (Caprez-Krompàk, 2010: 178)

Development of German language proficiency

To investigate whether the heritage language courses positively influenced German language proficiency, we compared the language achievement of the treatment and control groups (now without the Turkish subgroup) by using repeated measures ANOVA. The graph (Figure 8.6) confirms parallel language development for both groups.

The result of the analysis of variance reveals a significant effect of the factor time, F (1, 90)=121.9, eta^2=0.58, p<0.001, and of the factor group, F (1, 90)=5.2, p<0.05, eta^2=0.06, but no significance in the interaction of the two factors, F (1, 90)=0.8, n.s., eta^2=0.001. This means that, longitudinally, there is no significant relationship between the language growth of the treatment and the control groups (within the Albanian subgroup). The factors that influence language development in German were tested by further analysis of sequential regression (Caprez-Krompàk, 2010: 178–180).

Surprisingly, there are few differences between the results of Models 1 and 2 in the analysis of regression (Table 8.3). Model 1 and Model 2 can explain 80% of the variance. In both models, the achievement in German at T1 appears the strongest and is the only statistically significant predictor for the achievement at T2, accounting for 79% of the variance. On the basis of the analysis of regression, we can assume that the language achievement in the German c-test at T2 depends practically exclusively on language achievement at T1. The other control variables – SES, parental support, language orientation of parents, motivation and attendance of heritage language courses – have no impact on language achievement in the German c-test at the second point of data collection (T2).

To answer the main research question, we can conclude that pupils who attended the optional heritage language courses (treatment group)

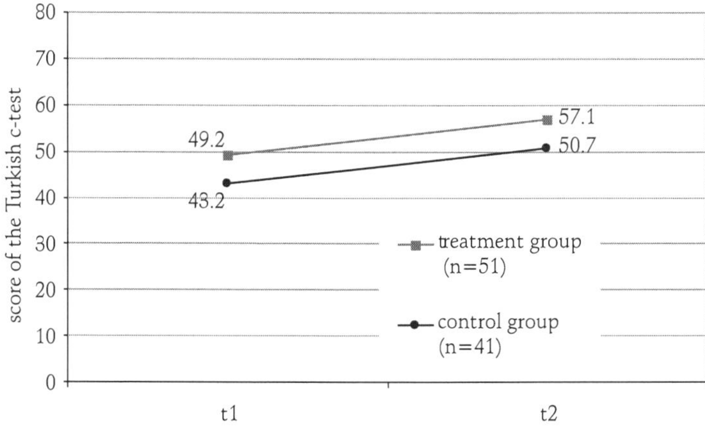

Figure 8.6 Development of German language proficiency (Caprez-Krompàk, 2010: 179)

Table 8.3 Sequential regression model explaining German language achievement

	n	*r*	*Model 1* R^2 *(p)*	*Model 2* R^2 *(p)*
Language achievement in L2 at T1	92	0.89***	79.0% ($p<0.001$)	79.0% ($p<0.001$)
SES	59	0.32*	0.6% (n.s.)	0.6% (n.s.)
Parental support for language learning	44	0.20 n.s.	0.1% (n.s.)	0.1% (n.s.)
Language orientation of parents	47	0.21 n.s.	-	0.3% (n.s.)
Attendance of heritage language course	92	0.21*	0.4% (n.s.)	0.2% (n.s.)
Intrinsic motivation for second language	83	0.12 n.s.	0.1% (n.s.)	0.2% (n.s.)
R^2 total			80.2%	80.4%
R^2 total corrected			77.3%	75.4%

Note: SES=socio-economic status; *r*=bivariate correlation with the criteria.

***$p<0.001$, **$p<0.01$, *$p<0.05$; n.s=no significance.

performed significantly better in the first language (Albanian) than pupils in the control group. Other crucial findings showed that the pupils in the treatment group made more progress in the first language than the pupils in the control group. The better performance and larger progress can be explained by the effect of the heritage language course. By contrast, there is no significant difference between the treatment group and the control group in the achievement in German. Thus, Hypothesis 1 can be falsified; the attendance of heritage language courses has a positive impact on first language acquisition but not on the acquisition of a second language. The result showed a significant growth in the development of Albanian by the treatment group who participated in the heritage language courses, but no significant growth in the development of German. Therefore, Hypothesis 2 can be falsified. Development of competences in the second language (German) was the same for the treatment and the control groups. Although the treatment group performed significantly better than the control group at both points of data collection, this growth cannot be explained with the impact of the heritage language courses. With respect to first language (Albanian) development, we can conclude that the language development of children who attend the heritage language classes was shown to be higher than the language development of children who did not attend heritage language classes.

Concluding Remarks

The implication of the results focuses on three key points: the measuring of multilingual children's language development; the empirical verification of the interdependence hypothesis; and considerations regarding the future of heritage language courses.

First, we had to respond to the absence of available language tests for multilingual children with immigrant backgrounds when developing German, Albanian and Turkish c-tests. Notwithstanding the satisfactory and high validity and reliability of the c-tests developed in this study (see the section 'German, Albanian and Turkish language achievement'), it is necessary to reflect critically on the limitations of these instruments. On the one hand, language tests in the traditional sense do not take into consideration aspects of multilingualism such as the limited literacy of many multilingual children and the possible dialectal form of language, as is the case in, for example, Albanian. As traditional language tests are often premised on the duality of right and wrong, they are deficit oriented. This deficit orientation may strengthen the contestable conclusions that some practitioners still draw. Where they fail to see multilingualism as a resource, they may continue to hold on to a problematic notion of semilingualism, i.e. the view that competences are fragmented across available languages. Although the semilingualist perspective has often been criticised in scholarly discussions (see Baker, 1993; Romaine, 1999), it still persists in daily educational practice to describe what is perceived as the deficient language competence of multilingual children. On the other hand, measuring language competence separately does not correspond to the recent translanguaging turn (García & Li Wei, 2014) in sociolinguistic and educational discourses. From the translanguaging perspective, the separating borders between first, second and third languages fade behind the 'multiple discursive practices in which bilinguals engage in order to make sense of their bilingual worlds' (García, 2009: 45). As the linguistic resources of which a multilingual individual disposes consist of a unity of linguistic practices, the centre of attention should be translanguaging rather than distinct languages in isolation from each other. For future investigation, the sociolinguistic approach of everyday language practices can and should bring deeper knowledge in exploring and measuring the linguistic potential of multilingual individuals.

Second, the positive impact of heritage language courses on language achievement and development in the first language (Albanian) warrants emphasis. This finding can appear trivial; however, in view of the limited instruction time (2 hours once a week), the results are more meaningful. Considering the adverse conditions impacting on heritage language courses – such as uneven funding and chronic changes in the classes – the impact of these courses actually appears encouraging (Caprez-Krompàk, 2010). Although the results of the study do not support Cummins' interdependence hypothesis, we can conclude that the heritage language courses do promote first language competence. Moreover, attending heritage language courses does not hinder development in the second language; in fact, it shows a positive tendency towards second language competence. Although the interdependence hypothesis does offer a sound basis for the investigation of the effect that heritage language courses have on language development, we would like to point out, as already discussed in Chapter 1, the questionable empirical testability of the hypothesis. Also, Cummins (2010) highlights the additional relevance of other concepts like the dynamic model of multilingualism expounded by Herdina and Jessner (2003) or the concept of multicompetence by Cook (1995), which capture the complexity of language interactions by multilinguals more elaborately than the interdependence hypothesis.[9]

The third key point concerns the future of heritage language courses. In German-speaking countries, heritage language courses are optional and, with some exceptions, are not included in the everyday timetable in school (Allemann-Ghionda, 2002; Reich, 2008). Furthermore, the financing of the courses is embroiled in difficulties: on the one hand, there are inequalities in the payment of fees; on the other, some of these courses depend in part on volunteer work. For example, in Switzerland, the responsibility for financing most Albanian heritage language courses lies with parents. In some cases, if parents are not able to pay the course fees, the Albanian language teachers volunteer their work (Caprez-Krompàk, 2010: 217; Schader, 2006: 102). All these factors complicate the already difficult situation of heritage language courses and their teachers, producing a legitimation crisis for these courses. Debates in current education policy about the relevance of heritage language courses centre largely on their effects. Many researchers (see Krompàk, 2015, 2016; Reich, 2016), however, criticise this legitimation pressure: 'This is a slightly unusual question: we do not ask whether the physics lesson makes a contribution to learning mathematics, or French instruction improves the achievement in English' (Reich, 2016: 168).[10] In this sense, Krompàk (2015, 2016: 174) pleads for a paradigm shift: multilingualism and plurilingualism should be taken as a norm – heritage language courses should be offered without instrumental concern for their effects on the language of instruction; and the focus in heritage language courses should be on their relevance to promoting plurilingualism instead.

Acknowledgement

The research project 'Development of first and second language in intercultural contexts' was conducted at the University of Zurich and was funded by the Swiss National Science Foundation. I would like to thank Professor Dr Kurt Reusser and Professor Dr Cristina Allemann-Ghionda, the supervisors of the research project. I am also grateful to Dr Mesut Gönç and Dr Nuran Kahyaoglu (Turkish c-test), Dr Naxhi Selimi and Nexhat Maloku (Albanian c-test) and Dr Basil Schader (Albanian and German c-test) for their valuable cooperation. I would also like to thank the editors and the authors of this book for their very valuable comments on this chapter and Stephan Meyer (University of Basel) for editing and commenting on an earlier draft.

Notes

(1) In this chapter, I consider the term 'heritage language' or 'first language' as the family language of children with immigrant backgrounds. The term 'second language' refers to the language of instruction in the school, which in the present case is German.
(2) A major part of this chapter (description of the project and the central results) is based on a doctoral thesis published in 2010 (Caprez-Krompàk, 2010).
(3) The first heritage language courses in Switzerland were founded in 1930 by Italian political refugees (Magnani, 1990; Serra, 1991).
(4) For the complete German c-test, see Caprez-Krompàk (2010: 268–269).
(5) For the complete Albanian c-test, see Caprez-Krompàk (2010: 270–272).
(6) Alternatives in parentheses are possible dialect versions of the Albanian word.
(7) For the complete Turkish c-test, see Caprez-Krompàk (2010: 273–275).
(8) For further statistical analysis of the c-test, see Caprez-Krompàk (2010:125–145).
(9) 'Although a dynamic systems view of multilingualism is obviously much more elaborated than the interdependence hypothesis, these constructs all share a

recognition that the languages of bi- and multilinguals interact in complex ways that can enhance aspects of overall language and literacy development' (Cummins, 2010: 18–19).

(10) In original: 'Das ist eine etwas ungewöhnliche Frage, man fragt ja auch nicht, ob Physikunterricht einen Beitrag zum Mathematiklernen leistet oder Französischunterricht die Leistungen im Englischen verbessert' (Reich, 2016: 168).

References

Allemann-Ghionda, C. (2002) *Schule, Bildung und Pluralität: Sechs Fallstudien im europäischen Vergleich* [*School, Education and Plurality: Six Case Studies in European Comparison*] (2nd revised edn). Bern, Switzerland: Lang.

Allemann-Ghionda, C. (2006) Klasse, Gender oder Ethnie? Zum Bildungserfolg von Schüler/innen mit Migrationshintergrund [Class, gender or ethnos? About the educational success of students with immigrant background]. *Zeitschrift für Pädagogik* 52 (3), 350–362.

Baker, C. (1993) *Foundations of Bilingual Education and Bilingualism* (1st edn). Clevedon: Multilingual Matters.

Baur, R. and Meder, G. (1992) Zur Interdependenz von Muttersprache und Zweitsprache bei jugoslawischen Migrantenkindern [About the interdependence of mother tongue and second language in Yugoslavian immigrant children]. In R.S. Baur, G. Meder and V. Previšić (eds) *Interkulturelle Erziehung in Praxis und Theorie. Bd. 15. Interkulturelle Erziehung und Zweisprachigkeit* [*Intercultural Education in Practice and Theory. Vol. 15. Intercultural Education and Bilingualism*] (pp. 109–149). Baltmannsweiler: Schneider Verlag Hohengehren.

Caprez-Krompàk, E. (2010) *Entwicklung der Erst- und Zweitsprache im interkulturellen Kontext. Eine empirische Untersuchung über den Einfluss des Unterrichts in heimatlicher Sprache und Kultur (HSK) auf die Sprachentwicklung* [*The Development of First and Second Languages in Intercultural Context: An Empirical Investigation into the Influence of Instruction in Heritage Language and Culture on Language Development*]. Münster: Waxmann.

Caprez-Krompàk, E. and Gönç, M. (2006) Der C-Test im Albanischen und Türkischen: Theoretische Überlegungen und empirische Befunde [The c-test in Albanian and Turkish: Theoretical considerations and empirical findings]. In R. Grotjahn (ed.) *Der C-Test: Theorie, Empirie, Anwendungen* [*The c-Test: Theory, Empiricism, and Applications*] (pp. 243–260). Frankfurt am Main: Lang.

Caprez-Krompàk, E. and Selimi, N. (2006) Zur Erstsprachkompetenz von albanischsprachigen Kindern in der Deutschschweiz. Eine vergleichende Fehleranalyse anhand des C-Tests [About language competences in the first language of Albanian-speaking children in German-speaking Switzerland]. In B. Schader (ed.) *Albanischsprachige Kinder und Jugendliche in der Schweiz. Hintergründe. Sprach- und schulbezogene Untersuchungen* [*Albanian-Speaking Children and Adolescents in Switzerland: Background and Investigations on Language and School*] (pp. 247–269). Zürich: Pestalozzianum.

Cook, V. (1995) Multi-competence and the learning of many languages. *Language, Culture and Curriculum* 8 (2), 93–98.

Cummins, J. (1981) The role of primary language development in promoting educational success for language minority students. In California State Department of Education (ed.) *Schooling and Language Minority Students: A Theoretical Framework* (pp. 3–49). Los Angeles, CA: Evaluation, Dissemination and Assessment Center, California State University.

Cummins, J. (1984) *Bilingualism and Special Education: Issues in Assessment and Pedagogy*. Clevedon: Multilingual Matters.

Cummins, J. (2000) *Language, Power, and Pedagogy. Bilingual Children in the Crossfire.* Clevedon: Multilingual Matters.

Cummins, J. (2010) Language support for pupils from families with migration backgrounds: Challenging monolingual instructional assumptions. In C. Benholz, G. Kniffka and E. Winters-Ohle (eds) *Fachliche und sprachliche Förderung von Schülern mit Migrationsgeschichte [Academic and Language Promotion of Pupils with Immigrant Background]* (pp. 13–23). Münster: Waxmann.

Creese, A. and Blackledge, A. (2010) Towards a sociolinguistics of superdiversity. *Zeitschrift für Erziehungswissenschaften* 13, 549–572.

Deci, E.L. and Ryan, R.M. (1985) *Intrinsic Motivation and Self-Determination in Human Behaviour.* New York: Plenum.

Deci, E.L. and Ryan, R.M. (1993) Die Selbstbestimmungstheorie der Motivation und ihre Bedeutung für die Pädagogik [Self-determination theory and its significance in teaching]. *Zeitschrift für Pädagogik* 39, 223–238.

Diefenbach, H. (2007) *Kinder und Jugendliche aus Migrantenfamilien im deutschen Bildungssystem. Erklärungen und empirische Befunde [Children and Adolescent from Immigrant Families in the German Education System. Explanations and Empirical Findings].* Wiesbaden: VS.

Dollmann, J. and Kristen, C. (2010) Herkunftssprache als Ressource für den Schulerfolg? Das Beispiel türkischer Grundschulkinder [Heritage language as a resource for school success? The example of Turkish primary school children]. *Zeitschrift für Pädagogik, Beiheft* 55, 123–146.

García, O. (2009) *Bilingual Education in the 21st Century: A Global Perspective.* Oxford: Blackwell.

García, O. and Li Wei (2014) *Translanguaging: Language, Bilingualism and Education.* Basingstoke: Palgrave Macmillan.

Gjinari, J. and Shkurtaj, G. (2000) *Dialektologjia [Dialectology].* Tiranë: Shtëpia Botuese e Librit Universitar.

Grotjahn, R. (1987) How to construct and evaluate a c-test: A discussion of some problems and some statistical analyses. In R. Grotjahn, C. Klein-Braley and D.K. Stevenson (eds) *Taking Their Measure: The Validity and Validation of Language Tests* (pp. 219–253). Bochum: Brockmeyer.

Grotjahn, R. (1997) Der C-Test: Neuere Entwicklungen [The c-test: New developments]. In M. Gardenghi and M. O`Connell (eds) *Prüfen, Testen, Bewerten im modernen Fremdsprachenunterricht [Examining, Testing and Evaluating in Modern Foreign Language Instruction]* (pp. 117–127). Frankfurt am Main: Peter Lang.

Grotjahn, R. (2002) Konstruktion und Einsatz von C-Tests: Ein Leitfaden für die Praxis [Construction and application of c-tests: A guideline for practice]. In R. Grotjahn (ed.) *Der C-Test. Theoretische Grundlagen und praktische Anwendungen [The c-Test: Theoretical Foundations and Practical Applications]* (Bd. 4) (pp. 211–225). Bochum: AKS-Verlag.

Haenni Hoti, A. and Schader, B. (2005/2006) The ignored potential of Albanian-speaking minority children in Swiss schools. *International Journal of Learning* 12 (7), 287–293.

Häusler, M. (1999) *Innovation in multikulturellen Schulen. Fallstudie über fünf Schulen in der Deutschschweiz [Innovation in Multicultural Schools. Case Study of Five Schools in German-Speaking Switzerland].* Zürich: Orell Füssli.

Herdina, P. and Jessner, U. (2003) *A Dynamic Model of Multilingualism. Perspectives of Change in Psycholinguistics.* Clevedon: Multilingual Matters.

Hetzer, A. (1995) *Nominalisierung und verbale Einbettung in Varietäten des Albanischen. Eine Untersuchung zur Geschichte der albanischen Schriftsprache am Beispiel erweiterter Verbalprädikate auf areallinguistischem Hintergrund. [Normalisation and Verbal Embedding in Varieties of Albanian. An Investigation Into the History of Written Albanian with Reference to Extended Verbal Predicates Against the Background of Linguistic Geography*]. Berlin/ Wiesbaden: Harrasowitz Verlag.

Krompàk, E. (2015) Herkunftssprachlicher Unterricht. Ein Begriff in Wandel [Heritage language instruction. A concept in change]. In R. Leiprecht and A. Steinbach (eds) *Schule in der Migrationsgesellschaft* [*School in the Migration Society*] (1st edn) (pp. 64–83). Schwalbach/Ts: Debus Pädagogik.

Krompàk, E. (2016) Herkunftssprachlicher Unterricht im Rampenlicht. Ergebnisse des For-schungsprojekts 'Entwicklung der Erst- und Zweitsprache im interkulturellen Kontext' [Heritage language instruction in the spotlight. Results of the research project 'Development of first- and second language in intercultural context']. In B. Schader (ed.) *Materialien für den herkunftssprachlichen Unterricht; Grundlagen und Hintergründe. Hand- und Arbeitsbuch* [*Materials for Heritage Language Courses: Foundations and Backgrounds. Hand- and Textbook*] (pp. 172–174). Zürich: Orell Füssli.

Kronig, W. (2003) Das Konstrukt des leistungsschwachen Immigrantenkindes [The construct of the poorly performing immigrant child]. *Zeitschrift für Erziehungswissenschaft* 6 (1), 124–139.

Kronig, W. (2007) *Die systematische Zufälligkeit des Bildungserfolgs. Theoretische Erklärungen und empirische Untersuchungen zur Lernentwicklung und zur Leistungsbewertung in unterschiedlichen Schulklassen* [*The Systematic Contingency of Educational Success. Theoretical Explanations and Empirical Investigations of Learning Development and Assessment in Different School Classes*]. Bern: Haupt.

Kronig, W., Haeberlin, U. and Eckhart, M. (2000) *Immigrantenkinder und schulische Selektion. Pädagogische Visionen, theoretische Erklärungen und empirische Untersuchungen zur Wirkung integrierender und separierender Schulformen in den Grundschuljahren* [*Immigrant Children and Selection in School. Pedagogical Visions, Theoretical Explanations and Empirical Investigation about the Effect of Integrative and Separating School Form in Primary School*]. Bern: Haupt.

Liu, N., Musica, A., Koscak, S., Vinogradova, P. and López, J. (2011) *Challenges and Needs of Community-Based Heritage Language Programs and How They Are Addressed.* Heritage Briefs Collection. Washington, DC: Center for Applied Linguistics (CAL). See http://www.cal.org/heritage/pdfs/briefs/challenges-and%20needs-of-community-based-heritage-language-programs.pdf (accessed 7 February 2016).

Magnani, F. (1990) *Eine italienische Familie* [*An Italian family*]. Köln: Kiepenheuer & Witsch.

Maluch, J.T., Kempert, S., Neumann, M. and Stanat, P. (2014) The effect of speaking a minority language at home on foreign language learning. *Learning and Instruction* 36, 76–85.

Moser, U., Bayer, N., Tunger, V. and Berweger, S. (2008) *Entwicklung der Sprachkompetenzen in der Erst- und Zweitsprache von Migrantenkindern. Schlussbericht.* [*Development of Language Competences in First and Second Language of Immigrant Children. Final Report*]. Zürich: Institut für Bildungsevaluation, Assoziiertes Institut der Universität Zürich. See http://www.ibe.uzh.ch/dam/jcr:00000000-6ff9-ac1b-ffff-ffffc6939460/NFP56_Moser_UZH_IBE_2008.pdf (accessed 26 July 2017).

Noels, K.A., Pelletier, L.G., Clément, R. and Vallerand, R.J. (2003) Why are you learning a second language? Motivational orientations and self-determination theory. In Z. Dörnyei (ed.) *Attitudes, Orientations, and Motivations in Language Learning: Advances in Theory, Research, and Applications* (pp. 33–63). Oxford: Blackwell Publishing.

OECD – Organisation for the Economic Co-Operation and Development (2010) *PISA 2009 Results: Overcoming Social Background: Equity in Learning Opportunities and Outcomes* (Vol. II). Paris: OECD.

Raatz, U. and Klein-Braley, C. (2001) *CT-D4. Schulleistungstest Deutsch für 4. Klassen* [*CT-D4. School Performance Test for the 4th Grade*]. Weinheim: Beltz.

Rauch, D.P., Jurecka, A. and Hesse, H.-G. (2010) Für den Drittspracherwerb zählt auch die Lesekompetenz in der Herkunftssprache [For third language acquisition reading competence in the heritage language also counts]. *Zeitschrift für Pädagogik 56/55*, Suppl., 78–100.

Reich, H.H. (2008) Herkunftssprachenunterricht [Instruction in heritage languages]. In B. Ahrenholz and I. Oomen-Welke (eds) *Deutsch als Zweitsprache (Deutschunterricht in Theorie und Praxis 9)* [*German as a Second Language. Instruction in German in Theory and Practice 9*] (pp. 445–456). Baltmannsweiler: Schneider.

Reich, H.H. (2016) Untersuchungen zur Wirksamkeit des herkunftssprachlichen Unterrichts. Forschungsstand, Forschungsprobleme, Forschungsbedarf [Investigations on efficacy of heritage language classes. Current state of research, challenges and research need]. In B. Schader (ed.) *Materialien für den herkunftssprachlichen Unterricht; Grundlagen und Hintergründe. Hand- und Arbeitsbuch* [*Materials for Heritage Language Courses: Foundations and Backgrounds. Hand- and Textbook*] (pp. 168–171). Zürich: Orell Füssli.

Romaine, S. (1999) Early bilingual development: From elite to folk. In G. Extra and L. Verhoeven (eds) *Bilingualism and Migration* (pp. 61–73). Berlin/New York: Mouton de Gruyter.

Ryan, R.M. and Deci E.L. (2000) Intrinsic and Extrinsic Motivations: Classis Definitions and New directions. *Contemporary Educational Psychology* 25, 54–67.

Serra, A. (1991) *Kurse in Heimatlicher Sprache und Kultur (HSK). Schlussbericht über die Versuchsphase gemäss Erziehungsratsbeschluss vom 8. November 1983* [*Courses in Heritage Language and Culture (HSK). Final Report about the Test Phase According to the Decision of the Education Department from 8th of November 1983*]. Zürich: Erziehungsdirektion des Kantons Zürich.

Schader, B. (2006) *Albanischsprachige Kinder und Jugendliche in der Schweiz: Hintergründe, Sprach- und schulbezogene Untersuchungen* [*Albanian-Speaking Children and Adolescents in Switzerland: Background and Investigations on Language and School*]. Zürich, Switzerland: Pestalozzianum.

Schuler, P. (2002) *Integrierter Fachbereich – „Kurse in heimatlicher Sprache und Kultur im Oberstufenschulhaus Limmat A" in der Stadt Zürich* [*Integrated Subject: Courses in Heritage Language and Culture in the Upper School Limmat A in the City of Zurich*]. Zürich: FS&S.

Stanat, P. (2006) Disparitäten im schulischen Erfolg: Forschungsstand zur Rolle des Migrationshintergrunds. *Unterrichtswissenschaft* 34 (2), 98–124.

Stanat, P. and Christensen, G. (2006) *Where Immigrant Students Succeed. A Comparative Review of Performance and Engagement in PISA*. Paris: OECD.

Stöckli, G. (2004) *Motivation im Fremdsprachenunterricht. Eine theoriegeleitete empirische Untersuchung in 5. und 6. Primarschulklassen mit Unterricht in Englisch und Französisch* [*Motivation in Foreign Language Instruction. A Theory-Based Empirical Investigation in 5th and 6th Grade Primary Classes with Instruction in English and French*]. Aarau: Sauerländer.

Vertovec, S. (2007) Super-diversity and its implications. *Ethnic and Racial Studies* 30 (6), 1024–1054.

9 The Development of Russian Heritage Pupils' Writing Proficiency in Finnish and Russian

Lea Nieminen and Riikka Ullakonoja

Introduction

The aim and background of the study

James Cummins (1979: 222) has stated that 'a cognitively and academically beneficial form of bilingualism can be achieved only on the basis of adequately developed first language (L1) skills'. In this chapter, we focus on bilingual writing development and its connections to learners' cognitive and linguistic skills in their L1 and second language (L2), as well as to background factors. Our participants come from Russian-speaking immigrant families living in Finland. All participants go to Finnish schools and are either integrated into mainstream classes or have started a preparatory class specially designed for recently arrived immigrant children. The basic aim of this chapter is twofold, and thus the study is introduced in two phases. In Phase 1, the aim is to follow the development of L1 Russian and L2 Finnish writing skills between two time points (T1 and T2). In Phase 2, we look for correlations and predictive relations between writing outcomes and the linguistic, cognitive and background variables to see what kind of factors may enhance bilingual writing development. In both phases of the study, special attention is paid to the relationship between the skills in the two languages.

The study introduced here is part of a larger research project, 'Diagnosing Reading and Writing in a Second or Foreign Language' (DIALUKI, 2010–2013; www.jyu.fi/dialuki; Alderson *et al.*, 2015; Alderson & Huhta, 2011: 45–48; Nieminen *et al.*, 2011), funded by the Academy of Finland, the University of Jyväskylä and the UK Economic and Social Research Council (ESRC). The aim of the multidisciplinary project was to investigate how literacy skills normally develop in a second or foreign language so that diagnostic tools for assessing learners' literacy skills could be developed. In DIALUKI, we tested many measures originating from the fields of psychology, special education and language assessment to predict strengths and weaknesses in reading and writing. The participants of the project came from two language groups: Finnish learners of English as a foreign language ($n=637$) and Russian learners of Finnish as an L2 ($n=264$). The pupils were recruited on a voluntary basis: pupils, their parents and the municipal authorities gave their written consent. In this chapter, the focus is on a longitudinal subsample of 47 pupils from the Russian–Finnish group.

Participants

The Russian–Finnish subsample consisted of 47 pupils (29 girls and 18 boys) from 25 different primary schools around Finland. The subsample included only those pupils who had completed Russian and Finnish writing tasks during the first data collection round (T1), and again two years later (T2). The basic information about the participants' age, schooling, mother tongue and languages used at home is presented in Table 9.1.

All participants came from families with a Russian background. At T1, they were between 9 and 15 years of age. The Russian–Finnish population was the target in the DIALUKI project as Russian is the biggest immigrant language in Finland with 26,900 families and 70,000 individuals in 2014. This represents about 26% of all inhabitants of Finland who have a language other than Finnish, Swedish and Sami as their mother tongue (Tilastokeskus, 2014).

Finnish and Russian are not related languages: Finnish belongs to the Finno-Ugric language family whereas Russian is an Indo-European language. Both languages have an alphabetic writing system, but Russian uses the Cyrillic and Finnish the Latin script. In terms of orthographic transparency, both languages are situated towards the shallow end of the transparency continuum, Finnish being among the most consistent orthographies with a bidirectional one-to-one correspondence between sounds and letters. (For orthographic depth, see Seymour *et al.* [2003].)

Linguistically, the participants form a heterogeneous group. For them, Russian is their heritage language or L1, which they use mainly at home, and Finnish is their L2, which is used at school and in their surrounding environment. A vast majority (70%) of the pupils considered Russian to be their mother tongue, 11% considered Finnish to be their mother tongue and 13% categorised themselves as Finnish–Russian. Similarly, a majority (70%) of the pupils reported using Russian most often at home, while 11% reported using Finnish and 15% Finnish and Russian. The use of Finnish at home – in some cases even as the major language – can be explained

Table 9.1 Study participants

Age at T1 (years)	*n*	*Gender*		*School at T1*		*Mother tongue (reported by child)*				*Home language (reported by parents)*			*Home language (reported by child)*			
		M	F	P	MS	R	F	R&F	?	R	F	?	R	F	R&F	?
9	8	2	6	1	7	5	0	3	0	7	1	0	5	0	3	0
10	11	3	8	3	8	8	0	1	2	11	0	0	9	1	1	0
11	12	5	7	1	11	9	1	2	0	9	2	1	9	0	2	1
12	9	4	5	0	9	7	2	0	0	6	3	0	7	2	0	0
13	6	3	3	0	6	3	2	0	1	4	2	0	3	2	0	1
15	1	1	0	0	1	1	0	0	0	1	0	0	0	0	1	0
Total	47	18	29	5	42	33	5	6	3	38	8	1	33	5	7	2

Note. M=male, F=female; P=preparatory education, MS=mainstream education; R=Russian, F=Finnish, R&F=Russian and Finnish, ?=information not available.

by several factors. In the parents' questionnaire, 11% of fathers reported Finnish as their mother tongue, indicating that some proportion of the families were actually bilingual. Second, there are studies that show how children, especially in bilingual but also in monolingual families living in a majority language environment, have a strong preference for the majority language, even at home (Montrul, 2008: 101). Siblings may also use the majority language in their mutual conversation (e.g. Mäntylä *et al.*, 2009). As can be seen in Table 9.1, the pupils and their parents differed slightly in their responses to the question about which language is mostly used at home.

At T1 of data collection, most of the children were already integrated into mainstream Finnish education but 21% studied in preparatory classes, indicating that they had arrived in Finland quite recently. By T2, all pupils studied in Finnish mainstream classes. According to the Finnish Basic Education Act (628/1998), immigrant children between the ages of 6 and 17 have the possibility to participate in 12 months of preparatory education before integrating into Finnish schools. According to the Finnish National Board of Education, the aim of this type of education is to prepare recently arrived immigrant children with inadequate Finnish (or Swedish) language skills for basic education in a Finnish-mediated pre-primary or basic education group. Education in the preparatory class will promote Finnish (or Swedish) language learning, the integration into Finnish society and the acquisition of different school subject content (National Board of Education, 2009). However, whether this facility is made available depends on the local authorities. When studying in Finnish-speaking mainstream classes, immigrant children have the possibility to participate in Finnish as an L2 lessons, but these are not offered by all schools (Latomaa, 2007).

The background questionnaires revealed language diversity in the participants' educational background: 53% of the pupils had first learnt to read in Russian and 17% in Finnish. Simultaneous learning to read in both languages was reported by 17% of the participants, and the remaining 13% did not answer the question. Participation in Russian lessons was reported by 64% of the pupils, and 47% said they had sometimes gone to a Russian-medium school in either Russia or Finland. In Finland, immigrant children can be offered lessons in their L1, but the lessons are not part of the curriculum for basic education. The pupils are not given grades or credits for these courses, which diminishes their motivation to attend L1 lessons (Latomaa, 2007). There are also other factors that negatively affect the motivation for attending the classes, such as parental pressure or the pupil's own desire to integrate into the Finnish-speaking environment and not to be identified as a Russian by others. All these factors related to language background, literacy learning and education make this group a heterogeneous literacy learner population with unique challenges, which is a common feature of immigrant learners of language (Hedgcock & Lefkowitz, 2011: 209).

How do background variables, linguistic proficiency and cognitive abilities relate to the development of bilingual writing proficiency?

The levels of bi- and multilingualism vary and so does the language dominance across contexts (Zecker, 2004). In addition, the style and genre knowledge as well as the level of accuracy may vary between the components. For example, stronger requirements for adequacy are set for writing in general than for speaking in informal contexts (Schoonen *et al.*, 2009). According to Cummins' (1979) developmental interdependence hypothesis, the level of a child's L2 competence is highly dependent on the level of his/her L1 abilities. High levels of L2 can be achieved only if L1 is strongly supported and promoted by the child's linguistic environment. In his later work, Cummins (e.g. 2010) separates basic interpersonal communication skills (BICS) and cognitive academic language proficiency (CALP), which refer to conversational fluency in everyday situations and the ability to express and understand the language genre of the school, respectively (cf. Chapter 1, this volume). In an L2, these proficiencies of an individual are commonly on very different levels. The situation is revealed when a student seems to have adequate conversational skills but performs at an unexpectedly low level in writing tasks. Cummins (1979) states that to create an effective educational programme for minority language children, teachers should take into account the varying level and quality of the linguistic input the children are exposed to. This is, however, not enough. Also, different background variables such as motivational factors and attitudes towards learning L2 and maintaining L1 need to be considered (Cummins, 1979).

When multilingual people use a language, it seems likely that all their linguistic resources are involved. Many studies (e.g. Hirose, 2006; Kobayashi & Rinnert, 2012; Rinnert & Kobayashi, 2009) suggest that novice L2 writers tend to depend more on L1 knowledge, but even at the early stage, transfer also occurs in the opposite direction. Laufer (2003) drew the same conclusion in a study about the lexical knowledge of immigrants who had only started to learn an L2 as adults. Their collocation patterns and lexical diversity in the L1 changed as the L2 exposure time increased. Usually, these findings are categorised as examples of transfer and manifestations of a multicompetence (Cook, 2002) – the knowledge of several languages and especially the use of that knowledge without language-specific boundaries. From this point of view, Kobayashi and Rinnert (2012) argue that advanced multicompetent writers do not transfer writing features across languages. Instead, they rely on a merged source of knowledge which is non-language-specific by nature (see also Chapter 1 of this volume for discussion).

According to Manchón (2013: 104), becoming a skilled writer requires automatised access to the linguistic knowledge needed for expressing intended meaning, genre specific knowledge, and the ability to pay attention to and solve all the relevant problems faced while composing a text. These also concern L2 writers who have to divide their attention between lower-level processes such as spelling, finding suitable words and building accurate syntactic structures, and higher demands such as creating a cohesive text (Manchón, 2013: 105). Thus, writing in L2, when it is the weaker language, is a cognitively demanding task. Any writing is dependent on linguistic knowledge and processing speed, but in the case of an L2, the dependence is found to be even stronger than in an L1 (Schoonen *et al.*, 2003), and the lower-level processes of grammatical and orthographical encoding are directly related to linguistic knowledge and processing speed (Schoonen *et al.*, 2009; see also Fitzgerald, 2006).

Working memory has also been found to have an essential role in literacy activities. For creating text, a writer needs to encode words into letters and ideas into sentences and text, and this process is constrained by the genre, the audience and the text itself (what is written before influences the following sentences and word choice). For all these purposes, working memory is an important tool, which functions more efficiently as the writing fluency develops and improves (McCutchen, 2000). When writers use their weaker language, the demands on working memory are obviously even greater and significantly influence the whole writing process (Manchón, 2013).

The borderline between language and cognition is very fine, if it even exists in the first place. While formal linguistic theories see cognition and language as separate modules, the functional theories treat language as an inseparable part of cognitive activities. From the functionalist view, the learning of several languages during childhood is a highly cognitive activity and must fundamentally affect the cognitive processes in general (Bialystok, 2002). The development does not happen in isolation. Bialystok (2002: 156) lists, among other things, the following background factors that affect the development: the parents' education, the literacy environment around the child, the child's L1 (heritage language) proficiency, the purposes for which the L2 is used, the degree and nature of support for that language and the extent to which the child identifies with the group who speaks that language. In the case of writing development, yet another factor has been emphasised in research, namely instruction in writing. For example, in Fitzgerald's (2006) meta-analysis of writing research, it is concluded that writers must create a special knowledge of writing as most of the problems they encounter in writing are not language specific, but more likely concern text and paragraph structure or other phases in a composition process. Additionally, the writers' genre knowledge and beliefs about what is good writing affect their text production (Manchón, 2013). Thus, the instruction that writers have previously received in writing either in an L1 or an L2 is important (Hirose, 2006; Kobayashi & Rinnert, 2012): in addition to writing-to-learn, learning-to-write is also needed (Manchón, 2011).

The interplay between linguistic proficiency, cognitive abilities and demographic background information is complex, and every factor seems to be connected to others. To tease the factors apart, we conducted a study on the writing development of bilingual Russian–Finnish pupils living in the Finnish environment. In Phase 1 of the study, we concentrated on the development of writing proficiency both in Russian and Finnish, and aimed to answer the following research question:

(1) How does the writing proficiency in Finnish and Russian develop in two years, assessed by a fine-tuned scale of the Common European Framework of Reference (CEFR)?

Phase 2 was dedicated to the investigation of the underlying background, linguistic and cognitive factors possibly explaining the development. The more precise research questions in Phase 2 are the following:

(2) What kind of relationships can be found between background factors and development in writing proficiency in Finnish and Russian?
(3) How do the linguistic and cognitive measures predict the writing performance at T1 and T2?

Based on previous studies, we expected to find clear connections between the writing outcomes in the L2 and background, cognitive and linguistic variables. The development in L2 Finnish writing is likely to be more rapid than the development in L1 Russian, as the pupils are surrounded by Finnish language and go to Finnish-medium schools where writing is an important part of learning and expressing what is learnt. The relationship between L1 and L2 writing development within the time period of two years may then contribute to the discussion of transfer, multicompetence and interdependence of linguistic skills in bilingual children.

Phase 1: The Development of Writing Proficiency in Russian and Finnish

Measures and data collection

The Phase 1 data consisted of writing tasks completed both in Russian and Finnish at two time points. To avoid confusion, Russian will be labelled as the L1 and Finnish as the L2 throughout the study, despite the fact that not all participants named Russian as their mother tongue. The first round of data collection was arranged during the school year 2010–2011 (T1) and the second round after a two-year interval in the school year 2012–2013 (T2). The tasks were administered during regular school hours at pupils' schools by trained researchers or research assistants with Russian language competence in case the participants needed more instruction in Russian.

The pupils wrote one L1 text and one L2 text, and the tasks were exactly the same at T1 and T2. The tasks originated from another research project (Topling; www.jyu.fi/topling), where they had been successfully used. In the L1 writing task, the pupils were able to individually choose between the following two argumentative topics: 'No mobile phones at school!' or 'Parents should decide how children are allowed to use the internet'. The pupils were instructed to express their opinion about the topic and also validate their arguments. In L2, the writing task differed depending on whether the pupils were in preparatory education or integrated into a regular class. The pupils in preparatory education were asked to write a message to a Finnish friend and explain what food, colours or music they liked and why. The pupils in mainstream classes were asked to write about a funny or scary thing that had happened to them. They were instructed first to explain what had happened, and then why they found the incident to be funny or scary. An easier writing task for the pupils in the preparatory education was chosen to make sure that the beginning learners of Finnish were able to respond to the task. All the writing task instructions were provided in both Russian and Finnish.

Method of analysis

Each essay was assessed by three qualified raters utilising the Finnish national curriculum scale for foreign languages. It is a fine-tuned version of the CEFR scale (2001), in which each CEFR level is divided into two or three sublevels (e.g. A1.1, A1.2 and A1.3; for more detailed information about the scale, see National Board of Education [2004: 278–295]). The raters discussed the rating criteria as well as looking at samples of essays before starting the assessment. The rating data were analysed with the multifaceted Rasch analysis programme 'Facets' and the final score for each essay was based on item response theory analysis (Linacre, 2009). This analysis allowed for the determination of the final score for each essay more reliably than, for example, a mean or median would.

Results

Figure 9.1 shows the pupils' performance in Russian L1 writing tasks at the two time points. The development in writing proficiency can be clearly seen in how the results at T1 and at T2 are centred in a different position on the scale. At T1, 39 pupils out of the group of 47 were graded at levels A1.3–B1.1 with a peak in A1.3 and A2.1 with 23 pupils. Two years later, the centre had moved to levels A2.2–B1.2 including the outcomes of 30 pupils. Also, the range of the outcomes of all 47 pupils changed from A1.1–B2.2 at T1 to A1.2–C1.1 at T2.

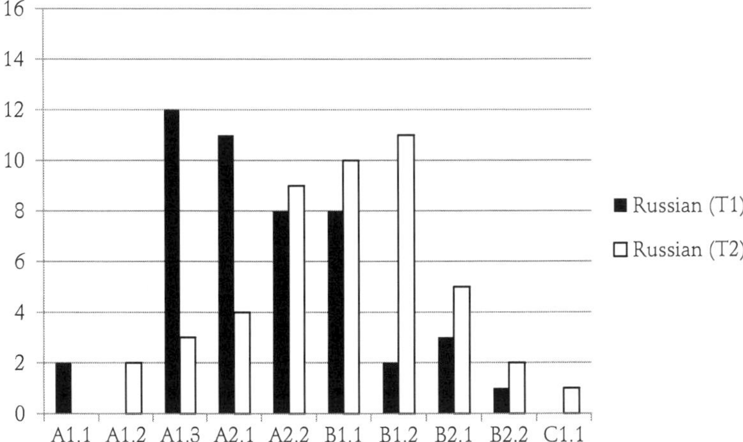

Figure 9.1 Writing outcomes in L1 Russian at T1 and T2: number of pupils reaching different proficiency levels on the Finnish national curriculum scale for foreign languages

The outcomes and development in Finnish writing during the two-year span is shown in Figure 9.2. In L2 Finnish, the writing development can be seen more clearly than in the case of L1 Russian. Although the peak of the outcomes at T1 is in A1.3–A2.1 (27 pupils), exactly as in Russian writing, the range of all pupils is now much narrower (A1.1–B1.1). Again, at T2 the peak performances coincide with those in Russian writing, but the volume is different: as many as 38 pupils reached the levels A2.2–B1.2 in Finnish writing. While none of the pupils exceeded B1.1 at T1 in Finnish writing, at T2 a total of 17 pupils reached B1.1 or a higher level.

The paired sample's *t*-test confirmed what is already shown in Figures 9.1 and 9.2: on the group level, the pupils had improved significantly in their writing in both languages during the 2-year period in Finland (L1 Russian writing: $t(46)=6.61$, $p<0.001$; L2 Finnish writing: $t(46)=9.99$, $p<0.001$). On the individual level, however, the picture was more complex. According to the gain scores (Table 9.2), most of the pupils improved their Finnish writing outcome by two (17 pupils) or three levels (14 pupils), the largest leaps being as much as five or seven levels. In L1 Russian, most pupils improved their performance by one (15 pupils) or two levels (12 pupils). The largest improvement was by four levels (4 pupils).

The results also show that there are pupils who remain at the same level in writing and those whose performance is poorer in one of the languages after a two-year period in Finland (Table 9.3). This kind of performance is more common in L1 Russian (5+7 pupils) than in L2 Finnish (2+4 pupils), which is rather understandable for the low amount of exposure to Russian texts and practice in Russian writing in the Finnish environment.

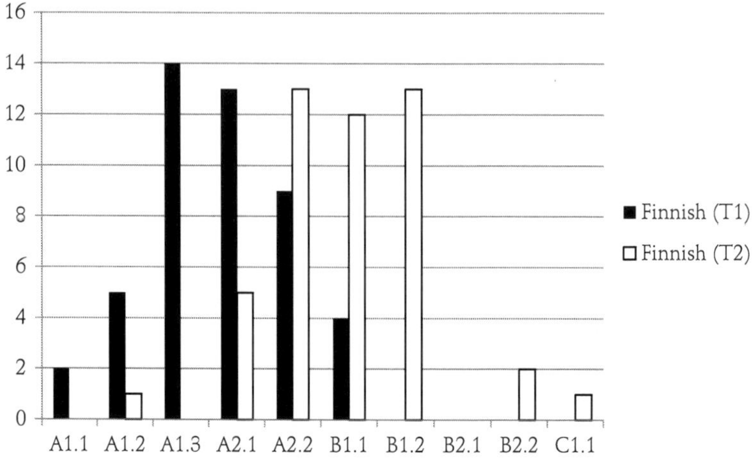

Figure 9.2 Writing outcomes in L2 Finnish at T1 and T2: Number of pupils reaching different proficiency levels on the Finnish national curriculum scale for foreign languages

Table 9.2 Comparison of individual results between T1 and T2 (gain scores) in L1 Russian and L2 Finnish writing tasks

Gain	*Difference in National Curriculum scales (T2–T1)*	*L1 Russian*	*L2 Finnish*
Negative gain	−1 level	5	2
No gain	0	7	4
Positive gain	+1 level	15	6
	+2 levels	12	17
	+3 levels	4	14
	+4 levels	4	1
	+5 levels		2
	+6 levels		
	+7 levels		1

The results shown in Table 9.3 reveal that only one pupil (ID 9) has not progressed in either Russian or Finnish writing. In all other cases, writing in the other language has improved one to five levels according to the CEFR. The interesting finding is that even if L2 Finnish writing does not seem to improve, those pupils are still progressing in their L1 Russian writing.

Table 9.3 Individual results (on the Finnish national curriculum scale) of those pupils whose performance did not improve between T1 and T2 in one or both languages

ID	*No progress in Russian writing (n=12)*				*No progress in Finnish writing (n=6)*			
	Results in L1 RUS		*Results in L2 FIN*		*Results in L1 RUS*		*Results in L2 FIN*	
	T1	*T2*	*T1*	*T2*	*T1*	*T2*	*T1*	*T2*
6					A1.2	A2.2	A2.2	A2.2
9	**B2.1**	**B1.2**	A1.3	A1.2	B2.1	B1.2	**A1.3**	**A1.2**
10	B2.1	B1.2	A2.1	A2.2				
19					B1.1	B2.1	B1.1	B1.1
21					A1.3	B1.1	A2.1	A2.1
27	A2.2	A2.1	A2.1	B1.2				
31	A2.1	A2.1	A2.1	B1.1				
33	A1.3	A1.3	A2.1	B1.1				
34	A1.3	A1.3	A2.1	B1.1				
35	A1.3	A1.3	A2.1	B1.2				
36	B1.1	A2.2	A1.3	A2.1				
37	B1.1	B1.1	A1.3	B2.1				
40	B1.1	B1.1	A2.2	B1.2				
42	B1.1	B1.1	A2.1	B1.2				
45	B1.2	B1.1	A2.1	B1.2				
46					A2.1	B1.1	B1.1	B1.1
47					A2.2	B1.1	B1.1	A2.2

Another finding is that 7 out of 12 pupils not progressing in Russian and 3 out of 6 pupils not progressing in Finnish have already reached the level of B1 or B2 at the first evaluation point, indicating fairly good existing writing abilities prior to the study.

Discussion

The results in writing development showed that the development has been greater and reached higher levels in L2 Finnish, the language of the school and environment of the children, than in L1 Russian. However, in most cases, writing skills in L1 Russian have also improved, although the progress has not been as rapid as in Finnish. With one exception, the participants showed progress in writing in at least one of the languages – usually in Finnish. It is not unexpected that literacy skills in the L1 are not developing if there is no education provided, if literacy in

L1 is not promoted at home or if the pupils are not motivated to attend L1 classes. It is also common that bilinguals seldom need to use their various languages in writing (Manchón, 2013), but are required to write in their L2 only. Thus, L2 writing is very likely to be improving at the expense of L1 writing skills, especially in genres which are practised at school. However, the six pupils who did not show progress in Finnish writing after a two-year period in Finland were the exception to these overall findings.

Phase 2: The Connections between Writing Performance and Cognitive, Linguistic and Background Variables

Methods

Data collection

During Phase 2, data of linguistic proficiency and cognitive abilities related to L1 and L2 literacy skills were analysed. The tasks were administered in both languages, although it is often argued that psychological abilities in particular should be assessed in a participant's L1 only, as the use of other test languages may skew the results (e.g. Lezak *et al.*, 2004: 313). However, in the case of bilingual pupils, it is not always the language learned first that is the stronger language or what is thought to be the mother tongue by the pupils themselves. Therefore, it is justifiable and fair to use both languages in testing.

The participants and their parents filled in separate questionnaires focusing on various background information. The linguistic tasks consisted of paper-and-pencil tasks and were administered to all participants from the same school simultaneously during normal school hours. The same was done with the pupils' background questionnaire. All instructions as well as the questionnaires were provided in Russian and Finnish to avoid difficulties in understanding the tasks or questions.

The cognitive tests were individually administered to each pupil via Cognitive Workshop software, which provided the stimuli and recorded the responses. Cognitive Workshop was originally designed for the purposes of the Jyväskylä Longitudinal Study of Dyslexia (JLD; www.jyu.fi/ytk/laitokset/psykologia/huippututkimus/en/research/JLD_main) in collaboration with the University of Dundee. All the measures introduced here were used at T1 only.

Background measures

The background information was collected from both pupils and their parents. The background questionnaires included questions about the child's mother tongue, parents' mother tongue, the language used most at home by the child, the length of the child's stay in Finland, the age of learning to read in Finnish and Russian, attitudes towards writing and writing habits in Finnish and Russian. For more information about the background measures in the DIALUKI project, see Huhta *et al.* (2016).

Linguistic measures

Vocabulary in Finnish and Russian

The vocabulary test in Finnish was a vocabulary size placement test (VSPT) from DIALANG. The test contained a total of 75 verbs: 25 pseudo-words with the remaining 50 real words. The task used a yes-no format to a question 'Is this a real word in Finnish or not' (Alderson, 2005: 79–81; Alderson *et al.*, 2015: 120–121). The Russian vocabulary was tested using a VSPT created by the DIALUKI team, as the DIALANG did not include a Russian language version. The test was created following the same principles as the DIALANG VSPT.

Reading comprehension in Russian and Finnish

Two Russian reading comprehension tasks (*A lump of clay* and *Antarctica*) were chosen from the Progress in International Reading Literacy Study materials (Foy & Kennedy, 2008; PIRLS, 2006). The test takers answered 10 multiple-choice and 11 open-ended questions based on the two texts, and the answers were scored according to the PIRLS guidelines (Alderson *et al.*, 2015: 92–93). The Finnish reading task was based on a reading comprehension measure from DIALANG. Ten items were chosen from different proficiency levels to be done as a paper-and-pencil test and scored according to the DIALANG principles. (For more information about the reading comprehension measure in DIALANG, see Alderson [2005: 119–137].) In most cases, answering the questions required retrieving explicitly stated information in the texts. The multiple-choice questions also used rephrased expressions which the test taker had to understand to be able to choose the right answer. Some of the questions required inference making as well.

Segmentation in Russian and Finnish

The segmentation tasks in Finnish and Russian were created for the purposes of the DIALUKI study. The Russian (51 words) and Finnish (40 words) text passages were chosen from school textbooks. The texts were manipulated by removing all spaces, punctuation and capital letters. The test taker had to re-segment the texts by finding and marking the word boundaries with a vertical line. The time to complete the task was measured and the number of errors calculated. Such tests have not been very frequently used in language testing, but in DIALUKI, this test type was shown to be successful in predicting second or foreign language reading comprehension (Alderson *et al.*, 2015: 106–107).

Dictation in Russian and Finnish

In a dictation task, the pupils first heard a story as a whole and it was then divided into short items which the pupils had to write down. The Russian task consisted of a story in two complex sentences which were divided into eight short items. In Finnish, we had two different tasks. The task for pupils in preparatory education had 6 simple sentences divided into 12 items to be written down. The task for the pupils in mainstream classes consisted of 5 complex sentences divided into 14 shorter items. The pupils heard the stories from a DVD recording, and the pauses provided for writing between the items were included.

Cognitive measures

The cognitive measures focused on literacy-related skills and resources such as phonological awareness, working memory capacity, word recognition and speed of lexical access. In the cognitive tasks, linguistic test items such as familiar words and pseudo- or non-words were used. However, the purpose of the tasks was to tap into the cognitive skills that are needed for processing linguistic items and not linguistic skills such as vocabulary knowledge or phonological abilities.

The following tasks were administered in both languages, unless mentioned otherwise. Whenever a Finnish standardised test was available, it was used, and a Russian counterpart was created based on it to make the tests as similar as possible, although the tests can never be identical when the stimuli are in two different languages. The same cognitive tasks were used regardless of the participants' age or language proficiency. Half of the pupils completed the Finnish tasks first and then the Russian tasks, and for the remaining participants, the task order was reversed. The whole test battery took approximately one hour. (For more information about the cognitive tasks, see Alderson *et al.* [2015: 134–140].)

In the phonological awareness tests, all sound stimuli were recorded beforehand to make sure that every test taker was provided with exactly the same stimuli. Phonological awareness was tested with the following five tests:

- *Non-word repetition.* A test taker hears 10 non-words one by one and, immediately after hearing each word, repeats it aloud. The words become longer and phonologically more complex towards the end of the task. The Russian version has one practice item before the actual test items; the Finnish version has two. The task requires accuracy in receptive skills and phonological memory.
- *Phoneme deletion.* A test taker hears a pseudo-word and repeats it aloud. Then he/she is asked to delete a sound in the initial, middle or final position of the word and to say aloud the resulting new pseudo-word.

The Russian test includes 3 items for practising and 12 test items, and the Finnish version has 2 practice items before 8 test items. The task requires the manipulation of items, together with good receptive and working memory skills.

- *Common unit in L1 Russian only.* A test taker hears pairs of pseudo-words and after each pair of words he/she is asked to name the common phonemic unit in the words. The test includes two practice word pairs and 10 actual test word pairs. The test requires good skills in segmentation, comparison and working memory.
- *Pseudo-word spelling in L1 Russian only.* A test taker hears a pseudo-word twice and is then asked to write it down. The test includes 12 pseudo-words. The test requires skills in working memory and the ability to apply knowledge of letter–sound correspondence to unfamiliar items.
- *Pseudo-word reading in L1 Russian only.* A test taker is shown 10 pseudo-words one by one on a computer screen and is asked to read them aloud. The test taker has to apply knowledge of letter–sound correspondence and decoding to unfamiliar items.

Working memory capacity was tested with a backwards digit span test (Wechsler, 1997). A test taker hears a random series of digits and has to recall them in reverse order. The test starts with two items including two digits, continues to two items of three digits, all the way up to items of eight digits. The test is stopped if the test taker has failed in two consecutive items with the same number of digits.

Word recognition was tested with the following two tests:

- *Rapidly presented words (RPW).* Ten words are presented one by one on the computer screen, each flashing for 80 milliseconds. Immediately after each word, a mask of non-letter characters (e.g. #&?€* following a five-letter word) appears on the screen. The participant's task is to recognise and say aloud each word when they flash on the screen. The task requires good recognition skills and rapid access to lexicon.
- *Word list reading.* A participant is given a list of 105 words and the task is to read aloud as many of the words as possible in 60 seconds. The words become longer and more complex towards the end of the list. The Finnish word list was a standardised test from the Lukilasse test battery created by Häyrynen *et al.* (1999). The Russian word list was created based on the model of the Finnish task. To complete the task successfully, good decoding skills and speed of lexical access are required.

The speed of lexical access was tested with rapid alternating stimuli (RAS; Wolf, 1986). In the Russian task, a test taker is given a matrix of 50 items representing letters, numbers and colours, and the task is to name them as quickly as possible. In the L2 Finnish task, there are 30 items representing numbers, colours and familiar objects. The time spent naming the stimuli is measured. The matrixes were based on those introduced in Ahonen *et al.* (2010). The task uses items which are very familiar to test takers to make sure that no time is needed to identify items themselves, so that words can be instead accessed from the lexicon as rapidly as possible.

Results

Correlations between the background variables and the writing outcomes

Spearman rank order correlations were computed between the writing outcomes in both languages at T1 and T2 and the following background measures: length of residence in Finland, attitude towards writing in general, time spent on writing during free time, age of learning to read in Russian and Finnish, frequency of writing in Russian and Finnish during free time, number of languages pupils reported to know and frequency of overall use of Russian and Finnish (reading, writing, listening and speaking combined). The significant correlations are presented in Table 9.4.

The frequency of use of Russian in general had a moderate positive correlation with Russian writing outcome at both T1 (rs=0.308) and T2 (rs=0.378), i.e. the more the pupils used Russian across the four skills (reading, writing, listening and speaking), the better their writing performance. Similarly, the overall use of Finnish had a positive correlation (rs=0.297) with Finnish writing performance at T1.

At T2, another two variables reached a significant correlation with Russian writing. Somewhat surprisingly, out of all possible background variables, the number of languages known by the pupil had a moderate positive correlation (rs=0.296) with Russian writing. This may indicate that the more you report to know languages, the more you are interested in languages, including your own heritage language, which may then

Table 9.4 Statistically significant correlations between background variables and writing outcomes in Russian (RusW) and Finnish (FinW) at T1 and T2

Background variables	*RusW T1*	*RusW T2*	*FinW T1*	*FinW T2*
Frequency of using Russian	0.308*	0.378**		
Frequency of using Finnish			0.297*	
Number of languages a pupil knows		0.296*		
Age of learning to read in Finnish		0.398**		−0.449**
Length of residence in Finland			0.532**	

* Correlation is significant at 0.05 level.

** Correlation is significant at minimum of 0.01 level.

contribute to your writing skills as well. The age of learning to read in Finnish has a moderate correlation with both Russian (rs=0.398) and Finnish (rs=–0.449) writing at T2. This indicates that the later the pupils learnt to read in Finnish, that is, the longer they had been exposed to Russian literacy only, the better they were in Russian writing, and the earlier they had become literate in Finnish, the higher their writing outcomes were in Finnish.

The length of residence had a strong correlation (rs=0.532) with writing in Finnish at T1. The same phenomenon has also been found in other studies with older students (Ullakonoja *et al.*, 2012, 2012a). The correlation between these two variables was no more significant at T2, perhaps indicating that the interval between the testing points had been long enough to balance the differences in writing between those who were newcomers at T1 and those who had already resided longer in Finland.

In Phase 1, we found that the participants fell into two groups: those who had improved at least one level on the writing assessment scale between T1 and T2, and those who had not improved or had even gone downwards on the scale. To find out some common features within these subgroups, we looked at some additional background factors, especially focusing on the languages of the family, the length of residence in Finland and attitudes towards writing and writing habits.

As the figures in Table 9.5 show, those who improve and those who don't do not clearly differ from each other in terms of background factors. With only a few exceptions, both mothers' and fathers' L1 is Russian. In pupils' L1, there seems to be a slight tendency towards bilingualism in the groups with a positive gain in writing in either language, whereas all participants in the groups with no progress identify themselves as monolinguals. The Russian language dominates in all groups when the pupils were asked which language they use most at home. However, some of the pupils in the groups of positive gain prefer Finnish over Russian, also when the positive gain was in Russian writing. The length of residence in Finland does not explain the differences either: those with clear development in writing in Finnish have not been in Finland much longer than the non-progressing pupils; and of those who progressed in Russian writing, there are pupils who have been in Finland for up to 12 years at T2. Probably the clearest difference between the groups can be found in the attitudes towards writing. The pupils who progressed in either or both languages seem to like writing more than the pupils with no progress. The attitude may be either a cause or a result. If you like writing, you may write more and with the help of the practice receive better outcomes. On the other hand, bad results may change this attitude in a negative direction. However, even here, the difference is not very clear, as there are also pupils in the no-progress group who like writing a lot and, again, in the positive gain group pupils who do not like writing at

Table 9.5 Background variables vs. the gain scores (T2–T1) in Russian and Finnish writing

Background variables	*L1 Russian writing*				*L2 Finnish writing*			
	Positive gain (n=35)		*No gain (n=7)* *Neg. gain (n=5)*		*Positive gain (n=41)*		*No gain (n=2)* *Neg. gain (n=4)*	
Mother's L1	Rus Fin Other	33 0 2	Rus Fin Other	12 0 0	Rus Fin Other	40 0 1	Rus Fin Other	5 0 1
Father's L1[a]	Rus Fin Other	27 4 1	Rus Fin Other	10 1 0	Rus Fin Other	32 5 4	Rus Fin Other	5 0 1
Pupil's L1	Rus Rus & Fin Fin Other	22 6 4 3	Rus Rus & Fin Fin Other	11 0 1 0	Rus Rus & Fin Fin Other	30 6 4 1	Rus Rus & Fin Fin Other	3 0 1 2
Language used most at home by the pupil[a]	Rus Rus & Fin Fin Other	25 4 5 1	Rus Rus & Fin Fin Other	8 3 0 0	Rus Rus & Fin Fin Other	30 5 5 0	Rus Rus & Fin Fin Other	3 2 0 1
Length of residence in Finland	T1 0–10 years T2 2–12 years		T1 1–8 years T2 3–10 years		T1 0–10 years T2 2–12 years		T1 2–8 years T2 4–10 years	
Attitude towards writing[a]	Don't like Like a bit Like a lot	3 23 7	Don't like Like a bit Like a lot	4 4 4	Don't like Like a bit Like a lot	5 24 10	Don't like Like a bit Like a lot	2 3 1
Time spent on writing per day in free time[a]	None ≤30 min 30–60 min 1–2 h >2 h	5 16 3 4 2	None ≤30 min 30–60 min 1–2 h >2 h	3 4 3 0 1	None ≤30 min 30–60 min 1–2 h >2 h	8 18 5 2 2	None ≤30 min 30–60 min 1–2 h >2 h	0 2 1 2 1

[a]Information was not provided in the questionnaires by all participants or parents.

all. According to the pupils' own reporting, the daily time spent on writing outside school unites these children. Most of the participants wrote less than 30 minutes per day, but surprisingly, it is in the no-gain groups where a bigger proportion of children claim to write more than that. The number of pupils is, however, very small, and thus, no far-reaching conclusions should be made based on this.

Linguistic variables predicting the writing outcomes at T1 and T2

To see how much the results in reading comprehension, vocabulary, dictation and segmentation tasks at T1 can predict the writing outcomes at T1 and T2, we conducted a regression analysis (Table 9.6). Only the variables showing a significant correlation with the dependent variable were entered into the analysis. Therefore, for example, the segmentation and dictation tasks in Russian were not added to the model when Finnish writing at T1 and T2 was the dependent variable, and segmentation in Finnish was left out from the model explaining Finnish writing at T2. Finnish vocabulary and Finnish dictation strongly correlated with each other (rs=0.892), which may indicate collinearity; we therefore only used dictation in the model.

The proportion of the variation in the writing results predicted with the chosen linguistic variables is considerably high, except for Finnish

Table 9.6 Time spent on segmentation, vocabulary, reading comprehension and dictation tasks at T1 predicting L1 Russian and L2 Finnish writing outcomes at T1 and T2

Dependent variable (DV)	*Variation explained by the predictors (Adjusted R2 converted into percentages)*	*Predictors*	*Correlation between the DV and the predictor*
Russian writing T1	60%	Dictation RUS	0.780**
		Reading comprehension RUS	0.614**
		Segmentation (time) RUS	-0.537**
		Segmentation (time) FIN	-0.379**
Russian writing T2	71%	Dictation RUS	0.847**
		Reading comprehension RUS	0.661**
		Segmentation (time) RUS	-0.362**
		Segmentation (time) FIN	-0.699**
		Vocabulary FIN	-0.320*
Finnish writing T1	63%	Segmentation (time) FIN	-0.377**
		Dictation FIN	0.763**
		Reading comprehension FIN	0.596**
Finnish writing T2	28%	Dictation FIN	0.476**
		Reading comprehension FIN	0.484**

* Correlation is significant at 0.05 level.

** Correlation is significant at minimum of 0.01 level.

writing at T2. The results in dictation and reading comprehension in Russian are the best predictors of Russian writing at both T1 and T2. Time spent in completing the segmentation task in Finnish and Russian are good predictors, too. The less time you spend to complete the task, the better you seem to be in Russian writing. Also, Finnish vocabulary is among the predictors of Russian writing at T2. However, the negative correlation (–0.320*) indicates that the smaller the vocabulary is in Finnish, the better the writing outcomes are in Russian. At T1, 63% of the Finnish writing outcomes are explained by Finnish segmentation, dictation and reading comprehension results. However, at T2, the prediction is much smaller (28%) and is based only on dictation and reading comprehension, which are both very close to the construct of writing. This is in line with the results in previous studies with a bigger Russian-speaking cohort (*n*=183) in DIALUKI (Ullakonoja *et al.*, 2012b).

Cognitive variables explaining the writing outcomes

To investigate how much of the writing proficiency can be explained with cognitive abilities, we administered nine different cognitive tests, six of them in both languages and the remaining three only in L1 Russian. The results of the regression analysis are shown in Table 9.7.

As Table 9.7 shows, the variation in L1 Russian writing outcomes was explained by the cognitive variables for 46% at T1 and as much as 73% at T2. For L2 Finnish writing, the proportions of prediction are 54% and 17%, respectively. Although the percentages differ, the trend in prediction is similar to the one with linguistic variables.

Table 9.7 Cognitive measures explaining the writing outcomes in L1 Russian and L2 Finnish

Dependent variable (DV)	*Variation explained by the predictor (adjusted R2 converted into percentages)*	*Predictors*	*Correlation between the DV and the predictor*
Russian writing T1	46%	RPW Rus	0.429**
		Word list reading Rus	0.662**
		RAS time Rus	0.528**
		NW repetition Rus	0.348*
		PW reading Rus	0.530**
		PW spelling Rus	0.646**

Russian writing T2	73%	RPW Rus	0.423**
		Word list reading Rus	0.728**
		RAS time Rus	0.627**
		NW repetition Rus	0.307**
		PW reading Rus	0.413**
		PW spelling Rus	0.771**
Finnish writing T1	54%	RPW Fin	0.542**
		Word-list reading Fin	0.598**
		RAS time Fin	0.314*
		NW repetition Fin	0.471**
		Phoneme deletion Fin	0.477**
Finnish writing T2	17%	RPW Fin	0.420**
		Phoneme deletion Fin	0.315*

* Correlation is significant at 0.05 level.
** Correlation is significant at minimum of 0.01 level.
Note: RPW=rapidly presented words; RAS=rapid alternating stimulus; NW=non-word; PW=pseudo-word.

Discussion

Only a few background factors seemed to correlate with writing outcomes in either language, and the correlations were moderate except for the one between the length of residence in Finland and Finnish writing at T1. Background variables did not explain the difference between the writers making progress and those who did not progress.

Linguistic and cognitive measures seemed to be more efficient in predicting the writing outcomes. The first regression analysis showed differences in which linguistic measures predict the outcomes in L1 Russian and L2 Finnish writing and how they do it. At both time points, only Finnish variables explain the results of Finnish writing, whereas for Russian the predicting variables come from both languages. However, the Finnish linguistic variables are all negatively correlated with Russian writing, indicating that poor skills in Finnish are likely to be connected to good writing skills in Russian. The other observable difference is that Russian writing outcomes are strongly predicted by the linguistic variables at both time points, whereas for Finnish writing the prediction drops notably at T2.

The second regression analysis investigating how the writing results could be explained by cognitive measures shows a similar pattern: the predictions are fairly high except for Finnish L2 writing at T2 (17%). For Russian writing, the variables emerging from the prediction are the same at both time points. Three of them (RPW, word-list reading and RAS) tap into word recognition and speed of word retrieval, which are aspects of vocabulary knowledge (Alderson *et al.*, 2015: 105). The remaining three variables have more to do with phonological awareness and especially letter–sound correspondence. For Finnish writing, five predictors emerge at T1, but at T2 only two of them are left. Also, here the predicting variables tap into vocabulary knowledge and phonological awareness, but this time the focus is on the manipulation of phonological information. The predicting variables also created a clear language division. Although all cognitive variables in both languages were involved in the analysis, only Russian tasks explained Russian writing and Finnish tasks Finnish writing, respectively.

The backwards digit span task measuring the working memory does not belong to the predicting variables for either of the languages. This does not, however, mean that working memory is not involved, as all phonological awareness tasks clearly require working memory functions. Therefore, it can be stated that working memory is tightly intertwined with the prediction.

Conclusions

In Phase 1, we focused on the development in writing skills over a two-year period in both L1 Russian and L2 Finnish. The comparison of the writing outcomes between T1 and T2 clearly showed that the majority of the pupils progressed in their writing skills, not only in L2 Finnish but also in L1 Russian, despite the fact that the children lived in a Finnish environment and went to Finnish schools. The tendency was detectable in data which covered only a small slice of the writing proficiency, with only one writing task in each language at T1 and T2. At school, the pupils were instructed in Finnish and learned the language from their surrounding environment. They were all also instructed in Finnish writing skills, and thus they both wrote-to-learn and learnt-to-write (Manchón, 2011) in their L2. Thus, it appears very logical that most of them showed more improvement in L2 Finnish writing, especially as writing skills were measured with writing tasks which resemble the typical school writing tasks. The development in L1 Russian writing proficiency needs an explanation, too. The progress was not as clear as in Finnish, but still some of the pupils had gone up as many as four levels on the evaluation scale.

Many of the children had also participated in home language instruction in a school setting. This participation, for example, was once a week for an hour and therefore was not likely to markedly improve language skills, particularly considering that the time was not dedicated to improving writing skills alone. However, in two years, all these children have matured in their thinking and cognitive abilities. They have had more experience with literacy, although not necessarily so much in Russian. It is possible that what they have learned about literacy in L2 Finnish has also widened their multicompetence repertoire and thus partly made their progress in Russian writing possible. Hedgcock and Lefkowitz (2011) have argued that to improve in their heritage language, children need to also develop rhetorical skills, discourse knowledge and genre awareness. This is closely connected to the assessment criteria we used. The Finnish national curriculum scale for assessing foreign language skills follows the CEFR assessment criteria, which focus more on functional aspects of language than grammatical accuracy. Thus, the progress of our participants indicates that they have developed the coherency of the texts they write, how well they can express and justify their opinions or thoughts, how well the text meets the genre criteria and how well they can tell a story. These things may have also been learned through the L2 (Rinnert & Kobayashi, 2009), especially when the literacy cultures or the L1 and the L2 are close.

If the results in writing development are looked at against the developmental interdependence hypothesis (Cummins, 1979), no support for the hypothesis can be found. This is most evident in pupils whose writing skills did not improve in one of the languages. If the interdependence hypothesis were to hold, these pupils should not have improved in either language between T1 and T2. However, with only one exception (pupil ID 9), those who did not improve in L1 Russian did still develop their writing skills in L2 Finnish, and those who improved in L1 did not develop in L2 writing, although that would have been expected according to the interdependence hypothesis. Thus, our results do not give evidence for transfer from L1 to L2 or for a straightforward connection between the writing skills in L1 and L2.

In Phase 2, our research interest was twofold, including, on the one hand, connections of the background variables to the writing outcomes and, on the other hand, the power of cognitive and linguistic variables to explain the variation in the writing outcomes. Only a few of the background variables had a significant although only small or moderate correlation with the writing outcomes: the use of Russian in general, number of languages a pupil knows and age of learning to read in Finnish correlated with Russian writing, and the use of Finnish in general, age of learning to read in Finnish (negative correlation) and time of residence in Finland with Finnish writing, respectively. The background variables were not able to shed light on why some of the participants progressed only in one language. The group was rather small and very heterogeneous for this kind of analysis.

For linguistic and cognitive variables, the situation was different. Both factors turned out to be very good predictors of writing outcomes, except for Finnish writing at T2. Both analyses also gave very similar results: vocabulary and segmentation skills and equivalent cognitive skills (speed of lexical access, word recognition) were among the predicting variables. On top of this, various aspects of phonological awareness partly explained the variation in the writing outcomes. These findings are very much in line with the results of previous research (e.g. Shoonen *et al.*, 2003, 2009). Together with the result that almost exclusively Russian tasks predicted Russian writing, and Finnish tasks Finnish writing, these outcomes also support the idea that language and cognition are inseparable and that they function together (Bialystok, 2002). At the same time, with the clear tendency towards language specificity, these findings do not support the interdependence hypothesis (Cummins, 1979). Neither do they give evidence about an overt transfer of skills or abilities from L1 to L2. Instead, they show a picture of development, where many things other than just language proficiency in L1 create different learning paths in L2 and writing skills.

References

Ahonen, T., Tuovinen, S. and Leppäsaari T. (2010) *Nopean sarjallisen nimeämisen testi* [*Rapid Serial Naming Test*] (3rd revised edn). Jyväskylä: Niilo Mäki Institute, Haukkaranta School.

Alderson, J.C. (2005) *Diagnosing Foreign Language Proficiency. The Interface between Learning and Assessment.* London: Continuum.

Alderson, J.C. and Huhta, A. (2011) Can research into the diagnostic testing of reading in a second or foreign language contribute to SLA research? In L. Roberts, G. Pallotti and C. Bettoni (eds) *EUROSLA Yearbook, Volume 11* (pp. 30–52). Amsterdam: John Benjamins.

Alderson, J.C., Haapakangas, E-L., Huhta, A., Nieminen, L. and Ullakonoja, R. (2015) *The Diagnosis of Reading in a Second or Foreign Language.* New York: Routledge.

Basic Education Act 628/1998, act of law. See www.finlex.fi/en/laki/kaannokset/1998/en19980628 (accessed 14 January 2016).

Bialystok, E. (2002) Cognitive processes of L2 users. In V. Cook (ed.) *Portraits of the L2 User* (pp. 147–165). Clevedon: Multilingual Matters.

CEFR (2001) *Common European Framework of Reference for Languages: Learning, Teaching, Assessment.* Council for Cultural Co-operation. Education Committee, Modern Languages Division, Strasbourg & Council of Europe. Cambridge: Cambridge University Press.

Cook, V. (2002) Background to the L2 user. In V. Cook (ed.) *Portraits of the L2 User* (pp. 1–28). Clevedon: Multilingual Matters.

Cummins, J. (1979) Linguistic interdependence and educational development of bilingual children. *Review of Educational Research* 49 (2), 222–251.

Cummins, J. (2010) BICS and CALP: Empirical and theoretical status of the distinction. In B. Street and N. Hornberger (eds) *Encyclopedia of Language and Literacy (2nd edn), Volume 2: Literacy* (pp. 71–83). New York: Springer.

Fitzgerald, J. (2006) Multilingual writing in preschool through 12th grade: The last 15 years. In C.A. MacArthur, S. Graham and J. Fitzgerald (eds) *Handbook of Writing Research* (pp. 337–354). New York: Guilford Press.

Foy, P. and Kennedy, A.M. (2008) *Progress in International Reading Literacy Study PIRLS): PIRLS 2006 User Guides.* See http://timss.bc.edu/pirls2006/user_guide.html (accessed 14 January 2016).

Häyrynen, T., Serenius-Sirve, S. and Korkman, M. (1999) *Lukilasse. Lukemisen, kirjoittamisen ja laskemisen seulontatestistö peruskoulun ala-asteen luokille 1–6* [*Lukilasse. Screening Battery for Reading, Writing, and Arithmetic for Primary School Grades 1–6*]. Helsinki: Psykologien Kustannus Oy.

Hedgcock, J. and Lefkowitz, N. (2011) Exploring the learning potential of writing development in heritage language education. In R.M. Manchón (ed.) *Learning-to-Write and Writing-to-Learn in Additional Language* (pp. 209–233). Amsterdam: John Benjamins.

Hirose, K. (2006) Dialogue: Pursuing the complexity of the relationship between L1 and L2 writing. *Journal of Second Language Writing* 15, 142–146.

Huhta, A., Alderson, J.C., Nieminen, L. and Ullakonoja, R. (2016) The role of background factors in the diagnosis of SFL reading ability. In D. Tsagari and J. Banerjee (eds) *Contemporary Second Language Assessment* (pp. 125–146). London: Continuum.

Kobayashi, H. and Rinnert, C. (2012) Understanding L2 writing from a multicompetence perspective: Dynamic repertoires of knowledge and text construction. In R. Manchón (ed.) *L2 Writing: Multiple Perspectives* (pp. 101–134). Berlin: DeGruyter.

Latomaa, S. (2007) Miten maahanmuuttajat kotoutuvat Suomeen – opinpolku varhaiskasva-tuksesta työelämään [How do immigrants integrate in Finland – educational path from early education to working life]. In S. Pöyhönen and M-R. Luukka (eds) *Kohti tulevaisuuden kielikoulutusta. Kielikoulutuspoliittisen projektin loppuraportti* [*Towards the Future Language Education. The Final Report of the Project in Language Education Policy*] (pp. 317–368). Jyväskylä: Centre for Applied Language Studies. See https://www.jyu.fi/hum/laitokset/solki/tutkimus/projektit/kiepo/projektin_loppuraportti/KIEPOn_loppuraportti.pdf (accessed 20 January 2016).

Laufer, B. (2003) The influence of L2 on L1 collocational knowledge and on L1 lexical diversity in free written expressions. In V. Cook (ed.) *Effects of the Second Language on the First* (pp. 19–31). Clevedon: Multilingual Matters.

Lezak, M.D., Howieson, D.B., Loring, D.W., Hannay, H.J. and Fischer, J.S. (2004) *Neuropsychological Assessment* (4th edn). Oxford: Oxford University Press.

Linacre, J.M. (2009) *Facets Computer Program for Many-Facet Rasch Measurement, Version 3.65*. Beaverton, OR: Winsteps.com.

Manchón, R.M. (2011) Situating the learning-to-write and writing-to-learn dimensions of L2 writing. In R.M. Manchón (ed.) *Learning-to-Write and Writing-to-Learn in Additional Language* (pp. 3–14). Amsterdam: John Benjamins.

Manchón, R.M. (2013) Writing. In F. Grosjean and P. Li (primary authors) *The Psycholinguistics of Bilingualism* (pp. 100–115). Malden, MA: Wiley-Blackwell.

Mäntylä, K., Pietikäinen, S. and Dufva. H. (2009) Kieliä kellon ympäri: Perhe monikielisyyden tutkimuksen kohteena [Languages around the clock: Researching multilingualism in families]. *Puhe ja kieli* 29 (1), 27–37.

McCutchen, D. (2000) Knowledge, processing, and working memory: Implications for theory of writing. *Educational Psychologist* 35 (1), 13–23.

Montrul, S.A. (2008) *Incomplete Acquisition in Bilingualism. Re-examining the Age Factor.* Amsterdam: John Benjamins.

National Board of Education (2004) *National Core Curriculum for Basic Education 2004*. Helsinki: National Board of Education. See http://www.oph.fi/english/curricula_and_qualifications/basic_education.

National Board of Education (2009) National Core Curriculum of Instruction Preparing for Basic Education. Helsinki: National Board of Education. Accessed 13 September 2016. http://www.oph.fi/download/138886_national_core_curriculum_for_instruction_preparing_for_basic_education_2009.pdf (accessed 14 January 2016).

Nieminen, L., Huhta, A., Ullakonoja, R. and Alderson, C. (2011) Toisella ja vieraalla kielellä lukemisen diagnosointi – DIALUKI-hankkeen teoreettisia ja käytännöllisiä lähtökohtia [Diagnosing reading in a second or foreign language – Theoretical and practical premises for DIALUKI research project]. In E. Lehtinen, S. Aaltonen, M. Koskela, E. Nevasaari and M. Skog-Södersved (eds) *AFinLA-e Soveltavan kielitieteen tutkimuksia [AFinLA-e Studies in applied linguistics] 2011(3)* (pp. 102–115). See http://ojs.tsv.fi/index.php/afinla/article/view/4470.

PIRLS (2006) Progress in International Reading Literacy Study, The Russian test. Tsentr Otsenki Kachestva, Obrasovania.

Rinnert, C. and Kobayashi, H. (2009) Situated writing practices in foreign language settings: The role of previous experience and instruction. In R. Manchón (ed.) *Writing in Foreign Language Context: Learning, Teaching, and Research* (pp. 23–48). Bristol: Multilingual Matters.

Schoonen, R., van Gelderen, A., de Glopper, K., Hulstijn, J., Simis, A., Snellings, P. and Stevenson, M. (2003) First language and second language writing: The role of linguistic knowledge, speed of processing, and metacognitive knowledge. *Language Learning* 53 (1), 165–202.

Schoonen, R. Snellings, P., Stevenson, M. and van Gelderen A. (2009) Towards a blueprint of the foreign language writer: The linguistic and cognitive demands of foreign language writing. In R.M. Manchón (ed.) *Writing in Foreign Language Context. Learning, Teaching, and Research* (pp. 77–101). Bristol: Multilingual Matters.

Seymour, P.H.K., Aro, M. and Erskine, J.M. (2003) Foundation literacy acquisition in European orthographies. *British Journal of Psychology* 94 (2), 143–174.

Tilastokeskus (2014) Suomen virallinen tilasto: Perheet. Vuosikatsaus 2014 (2). Perheistä neljä prosenttia kokonaan vieraskielisiä [Official Finnish Statistics: Families. Year Report 2014 (2). Four per cent of the families are foreigners], statistics. See http://tilastokeskus.fi/til/perh/2014/02/perh_2014_02_2015-11-27_kat_002_fi.html (accessed 20 January 2016).

Ullakonoja, R., Nieminen, L., Haapakangas, E-L., Huhta, A. and Alderson C. (2012) Kaksikieliset oppilaat suomea ja venäjää kirjoittamassa: Minun rakkaus väri – valeasininen ja violetti [Bilingual pupils writing in Finnish and in Russian: My love color – light blue and purple]. In L. Meriläinen, L. Kolehmainen and T. Nieminen (eds) *Monikielinen arki – Multilingualism in Everyday Contexst. AFinLa Yearbook 70* (pp. 113–134). Jyväskylä: Suomen soveltavan kielitieteen yhdistys AFinLA.

Ullakonoja, R., Haapakangas, E-L., Nieminen, L., Huhta, A. and Alderson C. (2012a) Двуязычность в сочинениях школьников на финском и на русском языках [Bilingualism in pupils' Finnish and Russian compositions]. In. L.G. Gromova (ed.) *Русский язык в мире: актуальные проблемы изучения и преподавания [Russian language in the world: current issues of learning and teaching]* (pp. 108–114). Tver: TvGU.

Ullakonoja, R., Haapakangas, E-L., Nieminen, L., Huhta, A. and Alderson C. (2012b) Влияние языковых и когнитивных факторов на формирование умений в чтении на финском языке и в финской письменной речи у русско-финских школьников [The influence of linguistic and cognitive features of Finnish-Russian pupils on the development of reading and writing skills in Finnish]. In I. Pavlovskaya (ed.) *Тестология – Материалы секции* XXXXI *международной филологической конференции [Testing - Materials of the session at the XXXXI international philological conference]* (pp. 61–70). Sankt-Peterburg: Fakul'tet filologii i isskustv Sankt-Peterburgskogo gosudarstvennogo universiteta.

Wechsler, D. (1997) *Wechsler Memory Scale – Third Edition Manual*. San Antonio, TX: The Psychological Corporation.

Wolf, M. (1986) Rapid alternating stimulus (R.A.S.) naming: A longitudinal study in average and impaired readers. *Brain and Language* 27 (2), 360–379.

Zecker, L.B. (2004) Learning to read and write in two languages. In C.A. Stone, E.R. Silliman, B.J. Ehren and K. Apel (eds) *Handbook of Language and Literacy. Development and Disorders* (pp. 248–265). New York: Guilford Press.

10 Assessing Heritage Languages and Interdependence: Why and How?

Raphael Berthele

Different language-related considerations and values have aroused interest in interdependence research during the last few decades. One of these values is the instrumental idea that skills in one language benefit the other language(s). In the first section of this concluding chapter, I discuss issues related to instrumental or other values underpinning scholars' and stakeholders' beliefs about linguistic interdependence.

Interdependence research requires tasks that allow measuring the same skills in different languages, which then allows correlating these measures across languages. In the second section, I address the difficulty in constructing equivalent tasks in typologically different languages, and in the third section, the influence of linguistic typology on second language (L2) learning is discussed.

In the main part of this concluding chapter (section 'Conclusions'), I discuss the different correlational patterns between bi- and multilinguals' languages and their possible interpretations as far as ideas of interdependence are concerned (section 'Interdependence: Data patterns and possible explanations'). Then, I review some of the main findings on interdependence from all studies presented in this book (section 'Possible theoretical explanations for crosslinguistic correlations'). The goal is to see whether it is possible, despite the variety of constructs, operationalisations and languages under investigation, to find converging evidence for the interdependence of languages. In the remainder, I draw conclusions based on this review of the results presented in this book.

Instrumental and Other Values of Heritage Languages

The value of a language and thus the value of proficiency in it can lie in very different aspects (Lehmann, 2006; Robichaud & de Schutter, 2012). A language can be valued from a cultural and symbolic, aesthetic, epistemological or communicative-instrumental point of view. After a period of deficit-oriented research on bilingualism and literacy competences, the current dominant discourse, influenced by seminal studies such as Peal and Lambert (1962), is shaped by a great deal of optimism regarding the beneficial effects of bilingualism on cognition and on the development of literacy skills. The main *topoi* in this discourse are the *direct* as well as *indirect* instrumental values of proficiency in a (first or heritage language, HL) language that is different from the language used as the language of instruction (school language, SL): by 'direct instrumental value', I refer to the communicative opportunities that skills in the language in question provide to the individual. An example of an 'indirect instrumental value' is the transfer-based theory, predicting that it is useful for the development of an SL that is a second or third language to invest in the HL. Such transfer theories form part of the standard repertoire of many researchers in bi- and multilingualism, and I suspect that they also appeal to those who fight for linguistic minorities because they come with a mercantilist flavour of a measurable benefit of being multilingual.

There is a trade-off between some of the values mentioned above. The epistemological value of a language, in the sense of Fishman's (1982) 'Whorfianism of the third kind', is arguably larger if this language encodes knowledge in a way that is substantially different from dominant languages such as English or other successful big languages. Seen from the interdependence point of view, on the other hand, larger typological distances between languages coincide with less positive transfer.

The main part of this concluding chapter focuses on the pertinence of interdependence claims based on the evidence presented in this book. To measure interdependence in a meaningful way, the linguistic distance between the languages involved needs to be looked at from two angles: firstly, from the point of view of operationalising the same skills in typologically different languages, and secondly from the point of view of the impact of typological distance on literacy acquisition.

The Difficulty of Testing the Same Skills in Different Languages

In all projects presented in this volume, the linguistic tasks were carefully constructed to operationalise skills. As argued in Chapter 1, our approach to literacy is a skill-based approach, as this is the view of language that is currently applied in our educational systems. We are, however, perfectly aware of alternative views on literacy and do not question their scholarly value (see Baker [2006] for an overview).

The tasks developed in the Heritage Language and School Language: Are Literacy Skills Transferable? (HELASCOT) project (Chapters 4 and 5) were modelled on the proficiency dimensions described in the national educational standards and in the curriculum elaborated for Portuguese HL classes. These standards describe skills that all pertain to higher language cognition (HLC) as described by Hulstijn (2015). Our goal was to measure these skills in a way that emulates currently used testing formats in the SL classrooms, to make sure that the tests score high on ecological validity. As described in the two chapters, the items developed did not turn out to measure certain subskills with sufficient reliability, which only allowed an analysis of a general score for reading comprehension and for the two writing tasks, respectively. A similar analysis of writing proficiency was also made in the project discussed in Chapter 9, where an overall score of writing was used as the dependent variable. The projects presented in Chapters 7 and 8, however, use rather different tasks in their operationalisations of language proficiency. The study in Chapter 8 uses the widely used c-test format, which is considered a good way to measure general linguistic proficiency. However, as documented by Krompàk in Chapter 8, the linguistic systems in question call for the careful adaptation of the tests: firstly, the typological properties of Turkish require an adaptation of the deletion principles for this language. In the case of Albanian, on the other hand, dialectal variation needs to be considered in the scoring procedure. In the study presented in Chapter 7, the investigators tap into enabling skills for HLC development, using independently validated standardised instruments. Again, care was taken to develop equivalent tests for the different HLs.

The different problems related to the measurement of linguistic skills across different languages show that test formats are not universally suited for all languages, and that typological and dialectal variation needs to be accounted for in the development of test instruments.

Language Typology and Language Use Typology in Biliteracy Development

Language typology plays a role not only in the development of the tests, but also in the learning task. As recent studies on L2 learning in migrant populations show (Schepens, 2014), the typological proximity between languages already in the repertoire and the target language is a predictor of learning difficulty. At first sight, this fits in with the differences between the migrant and comparison groups in the reading comprehension and writing tasks discussed in Chapters 4 and 5. However, as argued in Chapter 3, there are a number of other explanations that might play a role: there are measurable differences in parents' skills in the local languages due to the Portuguese school curriculum that involved French as a foreign language. There are slight but potentially relevant differences in parents' socio-economic statuses between the two language areas. Moreover, the Swiss–German context generally induces linguistic assimilation less strongly, as census data show. This may be related to the diglossic situation which makes local L2 acquisition more complicated. Given this cluster of potentially conspiring factors, the impact of language typology alone is difficult to assess. Language typology as a factor in language acquisition thus needs to be complemented with a typology of language use in the contexts under investigation.

The lack of valid test instruments for many HLs is a challenge for the researcher, and the fundamental question whether bilinguals and multilinguals should be tested with the same instruments and in reference to the same standards as monolinguals is frequently asked (see e.g. Krompàk in Chapter 8, but also Lenz and Berthele [2010] on assessing multilingual skills). Drawing on Hulstijn's distinction between basic and higher language cognition (BLC and HLC), we can ask whether the expectation that minority students need to develop HLC in their HLs and dialects is always adequate: especially if literacy activities simply do not form part of the cultural practices in the respective social networks, it is questionable whether the effort put into developing this language as if it were an SL is worth it. By considering the language use typology, we can avoid exaggerated expectations about biliteracy.

Krompàk therefore argues strongly in favour of a translanguaging perspective that would, in her view, allow us to get rid of the deficit-oriented view on multilingualism still shaping research and the policy debates. Her comments calling for a change of norms in the assessment of multilingual children's literacy go well beyond the scope of our book, and she explicitly appeals to values other than the instrumental transfer benefit as a legitimation of HL instruction.

At the risk of taking an outdated stance, however, we deliberately focused on the type of skills that correspond to standards that are currently in vigour in European and other countries. As long as children's and adolescents' educational success is measured from this perspective, it seems reasonable to investigate the acquisitional processes leading towards these goals. If, however, policy changes in the future, new questions would arise regarding whether such paradigm shifts towards multilingual education do indeed make a difference for the situation of migrant children from a pedagogical and sociological point of view.

Testing Interdependence Hypotheses

The idea that a bilingual's or multilingual's languages are interdependent is of key importance in the policy discourse on language education. Two pertinent questions, then, are *What, exactly, is interdependence?* and *Does it exist?* Some researchers in the field apply a falsificationist paradigm to theories related to basic and academic language proficiency (e.g. Hulstijn, 2015). Even if one accepts other theoretical stances that not only rely on the falsification of theories, but on the accumulation of knowledge that indeed allows us to scientifically confirm them (Sokal & Bricmont, 1997), I believe that researchers should formulate theories and then put them to a test that could, in principle, provide counterevidence to the theory, with the goal of coming up with a new, hopefully better theory that, in turn, can be put to the test. If interdependence is to undergo such a treatment, the relevant theories need to lend themselves to the formulation of testable predictions.

Most quantitative investigations of interdependence measure the linear link between skills in one language and skills in another language by means of correlation, regression or structural equation analyses. Such analyses rely on individual differences between participants, and individual differences can have multiple causes. Correlation coefficients or regression analyses allow us to estimate the strength of this linear association (with some underappreciated differences between the two measures, as discussed in Vanhove [2013]). Such links can be measured longitudinally (How well do skills at Time 1 [T1] predict skills at Time 2 [T2]?) or cross-sectionally (How well do skills in Language A predict skills in Language B?) Longitudinal measures can be taken within languages (auto-regressive effects) or across languages (cross-lagged effects). In all cases, the usual caveat that correlation is not causation needs to be made: causal explanations for good or bad skills in each language are formulated in the researchers' theories, and the data have a more or less good fit to the theory. To prove causality empirically, randomised experiments should be carried out, which is hardly ever possible in applied linguistics (see discussion in Chapter 1: 'On Testing Interdependence'). The only study in this book that comes close to this gold standard is the study presented in Chapter 7. Given these methodological limitations and the multifactorial nature of language learning, causal interpretations of data need to be made with great caution.

Interdependence: Data patterns and possible explanations

It is useful to think of possible outcomes of the empirical investigation of interdependence before looking at the data collected and analysed. If we had the luxury of unlimited and high-quality data, the relationship between first and second language skills (or, in our context between HL

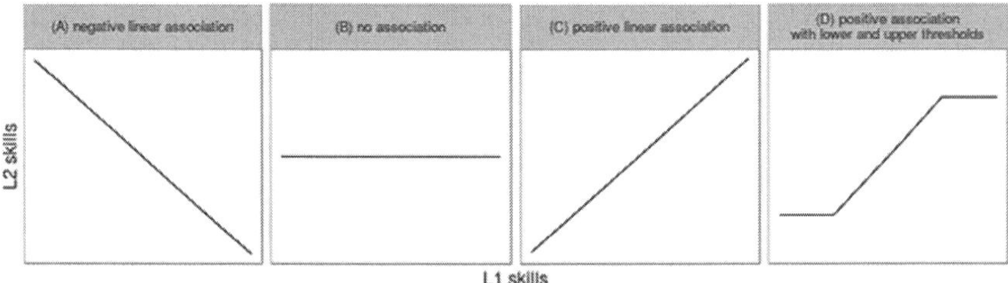

Figure 10.1 Four types of relationship between L1 and L2 skills

and SL skills) would need to correspond to one of four possibilities, i.e. the data could yield one of four general patterns (Figure 10.1):[1]

(1) Negative linear association of L1 and L2 skills (i.e. negative regression slopes).
(2) No association between skills.
(3) Positive linear association of L1 and L2 skills.
(4) Non-linear associations (modifying [1] or [3], e.g. due to thresholds).

Possible theoretical explanations for crosslinguistic correlations

There are at least four, mutually non-exclusive theoretical approaches that can be considered when studying interlingual correlations in language skills. The most successful framework in bilingualism research and educational linguistics is the interdependence approach discussed in Chapter 1 and in the literature reviews of all other chapters describing the empirical studies (Chapters 7 through 9). This approach, today, is generally combined with the idea of thresholds, as the simplest predictions made (see first column in Table 10.1) have been shown to be wrong for quite some time (Cummins, 1976).

The interdependence with thresholds approach predicts either a positive correlation between skills in two or more languages (above the threshold) and no correlation or maybe even a negative one (below the threshold). In this vein, studies often compare proficiency measures in two languages. If the measures are only correlated positively and significantly in subgroups that pattern above a minimal proficiency level, then this is often taken as evidence for a threshold (see Hulstijn [2015] and Chapter 3 for an overview of studies on reading comprehension). Even though this seems to be a reasonable way of investigating thresholds, the logic of such studies can be problematic, as we also discuss in Chapter 1. If the threshold is not set *a priori*, e.g. based on evidence from other, independent studies, then invoking a threshold effect as an explanation of results that do not positively correlate, even though it may make sense at first sight, is unsatisfactory: unless thresholds are defined independently, many possible results in correlational studies are compatible with the interdependence with thresholds theory, even the negative correlations. They would fit in with what Cummins (1976), in his earlier work, referred to as *semilingualism*, and to what is sometimes called *subtractive bilingualism*. A threshold theory might be interesting to put to the test if there is independent evidence for thresholds that can then be modelled in the empirical investigation. Drawing on the threshold idea *a posteriori* to explain the absence of linear relationships in certain groups or subgroups bears the risk of ending up with relatively uninformative theories of the type that skills in two languages generally correlate unless they don't. Another problem with defining thresholds a posteriori is that the probability of producing false positive test results is increased (Vanhove, 2014).

The aforementioned subtractive bilingualism is compatible with the *time on task* idea, i.e. the idea that the growth of the linguistic system is mainly a function of the time spent on tasks in that language and that the interlingual benefits are negligible. Time on task as a main explanatory factor for statistical patterns would be incompatible with strong positive correlations, assuming bilinguals don't spend more time on each of their languages than monolinguals do on theirs.

Language giftedness (see Bishop *et al.* [2006], Rimfeld *et al.* [2015] and Stromswold [2001] for studies on the genetic dimension of language giftedness) as an explanatory factor would be incompatible with negative associations and the absence of associations, but compatible with a positive function. *General cognitive skills* (e.g. measured in working memory and fluid or crystallised intelligence) as explanatory constructs of cross-language patterns would again be incompatible with the negative association of language skills in bilinguals, and it is also difficult to reconcile this explanation with the absence of any association, as these skills would predict that bilinguals relying on their domain-general cognition would show a positive association between those skills and abilities in both languages. Considering the tasks used in the projects described in this volume, a positive correlation in task performance in structurally similar tasks in two languages, if found at all (see Chapter 6 for detailed analyses of such correlations), can at least partially be caused by task-wiseness or other cognitive (non-linguistic) characteristics that the participant can deploy in both tasks.

Table 10.1 also shows that several explanations are incompatible with negative correlations and with the absence of an association across languages, whereas four out of five explanations cannot be ruled out if positive associations are found. In other words, positive associations across languages do not tell us much about which theory fits the data best. Moreover, as several causal mechanisms in Table 10.1 most likely

Table 10.1 Correlational patterns and theoretical explanations thereof

Association type found in data	*Interdependence without thresholds*	*Interdependence with thresholds*	*Time on task*	*Language giftedness*	*General cognition*
Negative association	Incompatible, theory rejected	Compatible, theory not rejected	Compatible, theory not rejected	Incompatible, theory rejected	Incompatible, theory rejected
No association	Incompatible, theory rejected	Compatible, theory not rejected	Compatible, theory not rejected	Incompatible, theory rejected	Incompatible, theory rejected
Positive association	Compatible, theory not rejected	Compatible, theory not rejected	Incompatible, theory rejected	Compatible, theory not rejected	Compatible, theory not rejected

Main explanation of statistical pattern (always assuming that minimal conditions providing learning opportunities and exposure are met)

influence literacy skills at the same time (giftedness, general cognition and interdependence are not mutually exclusive), we cannot make strong claims about which theory merits the most credit based on such correlational results. Survey studies producing positive correlations of scores that operationalise linguistic skills in multilinguals, thus, are non-informative with regard to whether interdependence exists.

Overview of the findings

Table 10.2 gives an overview of the findings of the four studies presented in this volume. The table focuses on the skills measured in the two languages in question.

Table 10.2 shows that there is a general positive relationship in skills across the two languages considered in the studies. This applies both to the cross-sectional measures (thus at a specific measurement time) and to the cross-lagged measures (e.g. HL at T1 predicting SL at T2, and vice versa). The notable exception is the finding in the study reported in Chapter 9, where a negative relationship between vocabulary size in Finnish measured at T1 and writing skills in Russian at T2 was borne out. The same study also suggests that an early age of onset of learning the SL has a positive impact on mastering the SL but a negative impact on mastering the L1 in writing. Both results are not compatible with the simple version of the interdependence explanation but rather with the time on task explanation in Table 10.1. However, most studies find positive relationships between the two languages measured. These findings are compatible with interdependence, with language giftedness and with general cognitive abilities as explanations for the patterns. Positive relations are, however, difficult to reconcile with the time on task idea. Two of the four studies

Table 10.2 Summary of the main findings of the four studies

Study	*Chapter 7: Moser, Bayer, Tomasik*	*Chapter 8: Krompàk*	*Chapter 9: Nieminen, Ullakonoja*	*Chapters 4 through 6: HELASCOT*
Language skills	Phonological awareness and elementary reading	C-test (general proficiency)	Writing skills (DVs), segmentation, reading, dictation (IVs)	Reading comprehension, writing skills
Association HL–SL (cross-sectional)	**Positive** (only measured at T1)	NA	SL–HL: reading and dictation **n.s.** SL segmentation skill – HL writing skills **positive** HL–SL: n.s.	**Positive**
Association HL–SL (cross-lagged)	**Positive** T1–T2, partially **positive** T2–T3 and T3–T4	**Positive** SL.T1–HL.T2 for Albanian	HL–SL: **n.s.** SL.T1–HL.T2: **positive** (segmentation skill) and **negative** (vocabulary)	**Positive**, weaker than within-language
Association within HL or SL (auto-regressive)	**Positive** (all measurements)	SL: **positive** (T1–T2)	HL: **positive** (3/3 variables) SL: **positive** (2/3 variables)	**Positive**, stronger than cross-lagged
Effect of instruction	Promoting HL: **n.s.** on HL, **n.s.** on SL	Promoting HL: **sig.** on HL, **n.s.** on SL	NA	Learning literacy in school language: **no significantly stronger** effect from SL on HL than from HL on SL
Cognitive variables	Intelligence **positively** correlated with intercept, not with progress	NA	Various constructs **positively** correlated (non-word repetition, WM, etc.)	NA
Sociolinguistic variables	Gender and parents' education (**positive** impact on intercept, not on progress)	SES, parents' language orientation, motivation: **n.s.**	Frequency of language use **positively** associated with language, respectively, size of language repertoire (pos. with HL at T2), length of residence	Parents show low levels of German proficiency in German-speaking Switzerland

Note: HL: heritage language; SL: school language (as second/third language); T1, T2, T3: measurement times; DV: dependent variable; IV: independent variable.

report positive associations of cognitive variables with the linguistic skills measured, which can be interpreted as being in line with explanations that emphasise the importance of general cognition for language learning and usage.

The attempt to summarise the results in Table 10.2 does not allow us to clearly state which explanation fits the patterns best. I do not discuss threshold-based explanations here as they fit all possible outcomes as stated in Table 10.1, and as the plots rendered in the figures in Chapter 6 do not suggest any abrupt changes in the slopes which would be required if a threshold explanation would fit.

No single explanation fits all results; in particular, the negative association found in Chapter 9 poses a problem for the explanations that otherwise seem compatible with the findings (interdependence, language giftedness and general cognition).

Effects of language pedagogy measures

Two studies explicitly provide evidence regarding the effects of educational interventions on the development of language skills. Both studies (Chapters 7 and 8) measure the impact of HL classes on HL and SL skills. It is common for applied linguists to recommend HL instruction as a means to reducing the 'language gap' between migrant students and non-migrants (Avineri & Johnson, 2015). One line of argumentation is based on Cummins' influential work on the transferability or shared nature of literacy skills across languages and more general claims on the positive effects of certain types of bilingualism. In many countries, HL instruction is thus promoted as it is seen as being beneficial for literacy development in the SL, too. In the two studies reported in Chapters 7 and 8, no evidence for such effects of HL instruction on literacy skills in the SL is found. One study (Chapter 7) even fails to provide substantial evidence for an impact of HL instruction on the HL itself. In Chapter 6, we have also investigated the question whether there is a beneficial transfer effect from the SL onto the HL, based on the idea that most of the work in the development of literacy is done in the SL. The analysis also shows that the data do not allow this conclusion to be drawn either.

Given these results, the popular claims about the beneficial transfer-effects of L1 instruction in migrant children seem overly optimistic, and the critical stance of sceptics (Esser, 2006; Hopf, 2005) seems justified. As Krompàk discusses in Chapter 8, the justification of HL instruction purely drawing on this instrumental idea of it being beneficial for the pupils' literacy development is insufficient. Other values that can legitimise HL instruction are discussed in the section 'Instrumental and Other Values of Heritage Languages'.

Complexity as an escape route

The approach taken in Table 10.1 does not do justice to the multitude of factors, be they linguistic, cognitive and social, that are known to be related to task performance in first, second and foreign languages. As shown in the chapters in this book, these factors can be included in the statistical models to assess their respective contributions to the variation measured in the outcome variables.

A more radical way to go would be to claim that multilingual language learning and usage is complex and dynamic (De Bot, 2007; Herdina & Jessner, 2002; Hufeisen, 2003), to enumerate all potentially important factors and to state that they may or may not play a role, depending on the particular time, context and case, as is done by certain researchers in multilingualism (see Chapter 1 for discussion). Such theories are seductive as they appear to do justice to the complexity of the phenomena that the applied linguist is interested in. On the other hand, they are not very useful for scholarly research and educational planning: they cannot be proven wrong because they do not make any clear predictions, or their predictions are on the level of the individual which means they do not meet the needs of educational policymaking and curriculum planning.

Thus, seen from the point of view of complexity theory or from a dynamic systems framework, the empirical investigation of interdependence effects may well be possible, but it remains unclear what the predictions are that could be tested. For such theories, other methods and epistemological stances than the one taken in this book might be considered. For language policymakers, however, the answer that multilingual language learning is complex and dynamic is not promising when evidence-based recommendations are expected. Therefore, in this book, we attempted to use quantitative empirical methods to test hypotheses that derive from different explanatory frameworks. We did this knowing that our research designs are always only partially capable of modelling all relevant factors. Proving or falsifying the interdependence theory turns out to be a challenge for quantitative testing, but our goal was nevertheless to contribute to the accumulation of knowledge that will allow ruling out theories and expectations regarding transfer and interdependence effects that are clearly not fitting the empirical results.

Conclusions

As the studies in this book show, the empirical evidence for the instrumental effects of HL on SL proficiency is not overwhelming. As argued above, finding positive correlations between measurements in two languages is not sufficient for strong claims about interdependence – there are simply too many other explanations that are equally in line with such correlations. As Krompàk states in Chapter 8, the HL courses are constantly under pressure regarding their legitimisation. In my view, the empirically unsupported claims on strong interdependence and transfer effects even raise this pressure, as such effects are spurious and weak at best. Expecting transfer miracles from HL instruction is therefore ultimately counterproductive to its legitimisation, as a massive transfer is unlikely to happen and one of the main arguments in favour of this instruction can thus easily be shown to be void. Maybe, as argued in Chapter 7 by Moser *et al.*, there would be more beneficial effects, at least on the development of the HL, if this language were used in immersion or content and language integrated learning (CLIL) settings. The logistic problems in countries such as Switzerland, where migrant populations come from many different areas, would be considerable, but if policymakers insist on the educational value of HLs, then such pedagogical scenarios would deserve further investigation.

For the time being, however, other values than the transfer-oriented instrumental value are more promising if HL classes should be advocated. I share the point of view that HLs are valuable from many different perspectives (culturally, socially and, why not, even aesthetically), but such opinions and values pertain to the social and political realms, not to the scientific models put to test in this book. Whereas, from the instrumental view on the transfer potential, the results in this book might be disappointing, the book should not be read as a pamphlet against HL instruction. However, it cannot be read as a pamphlet in favour of it either. All we intend to do is to contribute to the scholarly investigation of transfer and interdependence in bi- and multilingual migrant children. And the data discussed here do not lend themselves to support strong claims about beneficial interdependence effects.

Acknowledgement

Many thanks to Amelia Lambelet and Jan Vanhove for their very valuable comments on earlier versions of this chapter.

Notes

(1) I do not discuss experimental research designs here, as interdependence research is overwhelmingly longitudinal or cross-sectional.

References

Avineri, N. and Johnson, E.J. (2015) Invited forum: Bridging the 'language gap'. *Journal of Linguistic Anthropology* 25 (1), 66–86.

Baker, C. (2006) Literacy, biliteracy and multiliteracies for bilinguals. In C. Baker (ed.) *Foundations of Bilingual Education and Bilingualism* (4th edn) (pp. 320–345). Clevedon: Multilingual Matters.

Bishop, D.V., Laws, G., Adams, C. and Norbury, C.F. (2006) High heritability of speech and language impairments in 6-year-old twins demonstrated using parent and teacher report. *Behavior Genetics* 36 (2), 173–184. See https://doi.org/10.1007/s10519-005-9020-0.

Cummins, J. (1976) The influence of bilingualism on cognitive growth: A synthesis of research findings and explanatory hypotheses. *Working Papers on Bilingualism* 9, 1–43.

De Bot, K. (2007) Dynamic systems theory, lifespan development and language attrition. In B. Köpke, M.S. Schmid, M. Keijzer and S. Dostert (eds) *Language Attrition. Theoretical Perspectives* (pp. 53–68). Amsterdam: John Benjamins.

Esser, H. (2006) Wenig hilfreich. Zweisprachigkeit fördert die Integration von Zuwanderern nicht wesentlich. *WZB-Mitteilungen Heft* 111, 23–24.

Fishman, J.A. (1982) Whorfianism of the third kind: Ethnolinguistic diversity as a worldwide societal asset. *Language in Society* 11 (1), 1–14.

Herdina, P. and Jessner, U. (2002) *A Dynamic Model of Multilingualism. Perspectives of Change in Psycholinguistics*. Clevedon: Multilingual Matters.

Hopf, D. (2005) Zweisprachigkeit und Schulleistung bei Migrantenkindern. *Zeitschrift Für Pädagogik* 51, 236–251.

Hufeisen, B. (2003) L1, L2, L3, L4, Lx – alle gleich? Linguistische, lernerinterne und lernerexterne Faktoren in Modellen zum multiplen Spracherwerb. *Zeitschrift Für Interkulturellen Fremdsprachenunterricht* 8 (2/3), 97–109.

Hulstijn, J.H. (2015) *Language Proficiency in Native and Non-Native Speakers: Theory and Research*. Amsterdam/Philadelphia, PA: John Benjamins Publishing Co.

Lehmann, C. (2006) The value of a language. *Folia Linguistica* 40 (3–4), 207–238. See https://doi.org/10.1515/flin.40.3-4.207.

Lenz, P. and Berthele, R. (2010) *Assessment in Plurilingual and Intercultural Education. Satellite Study No. 2 for the Guide for the Development and Implementation of Curricula for Plurilingual and Intercultural Education*. Strasbourg.

Peal, E. and Lambert, W. (1962) The relation of bilingualism to intelligence. *Psychological Monographs: General and Applied* 127 (27), 1–23.

Rimfeld, K., Dale, P.S. and Plomin, R. (2015) How specific is second language-learning ability[quest]: A twin study exploring the contributions of first language achievement and intelligence to second language achievement. *Translational Psychiatry* 5, e638.

Robichaud, D. and de Schutter, H. (2012) Language is just a tool! On the instrumentalist approach to language. In B. Spolsky (ed.) *The Cambridge Handbook of Language Policy* (pp. 124–145). Cambridge: Cambridge University Press.

Schepens, J. (2014) *Bridging Linguistic Gaps: The Effects of Linguistic Distance on the Adult Learnability of Dutch as an Additional Language*. Utrecht: Utrecht University.

Sokal, A. and Bricmont, J. (1997) *Impostures intellectuelles*. Odile Jacob. See http://www.amazon.ca/exec/obidos/redirect?tag=citeulike09-20&path=ASIN/2253942766.

Stromswold, K. (2001) The heritability of language: A review and meta-analysis of twin, adoption, and linkage studies. *Language* 77 (4), 647–723. See https://doi.org/10.1353/lan.2001.0247.

Vanhove, J. (2013) The critical period hypothesis in second language acquisition: A statistical critique and a reanalysis. *Plos One* 8 (7), e69172. See https://doi.org/10.1371/journal.pone.0069172.

Vanhove, J. (2014, August 20) Calibrating p-values in 'flexible' piecewise regression models. See http://janhove.github.io/analysis/2014/08/20/adjusted-pvalues-breakpoint-regression.

Index